THE BASIC PRINCIPLES
OF
EURYTHMY

Collected and Compiled

by

ANNEMARIE DUBACH-DONATH

English translation by J. Compton-Burnett.

MERCURY PRESS

First published in 1937 by
RUDOLF STEINER PUBLISHING CO.
54 BLOOMSBURY STREET,
LONDON
&
ANTHROPOSOPHIC PRESS,
New York

Corrected American version
©2000
Mercury Press

ISBN 978-1-957569-45-1

MERCURY PRESS
an imprint of SteinerBooks
834 Main Street, PO Box 358
Spencertown, New York 12165
www.steinerbooks.org

IN MEMORY OF

THE CREATOR OF EURYTHMY

RUDOLF STEINER

PART III

XV	Group-Expression of Alliteration and Assonance	169
XVI	The Expression of Rhyme in Eurythmy	174
XVII	Musical Preludes and Studies: Studies in the Different Verse-Forms	194
XVIII	Forms for Children: Form for Poems Happy Mood Form for Poems Melancholy Mood: A Threefold Form (The Riddle of Destiny)	233
XIX	TIAOAIT: Form for Poems of a Cosmic Character	246
XX	Presentation of a Poem on Three Levels	252
XXI	A Dance of the Planets	254
XXII	The Origin of the Sounds in the Macrocosm	261
XXIII	Production of a Scene from a Play, preceded by the Mercury-Prelude (7th Scene from *The Portal of Initiation* by Rudolf Steiner)	271
Appendix		290

CONTENTS

Preface 7
Translator's Preface 15

PART I

I The Rod Exercises. 17
II Walking and Rhythmic Walking 24
III Vowels, Diphthongs, Modified Vowels,
     and their Expression in Eurythmy 31
IV Alliterations 42
V Educational Eurythmy Exercises 45
VI Eurythmy Soul-Gestures 75
VII Dionysian Forms 78

PART II

VIII The Consonants 93
IX Apollonian Forms 112
X Various Aspects of Artistic Expression 134
XI Certain Characteristic Exercises 146
XII The Colors 156
XIII Positions of the Head 161
XIV Positions of the Feet 163

PREFACE

It was in September of the year 1912 that Rudolf Steiner planted in the hearts of a small band of people ready to receive them the seeds of a new art, rich in forces for the future.

On many later occasions he stated that in doing this he was following the same laws of karma which he obeyed in all his deeds and which he always fully recognized. Certain questions had been put to him, and although, to begin with, these were connected with the narrower problem of a choice of vocation, they turned on this: How can the art of dancing be ennobled, spiritualized, renewed?

When the appointed time had arrived Rudolf Steiner answered with an abundance of concrete detail, of entirely new guiding lines, remote from any compromise with what is known as the art of dancing at the present time. He answered by giving innumerable and most detailed directions and suggestions, each of them being a path leading from the world of spiritual law into a newly-created domain, the joyous, sunny, life-giving domain of *eurythmy*.

To children also was this homeland—this well-spring of spiritual life and of soul-protecting, healing power—to be revealed. And so, among the first indications, were also educational exercises in eurythmy; for instance, the rod exercises described in the first chapter of this book, which work more upon the physical organism 'to correct awkwardness of carriage', and especially the exercises which remove and counteract weaknesses and disharmonies in the soullife of the child.

But the spirit of eurythmy is not abstract and moralizing, nor does it lead to states of over-intense mystical exaltation and ecstasy, as is the case with many a modern art of movement; it leads to the strong, living, primal forces of all that is *human;* it restores to man, and especially to the child, those divine creative powers whence he came forth, the powers which give him speech as a memory of the world-creative WORD.

How could he fail to feel himself in harmony with his own being and the world?

And indeed, it is the body and soul organism of the child which most quickly and surely responds to eurythmy. The beautiful movement of the etheric is still the natural life-element of the child, the formative power in harmony with which it invariably vibrates in all the activities of life. The child is not as yet wholly withdrawn from this formative power as is often the case with adults who may have been hardened and ossified by the errors of education and civilization.

But the primal truth and vitality that is wafted like a breath of the spirit from each movement of eurythmy takes hold of every human being, young or old, man or woman, who retains some measure of healthy feeling; and the more deeply he penetrates into the essential nature of eurythmy the more capacity he has for understanding and embodying it as an art, the more intensely will he be united with its own peculiar life-force, the more closely related will he feel it to be with his innermost being. And at last he will feel as if he were standing face to face with his own prototype, the prototype of man.

Only anthroposophy, the Wisdom of Man, could produce this 'wonder-child'. In other forms of art also it will be the task of anthroposophy to bring about a deepening, an expansion, a life-giving impulse. *Eurythmy* could only have sprung into being from the soil of anthroposophy; its impulses could only spring from direct anthroposophical vision.' (Extract from a lecture by Rudolf Steiner, Penmaenmawr, August 26th, 1923.)

Rudolf Steiner has told us what underlies the secret of this art, which has been awakened to life by him. 'The art of movement known as eurythmy takes its start from Goethe's view that all art is the revelation of concealed laws of Nature, which, without such revelation, would remain concealed. This thought may be connected with another Goethean thought. In each human organ there is an expression of the *whole* form of man. Each human limb is, as it were, the human being in miniature, just as, in Goethe's view, the leaf is the plant in miniature. We may reverse this thought and see in man a complete expression of what one of his organs represents. In the larynx and the organs connected with the larynx in speech and song, these activities set up the movements or tendency to movements, which are revealed in sounds or combinations of sounds, although the movements themselves are not perceived in ordinary life. It is not so much these movements themselves but the tendencies to them which are to be transformed by eurythmy into movements of the whole body. What occurs imperceptibly in the formation of sounds and tones in a single system of organs is to become visible as movement and posture in the whole human being. The movements of the limbs reveal what takes place in the larynx and its neighboring organs in speaking and singing; in movement in space, in the forms and movements of groups, there is portrayed what lives in the human soul as tone and speech. Thus in eurythmy, this art of movement, there is created something, at the birth of which those impulses ruled which have been active in the development of all forms of art.

Eurythmy is intended to lead the art of dancing back to the source from which it originated but from which, in the course of time, it has wandered far. It would do this not through imitation or mere revival of the old, but in the true sense of a truly modern conception of art.' These words were written by Rudolf Steiner as a short introduction to a performance of eurythmy during the West-East Congress in the Vienna Opera House, June 2nd, 1922.

What happened during the ten years which had passed since those first indications were given which laid the foundation for a cultural influence, the full possibilities of which were not to be gauged at the time—which at first were only before us as a fair vision of the future, without certainty of fulfillment?

Under the inspiring guidance of a great artist, Frau Marie Steiner, eurythmy has gradually developed into a really active branch of art. In 1914 she resolved to take this new artistic impulse, threatened as it was by difficulties and hindrances of all kinds, into her own nurturing and protecting hands. Beneath this art of movement she spread out the wings on which alone it would be possible to attempt high flight—the wings of a spiritual treatment of speech and a spiritual art of recitation.

Eurythmy as an art is unthinkable without the word spoken in the same spirit. The art of recitation cannot know renewal without living itself into the laws of eurythmy. The two arts start from separated points—the one rises from the hidden and invisible as visible movement in space; the other, by means of the audible word, creates and works into this spiritual element which is imperceptible to the senses; there they meet in the weaving of the etheric, where sound and movement issue in different directions, penetrate each other, become one.

It was a wonderful and unforgettable time for all eurythmists who had the privilege of living through it, this experience of being borne along on the spirit-illumined, sun-filled stream of speech which carried all with it, making possible life, success and growth. And all the evolutionary phases of eurythmy which grew out of this, down to the smallest detail, the smallest step forward, were followed by Rudolf Steiner with an untiring, kindly interest. He was present at countless rehearsals and performances, always helpful, always opening new doors, always bringing richer treasures to the students.—These were the years in which he produced the delicate wonders of the eurythmy forms—the *Standard Forms* as he called them later. He made a beginning with the cosmic poems of Fercher von Steinwand—the twelve *Urtriebe*. We were amazed when suddenly the difficult problem of group-distribution, of group-movements was solved in so unique a way. When we saw the sheets of paper on which were drawn the undulating lines of the movements of twelve to fifteen people, we dimly felt the artistic necessity that lay behind such a picture. This was no arbitrary choreography—a wonderful harmony and unity lived in each group-form and the whole picture breathed life. How significant and natural was the interweaving of the parts, how organic the connection! Some of these drawings were like opening blossoms, others seemed to be the wild zig-zag of uncanny elemental forces. Then followed single forms for poems more suitable as solos—each curve of the lines like an inner secret path into the thought and intention of the poet. Then, finally, came the musical forms. (Tone eurythmy, the combination of the movements with music, had evolved meanwhile.)

It almost took one's breath away to see the creation of such a form for tone-eurythmy. Rudolf Steiner had the piece played to him or simply took the score in his hand, and, while listening to the music, he let his pencil glide slowly, consideringly, over the paper, as if shaping a deeply significant design; and so there arose—often under the eyes of many curious bystanders—drawings, whose legitimate connection with the music was only understood by the eurythmists and musicians in the course of their studies, but whose beauty of line and inexhaustible variety enraptured one at first glance.

But these are domains on which the present book only touches. The feeling of *color,* as this should gradually enter into the formation of the sounds was only revealed to us later. In August, 1922, Rudolf Steiner gave to the students of Eurythmy (and all lovers of Eurythmy) a new object of study : the Eurythmy figures, carved in wood, each of which represented a single sound, composed of three colors. In a lecture given in Dornach on August the 4th, 1922, Rudolf Steiner spoke about the significance of these color combinations, and also about the artistic task of experiencing each sound as color. Now we had a clue to the understanding of the completely new style of lighting and costume which Dr. Steiner gave for the stage performances. An artistic color-experience was to be communicated to the spectator in the color-combination of dress and veil, in the rich play of the changing lights thrown upon them, everything being in inner harmony with the forms of eurythmy. Thus a rich orchestral 'symphony' of movement, color, form, the poetic structure of words, the musical tone, gradually came into being. And for a short time this interweaving of the arts developed under the domes of our destroyed Goetheanum. Here, where light, color, swinging movement, musical rhythm flowed into one another, eurythmy was inspired by the artistic powers of space, here eurythmy moved in her primal element.

On the night of the burning of the Goetheanum eurythmy was orphaned. We had to return to the temporary hail of the Schreinerei, where the first steps on the stage had been taken.

> Woe, woe, thou hast destroyed the world so fair!
> She falls headlong, she falls in ruins,
> A demi-god hath broken her.

Eurythmy had perforce to lament in the words of Goethe, to tell men—in her own language, in many places of the world—that they had been robbed of something most beautiful, most holy.

Since 1919 performances of eurythmy had taken place on many of the bigger stages of Europe and now this work in the outer world came more and more into the foreground.

In spite of repeated malicious partisan attacks, the young art gradually attracted attention, frequently even enthusiastic recognition.

And in quiet unbroken work this artistic development was accompanied by the actual teaching carried out in accordance with the first curriculum as given by Rudolf Steiner in the autumn of 1912, and further developed by him in Dornach in the summer of 1915.[*] A rich field of work opened out for many whose strivings were in this direction. Certainly this teaching activity was not organized from

---

[*] A third branch—Curative Eurythmy—was entrusted by Rudolf Steiner to the Anthroposophical doctors in the summer of 1921, and has since been applied in the treatment of illness with noticeable success.

the beginning, as is the case now, when all schools and single courses of Eurythmy are grouped together under the guidance of Marie Steiner. And so in the course of the passing years—by very reason of the speed with which Eurythmy evolved and of the ever-growing stream of pupils and those intent upon the teaching—the danger grew that the individual liberty that was left to every teacher (for pedantry lies far from the nature of Eurythmy) might give rise to an undesirable element, namely that the 'after-growth' no longer knew the basic exercises and could not judge of the legitimacy of amplifications made by the numerous teachers. It is necessary for the future that the kernel should remain intact and pure, so that the younger ones may always form their own independent judgment and be able to correct it.

A second danger was equally great—that of the neglect, indeed the forgetting of certain details, which may have appeared insignificant to certain people, but which a later Eurythmy generation would first be able to understand and use to their full extent.

Once again Rudolf Steiner declared himself ready to establish the 'tradition' of Eurythmy. This was to take place in the lectures of the Speech Eurythmy Course, which he gave in the summer of 1924 to a large audience of Eurythmy students and those interested in the arts. But these lectures went far beyond the range of mere repetition. What had already been given was indeed constantly touched upon, but with mighty steps Rudolf Steiner led us far, far out beyond the preliminary stages. His spiritual gaze passed over the whole field of Eurythmy. Many seeds had come forth, some blossoms had opened—lovingly he took the one or the other in his hand, freed them from the deposit which had collected in the course of time, narrowing and hindering— and then he embarked on an abundance of new possibilities which took away one's breath. It almost seemed as if those who wished to devote themselves to Eurythmy now had a gift in their hands, which, through its very superabundance of the new, might once more lead them astray by a too speedy application, by a superficial passing-over of the old.

In many of the introductory talks which Dr. Steiner used to give before the performances of Eurythmy, he had spoken of 'those others to whom it would probably fall to develop further what at present exists in germ'.

It was especially of these 'others', those who were to come after us, that Frau Marie Steiner was thinking when she gave me the joyous task of writing this book.

I have striven as far as possible, to give a scrupulous reproduction of the original groundwork—in which Frau Lory Maier-Smits was my teacher. The expressions used by Dr. Steiner himself—in explanation of the sound-content, in dealing with the educational effect of certain exercises, and so on—I have indicated by italics or inverted commas. For much I have had to rely upon. my own memory. Much again would have been difficult to put down in words with the necessary clarity, if I had not been able—during the writing of the description—to have certain examples demonstrated, thus gaining help from observation and the experiences which were revealed of themselves in the practical application.

I am deeply grateful that I was able to lay the questions and problems which arose in the course of this work before Frau Marie Steiner herself and to receive her advice.

Heartfelt thanks are also due to Frau Tatiana Kisseleff for her friendly assistance; I am indebted to her and Frau Lory Maier-Smits for the verbal quotations. Thanks also to Frl. Annemarie Groh for many interesting ideas for the working out of what had already been given; to Frau Alice Fels, Frau Erna van Deventer, Frau Lucie Neuscheller, Frau Dr. Husemann, heartfelt thanks must be expressed for their friendly replies to many questions in the domain of poetry, etc.

I should like to take this opportunity of expressing special thanks to Frau Erika Klug-Schilbach for her execution of the diagrams illustrating the educational exercises and the preludes and studies in Part III.

ANNEMARIE DUBACH-DONATH.

TRANSLATOR'S PREFACE

In order to make the translation of this book quite clear to the English reader, it will be well to make a few short comments.

One difficulty which always arises is the transference of the vowel-sounds from one language to the other. In this translation, as many German examples have had to be retained, the German pronunciation has been used throughout, the sound of the English *ah* being written a; *eh, e ; ee, i; ow, au; oi, eu ; i, ei,* and so on. If this is borne in mind no confusion will ensue, for the movements correspond to the actual sounds and the way in which they are written is quite immaterial.

Another difficulty was the inclusion of the many German poems. These are sometimes quoted merely for their soundcontent, as examples of rhythm, alliteration, certain vowel-sounds or consonant-sounds; in such cases translations are useless and no attempt has been made to include them. Sometimes the meaning of the text plays an important part, as in the Dionysian and Apollonian forms, and here a translation has been included in every case. The names of the different exercises have, where any doubt could arise, been given in English and German. In most cases these exercises were already being practiced during Dr. Steiner's lifetime, and when uncertainty was felt it was possible to ask him personally for advice. This was also the case with certain sounds peculiar to the English language. Dr. Steiner gave special movements for these sounds and they have been described in footnotes as opportunity arose.

One other point must not be omitted. It is customary in eurythmy to draw the diagrams with the foreground facing the reader. The book should be reversed for the diagrams to be more easily read. If this is not remembered the forms may well be practiced upsidedown.

I should like to take this opportunity of paying tribute to Frau Annemarie Dubach-Donath for the way in which she has carried out this book. She speaks in her preface of the nature of the task set her, and it would be difficult to imagine a task more perfectly fulfilled. The depth of understanding, the detailed accuracy, the delicate beauty of writing shown in all her explanations makes their study sheer delight. The book covers the whole groundwork of speech-eurythmy and forms a rich mine of treasure for teacher and student alike. Its translation has indeed been a labor of love.

JULIET COMPTON-BURNETT.
January, 1937.

PART I

I

THE ROD EXERCISES

In the first of the Lectures on Speech-Eurythmy given by Dr. Steiner in the year 1924* he drew attention to the fact that this art, which must be *through and through a creation out of the Spiritual,* serves as a means of expression for *that part* of *the human being which can manifest as movement.* Hence in the teaching of eurythmy a beginning is made with certain preparatory exercises which give the pupil a means of developing himself, his own human bodily form, into an adequate instrument or means of expression.

First and foremost in this Connection are the *Rod Exercises,* which, by nature of their inherent laws and given time and constant repetition, enable such forces to be developed as will transform the human body from more or less of a hindrance into an organ of soul capable of transmitting the spirit. These exercises should, as indicated by Dr. Steiner, always be practiced with copper rods, and the vitalizing effects of this metal soon make themselves apparent. Hands which frequently touch and handle these copper rods become skilful and dexterous; they quickly find what is being looked for and acquire a lively sense for delicacy of detail.

The first of these exercises is specially adapted to giving the human being a feeling for the directions of space: Right, left, above and below. The way in which it is to be practiced may shortly be described as follows. The exercise consists of seven beats, which may be accompanied by counting or suit-

---

* This course of lectures, entitled *Eurythmy as Visible Speech,* has appeared in book-form, Anthroposophical Publishing Co., London

able music.* With the first beat the rod is held in a horizontal position, the distance between the two hands corresponding exactly to the width of the shoulders and the direction of the arms downward. With 2 the arms are raised up and held vertical over the head. With 3 the right arm is brought downwards and stretched forwards at shoulder-level, the left arm crossing over towards the right until it is directly below the right arm; the rod is now vertical on the right side. With 4 the same position is taken up on the left side; the left arm is now at shoulder-level, the right crossed over to it. With ç the arms are brought to the right side (as 3); with 6 the arms are again vertical over the head; and 7 corresponds to the first position the arms held vertical in a downward direction.

This exercise can first be done standing still, then walking, one step to each movement; later it may also be practiced to walking both backwards and sideways. The figure described in the air by these movements up, down, right and left, is rectangular and must be shown with great precision. The arms must always adapt themselves to the straight lines —for instance, they must not be swung backwards over the head. With the third and fifth beats the right arm must be held stretched forwards exactly at shoulder-level (the same applies to the left arm with the fourth beat), while with 1 and 7 the arms must not be allowed to hang limply but must be stretched downwards with a certain feeling of inner tension. This exercise has a specially beautiful effect when two pupils stand facing each other, *for* then the crossing at 3, 4 and 5 is given full value and a new figure is brought about by the combination of the two movements.

Another exercise consists of passing the rod from below upwards and again from above downwards, thus describing a

---

* Musical accompaniments to this and the following exercises have been composed by L.v.d. Pals and by Max Schuurman.

THE ROD EXERCISES

moving *spiral* round the body. This exercise also can be carried out in seven beats. With 1 the rod is again grasped in both hands, the backs of the hands turned outwards. With 2 the left hand releases its hold and the right hand carries the rod (departing from its horizontal position as little as possible) in a slight curve backwards, where it is immediately grasped again by the left hand. The position of the hands is not altered, so that now the backs of the hands lie on the inner side. With 3 the right hand leaves go, the left describing a slight curve forwards and the right again takes hold ; 4 is once more behind as with 2, and thus it proceeds till 7. Now every time the rod is grasped care must be taken that it is raised a regular if only slight degree higher; in this way the arms are drawn from their original downward position upwards. Having arrived at the top—nearly at shoulder-level, that is to say—the backward journey begins; the spiral continues to move in the same direction (from left to right) in similar stages downwards, so that at the end of the exercise the rod has again reached the position from which it started. This exercise also should first be practiced standing still and later to walking. The necessary exactitude is obtained when the rod is raised and lowered with a certain inner tension, the rod being carried round in a horizontal position, while the hands are never allowed to approach nearer together than corresponds to the width of the shoulders.

A third exercise is more adapted to the development of lightness and grace. Here the rod is held at the extreme finger-tips, with the arms stretched slightly forwards at about shoulder-level. At first the thumb lies under the rod, the four fingers above it; then, without allowing the rod to move, the position of the hand is quickly reversed, so that the four fingers lie beneath it, with the thumb above—and so on, rhythmically to and fro. When changing the position of the hand the four fingers must always be kept together, and it must be done so quickly and skillfully that to an onlooker it would seem as though the rod were stationary, floating freely in the air, while the fingers play around it. To attain this one must practice exerting a definite tension of the fingers, the wrist being left quite relaxed.

Dr. Steiner was once asked what should be felt or pictured when practicing this exercise. Whereupon, drawing attention to the note of a bird, he replied: 'Tweet, tweet' (Qui. Qui). This sound, he said, should be present in the ear while the exercise is being practiced—and one will, indeed, soon realize that there is a certain similarity between this thin, chirping note and the dainty movement of the fingers demanded by this exercise. As the lessons proceed the same lightness can be transferred to the whole manner of walking, the steps which accompany the rhythmic action of the fingers being worked up from a gentle rocking movement to the point of jumping.

The strength and mobility of the wrists may be further increased by the so-called 'S-exercise', in which the rod is made to rotate in a circle with great rapidity, describing, as it were, the coils of an *s* in the air. In this case the middle of the rod is grasped by the finger-tips of one hand and made to revolve in a circle by means of a movement of the wrist. The more one can avoid any wobbling up and down in this rotary movement of the rod, keeping it steadily in a horizontal position (the coiling s-line is described even when one tries to keep the rod as level as possible), so much the better it is. When this exercise is done with dexterous agility—perhaps even with a rod simultaneously turning in each hand—there really is an impression of the eurythmy *s*. In the fourth Eurythmy Lecture, where Dr. Steiner is discussing the s-sound, he gives, as one among other characteristics of this consonant, the *putting something out of one's way with a sense of mastery—and,* indeed, this impression can be created by the pronounced yet unforced movement of the hands gradually developed by this exercise.

From a certain point of view each rod-exercise may be regarded as a eurythmy *s,* for, as will be seen later, an *s* is inherent in every 'bringing about of form by means of a• foreign object'.

There are two more exercises adapted to the development of a strong feeling for the space into which man with his body is placed, for that part of space also which lies behind him. This feeling is already strengthened by the spiral exercise, or encircling the body with the rod, previously described; but a real mastery over the movements carried out behind the back is only arrived at by means of the following exercise. The rod is grasped as in the first and third exercises and is then thrown upwards with a slight jerk (on to the inner side of the arm) the arms being simultaneously bent round it. It now lies at breast-level, balanced on the thumbs of the inward-turned hands. A similar movement must now be carried out at the back. The necessary intermediate movements must be rhythmically divided so as to fall into twelve beats. Thus, with *i* the rod is thrown upwards, with 2 and 3 this position is retained, with 4 the rod is allowed to descend, with 5 the right hand carries it backwards where it is grasped by the left hand (with the back of the hand outwards), with 6 the grasp of the right hand is reversed so that it is brought into the same position, *and* now, with the 7th beat, the rod is thrown up at the back and enclosed in the arms. Here at the back the rod is supported in the angle formed by upper arm and forearm. The back must be held very erect so that the rod may be thrown right up under the shoulders. With 8 and 9 this position is retained, with *io* the rod is again allowed to descend, and with *ii* it is carried forwards by the left hand, where, with the twelfth beat, the right hand again takes hold.

This exercise is easy and serves as *a* preparation for the next which demands considerable dexterity. This next exercise may be varied as to time: for instance, the rod may be slowly raised over the head, accompanied by five beats of music, then, with the sixth beat, the arms are drawn backwards and downwards by means of a bending of the elbows.

The rod now lies securely, not at the nape of the neck, but as far as possible down the back with the shoulders held well together. With the seventh beat the rod is released and the hands make a rapid grasping movement downwards in order to catch it—for which a certain amount of practice will probably be necessary.

The exercise can also be divided thus: *i*, Rod down; z, rod raised to shoulder-level; 3, vertical over the head; 4, lying at the back (as previously with 6); *5,* dropping and catching.

Mention must be made of another exercise, only indicated in principle by Dr. Steiner and as yet not very much applied. Here the rod is thrown upwards and allowed to revolve once or twice in the air before it is caught.

This exercise. like the previous one can be carried out in seven beats and divided in space accordingly.[*] Thus for example: 1, Grasping the rod with the right arm stretched forwards; 2, throwing and catching; 3, leading the stretched arm over to the right; 4, throwing and catching; 5, arm once more forwards; 6, throwing and catching; 7, arm down. The same thing may be done with the left arm on the left side, and, when this is perfected, even with two rods to right and left simultaneously. Dr. Steiner often emphasized that this and the following elementary exercises can be amplified and varied

---

[*] See Appendix.

in detail. They can also be practiced to forms, arranged either for one eurythmist or a group. It is, however, necessary first to master with strict exactitude the beautiful laws upon which the exercises are based, so that there may be no danger of any arbitrary or trivial developments which might lead away from the spirit of eurythmy. If the pupil, by means of intensive study, has become really impregnated with the mathematical exactitude, the magnificent simplicity of the rod-exercises, which are never aesthetic merely, a sure and certain feeling for the true laws of eurythmy will develop in him. He will gain the faculty of differentiating between anything devised or trivial, in contradistinction to the natural developments which may arise from the basic laws which have here been indicated.

II

WALKING AND RHYTHMIC WALKING

Now the teaching of another element of eurythmy must run parallel with the rod exercises—the necessity for this arising as soon as the pupil ceases to do the exercises standing still—and that is the art of correct eurythmy walking. In the ninth Eurythmy Lecture[*] we find an explanation of the significance of the step, of walking. Here, however, in order that the sequence of instruction may not be interrupted, mention shall be made of Dr. Steiner's earlier indications as to how eurythmy walking should be taught.

The pupil must first take up a preliminary position, with one foot placed in front of the other. Then the foot which is behind must be raised, not with a jerk, but with a gradual tension of the muscles, so that first the heel and then the toes are released from the ground. This is the first phase of the step; here the *'will-impulse* inherent in the action of walking' is brought to expression (Lecture IX). The second stage is the carrying of the foot forwards. This part of the movement must be felt as representing the *thought* contained in the impulse of will.—Indeed from a certain point of view the step in eurythmy. is that which raises up into the consciousness the various elements comprised in each single movement.—In the third phase of the step, the placing of the foot (toes first, then the whole foot), the process is completed with the *deed*. The foot is once again united with the earth, from which at the moment of the will-impulse it was previously released.[†]

This eurythmy walking can also be practiced backwards and sideways. The latter is particularly necessary, for, in the exer-

---
[*] *Eurythmy as Visible Speech*
[†] See Appendix.

cises later to be described and in the moving of the first simple forms used for the expression of poems in eurythmy, the whole posture of the body must remain turned in a certain direction, generally facing either forwards or towards the center, no matter where the form may happen to go. When walking in a sideways direction the step must be taken in such a way that one foot is placed over the other. (This static posture of the body in the form is an essential foundation for the beginner, in order that later, when freely following the lines and curves of a form, the necessary restraint may be observed.)

In Lecture IX Dr. Steiner also speaks of how, in the artistic expression of poems, effect can be given to the most varying moods by the way in which these three phases of the step may be more or less emphasized, accelerated or retarded. It is advisable to make a systematic study of these subtle variations of feeling, to choose, for instance, certain poems of absolutely different mood and content and then endeavor to pour the feelings they arouse right into the foot, into the whole way in which the step is taken. This can be still further elaborated, for instance, in poems of a thoughtful, contemplative nature, by timing the *carrying* of the foot to fall on the accented beat (the other phases being correspondingly apportioned); or, in more vigorous poems, by *lifting* the foot with the accented beat.

When walking the whole body must, however, also express the underlying mood. If the poem in question bears the character of will-activity, the quick *lifting* and decided *placing* of the foot may be accompanied by a swinging, or in special cases even spasmodic, movement of the body. When quieter, more delicate poems are to be expressed, one must learn to merge together the three movements carried out by the foot, to lead the one so harmoniously over into the other that an impression of quiet gliding is created.†

An exercise which directs particular attention to the feet and movements of the feet is as follows: First an energetic step must be taken, which is pulled up suddenly with determined conviction; this is succeeded by two consecutive steps checked in like manner, then three steps, then four and so on up to seven. Now the process is reversed: Six steps, five, four, till one step is again reached. (This reversed order may also be practiced walking backwards.) As the number of steps increases, the tempo must be correspondingly accelerated, so that the last seven steps take no longer (as respects the beat) than did the first one. Thus the beginning is quite slow, followed by a gradual acceleration and retardation of tempo, until the time of the first step is once more reached. This exercise should be specially used as an educational exercise for lively, excitable children, who are easily distracted by the impressions of their surroundings. For by the very fact that this running—which would, as it were, like to be carried ever further by its own impetus—has to be consciously checked, a restraining, self-strengthening force of will is brought into activity, the influence of which gradually finds its way into the whole soul-life.

The swinging or restrained movement of the body in walking, of which mention has already been made, also plays an important part in the marking or beating time to the rhythms of verse—which at a later stage forms the preliminary basis to every attempt towards the artistic working out of a poem in eurythmy. The interpretation of poems by means of eurythmy, side by side with the educational results aimed at by certain of the exercises, is the goal towards which the whole teaching is directed. Everything audible in the recita-

---

† See Appendix.

tion of a poem—the tone, the sounds of speech and also the rhythm—must be translated into visible movement. Rhythm can of course be reproduced quite freely when it is a question of artistic interpretation; but in order that the pupil may become accustomed to experiencing and giving expression to metric rhythm, a preliminary practice is made of definitely beating time. Let us first describe the movements made by the arms.

We will assume that the metric rhythm of the following lines from a poem by C. F. Meyer is to be expressed in movement:

∪ — ∪ — ∪ — ∪ —
Bemesst den Schritt, bemesst den Schwung,
∪ — ∪ — ∪ — ∪ —
die Erde bleibt noch lange jung;
∪ — ∪ — ∪ — ∪ —
hier fällt ein Korn, das stirbt und ruht,
∪ — ∪ — ∪ — ∪ —
die Ruh ist süss, es hat es gut...

In this example the long, emphasized syllable always follows the short, unemphasized syllable. The rhythm is Iambic, and may in the first place be shown thus: With the unaccented syllable the arms, which are raised upwards from the elbow, make a light movement towards each other so that the fingers almost touch, and are again withdrawn—a free, floating movement, about level with the shoulders. With the accented syllable the arms make a firm movement downwards. Diagrammatically the whole movement may be drawn as follows:

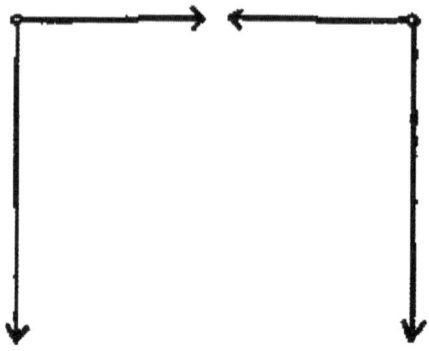

The starting point of both these movements is, as may be seen, identical; hence it is always necessary, even after the downward movement, to return to this same point. The converging movement of the arms with the short beat should not be carried out with the upper part of the body rigid, but lightly poised and swaying; the movement must start from the shoulders, every muscle being gently brought into play. With the accented syllable, on the other hand, the upper part of the body must be held consciously erect, with the muscles tense. In this way the breathing element inherent in rhythm is carried over into the movements employed for the expression of the rhythmic beat.

The Troche, where the unaccented beat follows the accented, is correspondingly shown: First the movement downward, then the light movement hovering over it.

The Anapest—two short beats followed by one long—(a metre which underlies most of the educational exercises) is shown in eurythmy by repeating the horizontal movement twice in succession, followed by the vertical movement; with the Dactyl (— ∪ ∪ — ∪ ∪) the process is reversed.

When in the more complicated metres of poetry two or three long beats fall into one group, one of these beats must stand out as the strongest, while the other (or both others) must be somewhat weaker. This occurs naturally in recitation and must—in proportion to the recitation—be shown in eurythmy by a lesser stress on the downward movement of the arms. Epimeleia's monologue from Goethe's *Pandora* may serve as an example. Here the metre is the so-called Ionicus a minore (∪ ∪ — —). In this rhythm the third syllable bears the strongest emphasis, whereas the fourth, though also a long beat, is somewhat weaker :

∪ ∪ — —
Meinen Angstruf,
∪ ∪ — —
um mich selbst nicht,
∪ ∪ — —
ich bedarf's nicht
∪ ∪ — —
aber hört ihn !..., and so on.

Although the same arm movement is employed for the two successive long beats, a difference in the degree of emphasis must be made apparent.

Now rhythm must also be expressed by walking, by the step, and this is done in such a way that the unaccented beat is accompanied by a small and not too vigorous step, while with the accented beat the step must be wide and the tread of the foot on the ground firm and determined. This marking of the rhythm with the feet is later carried out simultaneously with the movements of the arms, whereby an indication of the rhythm is brought into the whole body through the greater or lesser tension of the muscles and the slight raising and lowering of the body which results.

This rhythmic action of the feet may of course be varied in many ways.*With a Troche, for instance, instead of the short beat being shown by a whole step, this beat may just be indicated by slightly raising the back foot and lightly retouching the ground on the same spot, or even drawing the

---

* The rod-exercises can also be practiced to metric rhythm.

foot somewhat forwards. Similarly, with the Iambus, the foot which is in front can indicate the short syllable by just touching the ground with the toes, then treading vigorously with the long beat. For the practice of the Anapest a light springing movement is well adapted; the two short beats are shown by two little steps, and the following long beat by a wide, flying jump forwards, at the same time throwing the other foot out behind. Here, however, special care must be taken that, in the jump, the movements of the whole body are skillfully and not inharmoniously carried out. With such a jump as this a strong backward throw of the head and upper part of the body may be said to come about of itself. This is the necessary counter-movement, a contrary impetus enabling one to spring forwards freely and far. A similar movement can be carried out with the arms: during the two short beats —the run before the jump, so to speak—the arms are held lightly curved over the breast (the head also being slightly bent), and are then thrown freely outwards at the moment of jumping. This bending and, stretching of the arms already approaches that method of marking the rhythm in which the unaccented beat is expressed by an *o*, and the accented beat by an *i*. Before this can be explained in detail, however, the vowels and their equivalent movements must first be described.

III

VOWELS, DIPHTHONGS, MODIFIED VOWELS, AND THEIR EXPRESSION IN EURYTHMY

The origin of the eurythmy-gestures for the sounds of speech was a subject upon which Dr. Steiner spoke frequently and from ever differing points of view. In a short foreword given before a eurythmy performance in Vienna, June 12th, 1922, he threw light upon the genesis of this most fundamental part of eurythmy in the following words: 'The gestures which succeed in manifesting themselves outwardly in eurythmy are also present in germ (as organic and will-tendency) in both song and speech; there, however, at the moment of arising they are transformed into what is produced by the organs connected with singing and speaking. In eurythmy these *tendencies,* as perceived by sensible-super-sensible vision, are arrested, whereby the entire human being (finding expression in the visible) becomes an organism of song and speech.'

And in a foreword, April 5th, 1920, in Dornach: 'The element of *music,* which is more particularly present in the vowel-sounds of speech, this musical element, is inwardly connected with the laying hold of the Spiritual in the individual human soul. When the human being grows together, as it were, with the Spiritual *within himself,* and experiences within himself the impressions which outer Nature can make upon him, this brings about, expressed in the musical element of the vowels, a unison, an inner unison of experience, between the human being and the things and processes outside him....On the other side we have the consonantal element, that element wherein man penetrates less into himself, and for this very reason plunges down and surrenders himself to outer processes and things. This is the plastic element, the inner element of painting. It is a fact that two creative artistic elements in the human being stream together, albeit unconsciously, in the sounds of speech. Eurythmy gives outer form to what is here experienced by man through the image itself.'

In the impressive and magnificent words, with which, in the Eurythmy Lectures of the year 1924, Rudolf Steiner once again called up into consciousness these significant human experiences underlying the sounds of speech, we have the most comprehensive and detailed survey he ever gave of this subject.

The following brief explanation of the *vowels* is merely intended to show the way in which the eurythmy movements are formed, and hence it will only point out what is absolutely necessary in order that the beginner may learn to permeate the gestures with these primal experiences of the sounds.

With the sound *a**, where this is used as an interjection, we are indeed still conscious of this underlying experience. When something amazes us, when the grandeur, the sublimity of something outside us calls up in us the mood of wonder, perhaps even of awe or dread, we pour this feeling into the exclamation *Ah!* Thus, wherever an *a*-sound is to be expressed in eurythmy, the eurythmist must awaken this inner mood of *wonder,* of *amazement.** A feeling of being on the

---

Owing to the fact that certain German examples have had to be retained in the translation of this book, the German pronunciation of the vowel-sounds has been consistently used throughout.
German *a*, English ah (as in father)
German *a*, English *a*, (as in say)
German *ee*, English *ee*, (as in feet)
German *ei*, English *i*, (as in light)
German *au*, English *ow* (as in how)
German *eu*, English *oi* (as in joy)

* As already mentioned in the preface, the expressions employed by Dr. Steiner himself in his explanations are here printed in italics.

defensive may also be experienced here; the soul frequently seeks to defend itself against being overwhelmed by a mighty impression. (The activity of the genius of language in the formation of words, and how this can still be demonstrated in the experiences revealing themselves in eurythmy, and even in modern languages—on this subject also we find elucidation in Dr. Steiner's Course of Lectures: *Eurythmy as Visible Speech*, and also in the Course: *Speech-Formation and Dramatic Art*.)

The movement for a is the *angle;* it is a 'reaching-out in two directions '—usually with the arms (see Lecture III). But, indeed, an a can find expression in 'every angle', for example, in the angle formed between hand and forearm by means of an 'upward bending of the hands or in the angle arising between two fingers when they are stretched apart,[†] and so on. With the feet also an angle can be formed. When only one arm is raised, either sideways or in any direction, the angle thus arising between body and arm can also form a quite correct means of expression for the sound *a*. Now in language the *a*-sound can be either prolonged or short, with every possible gradation between. These differentiations must naturally be taken into account and reproduced. In the word *atmen* (to breathe), for instance, the formation of the *a* would be slower and more sustained, the movement would, as it were, have to be wider in sound than in the word *rasch* (quick). In the vowel-sounds especially one must be able to listen to one's own movements, to exert a greater or lesser tension of the muscles, just as though playing on an instrument; for it is in the vowel-sounds that the musical element of speech lies.

In order to enter completely into the experience of the *a*, Poems must be chosen and practiced into which this mood of

---

[†] See Appendix.

wonder, of amazement, has been conjured by the introduction of many *a*-sounds, either consciously on the part of the poet, or through an artistic instinct for language. We find an example of this in a poem by Christian Morgenstern, where just this very mood of dread in the presence of an unimagined greatness is expressed by a remarkable number of *a*-sounds:

Du hast die Hand schon am Portal
und tastest nach der Klinke Hand,
(denn noch erhellt sie dir kein Strahl.)

Du wirst erst wach, wenn sie sie fand,
sei's dieses, sei's das nächste Mal;
dann wirst du weiss stehn wie die Wand

davor du lange dumpf geirrt;
und wie ein Leichnam hinfällt, wird
dein Leib hinfallen in den Sand.

When in listening to this poem the pupil is only concerned with the a-sounds and brings these only to expression in movement, the opportunity arises of entering with the whole soul into the inner being of *a*

The *e* is expressed in eurythmy by 'every—though only indicated—crossing of the limbs', whether it be arms, hands or feet that are crossed, or whether the arm forms a cross with head, breast or back. Dr. Steiner originally said that this gesture is connected with *fear,* but also with *holy fear* or *reverence,* and passing, so to speak, to the opposite extreme in the scale of feeling, with *disgust.* These brief indications gain clarity from the Speech-Eurythmy Lectures. It is there emphasized that everything depends upon the *touching* of the limbs when forming the cross. To quote: '*The touching ex-*

presses the feeling that something has been done to one; the holding the cross-posture is the resultant standing-up-against-it.[*] Here, as is so often the case in what was later said, the inner process is elaborated more in detail. The *fear* is, as it were, present in the experience as an undercurrent, and the human being gains resistance in *reverence* or hardens himself in *disgust*. This is only brought forward as an example to show that one must not cling in *a* one-sided manner to any single description. A whole series of feelings befits each single sound. And it is only by inwardly uniting these relative, mutually complementary experiences that one may attain to fullness of perception for the sounds of speech.

The *e*-mood can be entered into by taking poems expressing inner steadfastness or religious poems such as call forth a pronounced feeling of reverence, and directing the attention to all the *e*-sounds they may contain. If one seeks for single words possessing these characteristic moods many examples are to be found. For the purpose of practicing one can build sentences for oneself, as, for instance : *betend werden Seelen fest*, and so on. In the prefixes *ver—, er—, zer—, be—*, etc., all of which contain the *e*-sound, this strengthening, self-maintaining element, this determination and intensification, is always to be found: *verdoppeln, vermehren, bemächtigen, zermürben*, and so on.

In cases where it appears suitable to imbue the *e*-movement with especial solemnity and power, the crossing may be brought about by stretching out the arms in such a way that the whole body produces a cross. Should, for instance, the word *Mensch* (man) occur in a poem and shortly afterwards the word *Welt* (world) the comprehensive nature of the latter word could be brought to expression by means of

[*]Lecture III

the big cross.

In *i* man experiences his own *prototype;* it is the sound of *self-assertion* (see Lecture III). This strong consciousness of the personality finds expression in every stretched line—whereby one accentuates the feeling of being firmly within one's own bony system. The *i*-line may be most definitely experienced when both arms are stretched out sideways, not quite horizontal, but pointing diagonally from below upwards, so that the straight line passes unbroken from the finger-tips of one hand, through arm and shoulder, to the finger-tips of the other hand. This is the clearest impression of the sound *i*. But the stretched line can also be described with one finger, or with the direction of the gaze of the eyes.

In the word *ich* (I) this *i*-character is already present, but it is still more strongly emphasized in the sentence: *ich bin da* (here I am).[*] Here the 'self-assertive' *i*-sound occurs twice, followed by the *a*-sound, with its 'wonder at one's own being'. This sentence is expressed in the following way: first the left arm and left leg are stretched out sideways (so that both limbs lie parallel), and are then drawn back again; now the same thing is carried out with right arm and right leg. When these successive movements are, as it were, arrested, this form[†] arises: (see diagram).

---

[*] In an English class the vowel-sounds may be kept the same as the German by putting the sentence in plural-form: *Here we are.* (Translator's Note.)

[†] See Appendix.

VOWELS, DIPHTHONGS, MODIFIED VOWELS, AND THEIR EXPRESSION IN EURYTHMY

Just as the stretched line is felt to be the essential expression for the sound *i*, so the sound *o* is experienced wherever the limbs are brought together in an encircling movement.

The feeling of 'slipping out of oneself', of 'loving affection' also 'of embracing something in wonder' lies in this movement. The arms form a gesture similar to that carried out by the organs of speech, larynx, mouth and lips, in the pronunciation of the sound *o*.* This is true indeed of all the sounds. It can be very clearly noticed when the eurythmy movements for the vowels *a, o, u,* are formed one after the other. First the widely opened angle of the arms, corresponding exactly to the position of the mouth, of upper and lower jaw, when uttering *a*; then the rounded movement of the arms

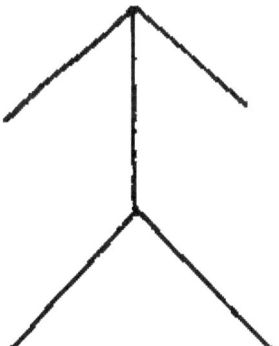

similar to the rounding of the lips in *o* ; and then the closing in of the arms in the close, firm pressure of the eurythmy *u*, just as the lips come together to let this sound emanate from them. With *u* the arms are drawn close to each other in a thin, nar-

---

* There is an English sound: *o* as in *love,* which Dr. Steiner described as the open *o* It has a slight tendency to become a, and the movement is the circular movement for *o*, which finally opens out towards the angle in an upward direction. The coloring of a must remain in indication only.

row movement. It suffices indeed when this is in so far indicated that the arms lie parallel with each other, but they may also be firmly pressed against the body, as though with a feeling of *fear* or *chill*. The movement first emphasized by Dr. Steiner as the movement for *u* was a *reaching-upwards* (keeping the arms in the aforesaid position). 'The mystic union with the Divine' can be suggested in this way by the *u*-gesture, while *amazement* (a dimmer, vaguer amazement) may also be experienced.

There yet remains the description of the modified vowels and diphthongs: *ä, ü, ö, du, eu, au, ei.**

The *ä* is similar to a, but the movement is such that either both hands or both feet *are placed one behind the other*. Ü is a *narrow pressing together of arms or legs;* the arms must be slightly twisted so that the inner side of the forearm is turned outwards. This movement is, as it were, of a sliding nature, one arm stroking down the other. Two people can express the *ü* by 'dancing past one another'. As something joyful lies in this sound, a *joyous wonder*, it may also be accompanied by a little spring into the air. (Where desirable this may also occur with the sound *u*, in the word *Juchhe!* (hurrah), for instance.) Another type of spring makes its appearance in the sounds *ö* and *äu*. With *ö*, when really correctly carried out, the jump must be *from the circumference towards the centre*. This sound is, as it were, torn asunder; it is *dissonant*. This is indicated in the manner of jumping, and also with the arms, in that the movement for *o* in the air is speedily 'torn apart'.

---

* ä is equivalent in English eurhythmy to the sound *a* as in and.
ü may be used where *ee* is preceded by *w* as in *sweet*.
ö as in *bird*.
äu has no English equivalent.
eu as in *joy*.
au as in *how*.
ei as in *eye*.

With *äu* the jump is firmly on to the ground; something 'oppressed', something heavy must here come to expression. The limbs are constricted, the arms are held to the side, bent back towards the shoulder, the elbow in the hand, and so on. *Eu* is an indicating gesture; the left hand is laid on the heart, while the right points towards some definite spot. *Au* is expressed by every 'touching of one's own body'; *ei* by 'every movement of the whole body'. With the latter sound a tender, affectionate feeling is expressed, as though saying to a child: 'How nice.'

In Lecture VII of the Speech-Eurythmy Course Dr. Steiner showed us a new way of forming the diphthongs, namely this, that the two component vowels—the first in its beginning, the second in its terminating stage—should both be represented in the movement. It seems apparent, however, that the possibilities of expressing the diphthongs originally given still hold good, and that it is a question of discovering in each separate case which type of movement to use.

Now when the pupil has practiced these single sounds, when they have been fully explained and combined in various sequences, he may then pass on to the expression of poems by means of the vowels, to reproducing in movement, that is to say, either all, or at least the most emphasized and prominent vowels contained in a certain poem. One will naturally choose poems where the vowel-element predominates, and these will be such as express intimate moods of soul, or indeed anything of a feeling nature. Contemplative, descriptive or dramatic poems make more demand upon the movements for the consonants. When making use of the movements for the vowels, the aim must be to impart to these movements the musical line of the vowels themselves ; they must be increased or decreased with the flow and ebb of the vowel-sounds, and this inner intensity must be brought to such a pitch that the movements are actually experienced as sound.

This realization of the musical element must be combined with a feeling for light and darkness, warmth and cold in the movements. Every *stretched movement* of the arms must be accompanied by the feeling as of *light* radiating outwards; the world around becomes lighter. In *curved movements* the 'light is inwardly consumed' and *darkness* arises in man's environment. From this point of view *a* and *i* are *light sounds,* whereas *o* is dark.* Similar to light and darkness is it with warmth and cold. *Warmth* (in the sense of soul and spirit) streams outwards in movement; the closer the sounds are kept to the body the more are they imbued with *cold.* These different shadings must be taken into consideration when it is a question of representing the inner mood and feeling of a poem; but even in the simple, rhythmic marking of the vowels in a text, this interchange of light, warmth and increasing tone on the one hand, and darkness, cold and decreasing tone on the other hand, can be expressed in the ebb and flow of the movement.* For instance, the emphasize vowel-sound may be formed with a wide movement outwards or upwards, while the un-emphasized vowel is drawn back and the movement made smaller and close to the body. The *e,* for instance, which occurs so frequently at the beginning or end of words, may be formed close to the breast and with the hands only. This outspreading (or vigorous outward-thrusting) of the movement and its subsequent withdrawal brings the rhythm into which the vowels are woven to visible expression.

It has already been mentioned that one definite way of marking the metric beat consists in accompanying the ac-

---

* See Appendix.
* For rhythm, with its up and down beats, may well be felt as an interplay between light and darkness, warmth and cold, and expressed accordingly.

cented syllable (no matter what the vowel-sound may be) with *i,* the unaccented syllable with *o.* Here we have a clear example of the alternating stretched and curved movements. (In indication this is indeed already contained in the simple method of marking the rhythm first described.) This metric movement in *i o* creates a beautiful impression when carried out by a whole chorus ranged in a half-circle. The vowel-sounds contained in the poem, the soul-element, are represented by a solo-eurythmist standing in the center front of the group. The chorus does the movements either standing still or rhythmically stepping up and down, forwards and backwards. When the *i* is formed in such a way that one arm is directed more upwards, the other more downwards, a harmonious effect is produced by doing the movements with alternate arms; thus once with the right arm up, the next long beat with the left arm up, then the right arm, and so on. The *o* is taken somewhat lower, so that a difference is also made in the zone of the two movements.

We have here mainly dealt with the movements of the arms, and it must be added that everything carried out by the arms represents the expression in movement of the *soul* element (the element of feeling). The way in which the head is held expresses, as we shall learn later, the relationship with the *spiritual;* and what is done with the feet is bound up with the *earth,* with the evolution of the *will* in the realm of the earthly. Such exercises, for instance, as the previously mentioned walking-exercises, in which the feet especially have to exert activity, which entail a special activity of the feet, will always work particularly strongly upon the development of the will. A further exercise which exerts and strengthens the will-forces will be described in the next chapter.

IV

ALLITERATION

Alliteration, or the initial rhyme, is, as is well known, the old form of Nordic poetry. It may be helpful to quote here a short passage from the Explanatory Notes to Simrock's translation of the Edda: 'Just as the rhyme at the end of a line depends upon similarity of sound in the terminal syllable ... so alliteration, or the rhymed first sound, demands similarity of sound in the initial syllable; that is to say, the alliterative rhyme simply consists in the sameness of the initial letters, in which case any vowel-sound serves the purpose, one being interchangeable with the other. For example: Einst war das Alter, da Ymir lebte. As a general rule three of these rhymed initial letters go to make up one rhyme. One of these bears the strongest accent, the other two being regarded as secondary. These latter are introduced into the first half of the line, and the main alliterated syllable, which occurs in the second part of the line, is led up to, as in the example just quoted or in the following example: Sie wollen, dass ich Walwaters Wirken künde. When this main alliterated sound is not a simple sound but the combination of *St* or *Sp,* this must also be the case with the secondary syllables. For example: '*Am starken Stamm, im Staub der Erde...*'(Eddische Verskunst.)

We know from Rudolf Steiner's spiritual scientific researches into history that the war-cry with which the old Germanic peoples hurled themselves into battle took this alliterative form, for instance, *Ziu zwing Zwist*. On the march, too, alliterations were uttered—one must imagine an immense roaring and thundering of voices—while every alliterated sound was accompanied by a blow on the shield.

Something of this feeling must be recaptured to-day when marching to alliteration. One must transport oneself into the wild climate of the north and picture the raging storm against which the battle hordes had to contend. Thus the vigour and determination with which one foot is set down in front of the other gives the alliteration its character. The step which accompanies each alliterative sound must be stamped (not with the whole foot at once, however, but with the ball of the foot first), the body remaining immovable and unflinching, and the gaze of the eyes directed straight ahead with a steadfast impulse of will. The accented syllables which are not alliterative are marked, not with a step, but with the gesture for the vowel-sound contained in the word.

Let us take as an example an alliteration from the *Song of the Nibelung* by Wilhelm Jordan :

Da schollen die Schilde von den Schäften der Lanzen,
Da klangen und klirrten die Klingen der Schwerter.

Here we should have to take a step with: *schollen, Schilde, Schäften*, and then with the word *Lanzen* make the gesture for a standing still; again three steps with *klangen, klirrten, Kling*en and with *Schwerter,* once more standing still, the gesture for *e.*

(It must also be mentioned that in the case of German compound words the root-syllable only should be alliterated.)

In this marching to alliteration equal attention and emphasis must be given to each step, and by this means one accustoms oneself to taking steps of the same length with both right and left foot. As a general rule the right foot takes longer steps, which is the cause of the well-known fact that people in a mist walk round and round in a circle.

When this marching to alliteration is carried out by several together, care must be taken that no one, either through too large or too small steps, gets out of the line— whether marching forwards or backwards. In this exercise a military discipline must always hold sway.

This is the simplest way of expressing the alliteration. More complicated methods only come into consideration when the movements for the consonants have been learned and they will then be described.

V

EDUCATIONAL EURYTHMY EXERCISES

Nearly all the educational eurythmy exercises are intended to be practiced by a number of people together; this also applies to the rod exercises, to walking and to the exercises for beating time. In cases where private tuition is necessary, or where, as frequently occurs, the pupil wishes thoroughly to practice the exercises by himself, it must be realized that the effects, even if no less strong, will be of quite another order than when these same exercises are worked at by several people together. The fact is that when they are carried out by one person alone it is the *etheric body*[*] (or body of formative forces) which is most strongly influenced; whereas it is the *astral body*[†] in particular which is ennobled, harmonized and developed when they are practiced by several people at once.

In the teaching of children (in so far, at least, as this is not a question of specialized cases, either sick or very difficult children) one can hardly conceive these exercises as being taught except in a class. Indeed the following exercises, which with their harmonizing and educative influences were specially given for children, are definitely built up on the working-together of a group.[‡]

The first exercise here described is based upon what takes place in the human being—whether child or adult—when he *weeps* or *laughs*. A really satisfying explanation of the inner processes taking place in man's being when he falls into these two states can only be furnished by Spiritual Science. The following sentences from a lecture on this subject, given by

---
[*] See Appendix.
[†] See Apeendix.
[‡] See Apeendix.

Dr. Steiner in Berlin in the year 1909, are here quoted in order that one may grasp the concepts necessary to the understanding of this eurythmy exercise :

'....For laughter and weeping are in reality nothing other than a finely organized, intimate expression of the ego-being in the corporeal being. What happens, for instance, when anyone weeps? Weeping can only come about when in some way or other the ego feels itself weak in comparison to its environment. When the ego is not within the organism, when it is not really individualized that is to say, this feeling of weakness over against the outer world cannot make its appearance. Man as the possessor of an individual ego feels a certain element of discord, a certain disharmony in his relationship to the outer world; and this feeling of disharmony manifests itself in an attitude of defense, in a sort of counter-attack. *How* is this brought about ? By the ego causing the astral body to contract. It may be said : In grief, which finds expression in weeping, the ego feels a certain disharmony with the outer world and it seeks to compensate for this by contracting the astral body, by, as it were, concentrating its forces. This is the spiritual process underlying weeping.... What is laughter ? The process underlying laughter is exactly the opposite. The ego, so to speak, leaves the astral body relaxed, allows its forces to spread outwards, to expand. Whereas the state of weeping is brought about by the contraction of the astral body, laughter is induced by its relaxation, its expansion. This may be spiritually observed. In every case of weeping clairvoyant consciousness can definitely state that there is a contraction of the astral body through the ego. In every case of laughter there is an expansion, a spreading outwards, an inflation of the astral body brought about by the ego....'

'....Laughter is, in a certain sense, an expression of egotism, of the ego-being, and this comes about through the fact that laughter, if one really looks into it, may always be traced back to the human being feeling himself superior to his surroundings, to what is happening in his environment.'

'....This is why laughter can be so healthy, and one should by no means condemn outright all egotism, not even this puffing-up-of-oneself; for laughter can be very healthy when in a justifiable way it strengthens a person in his feeling of self, when it raises him up over himself....'

'....It is just the happy medium between grief and joy which can contribute so infinitely much to human evolution. When grief and joy find their justification in the outer world, not depending on the inner life alone, when the ego, alternating between these two states, continually finds its right relationship to the outer world, then pain and joy can become real factors in the evolution of mankind.'

Now we shall be able to understand the whole moral and educational significance of this exercise, which has as its aim the harmonizing, in artistic form, of these two states. It runs as follows: The children - or grown-up people - stand in pairs facing each other a considerable distance apart; and now each individual tries to conjure up a vivid impression of having been attacked by the other one; he feels himself threatened from outside and at first is conscious of his own weakness; then, gathering all his forces together, he clenches his flats, presses them against his breast, tightens the muscles of arms, shoulders and neck with an almost convulsive intensity, bends the head as if to gather strength, and in this position—an externally visible expression of the contraction which takes place in the astral body in weeping—advances upon the other with firm, self-assertive steps. The two are now standing close in front of each other and each one must consciously conjure up the feeling: But it is I who am really superior in strength; my opponent cannot harm me! This strength; my opponent cannot harm me! This mood calls forth quite another posture; the head is raised, the chest expands as the breath is inhaled, the clenched fingers are relaxed, the arms stretched outwards—the whole body has become the expression of *laughter,* of the feeling of *superiority,* of healthy self-assurance. At this point the two turn round back to back and run to their first places.

This *exercise—Contraction* and *Expansion* as it is called, brings about a continuous inner alternation between the two states of *weeping* and *laughter,* conjuring them forth in artistic form, and at the same time, by means of strengthened self-assurance, develops in the children 'increased intelligence and the faculty of taking initiative.'

These educational eurythmy exercises have a direct bearing upon life itself and should therefore be introduced into its daily routine. In this connection Dr. Steiner once mentioned how refreshing and health-giving it would be for school-children if in the pauses between their ordinary lessons, they were made to practice for a few minutes a certain exercise which later became known as the *Energy Dance.* The *Power of communal work* would result from the practice of this exercise.

What is the nature of the *Energy Dance* and its companion exercise, the *Peace Dance?* Let us think of two different triangles, the one developed out of the equilateral triangle in such a way that it is pulled out lengthways, having two long side lines and a short bottom line; the other pressed out into width, with a long bottom line and the two side lines short.

I.

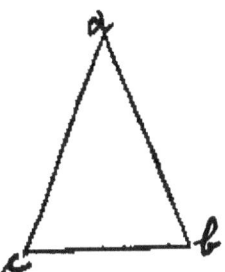

Taking the first triangle and moving its lines beginning from point a there will be a distinct feeling of striving towards the bottom line (which is indicated by placing a rod on the ground). One is moving towards a goal and energy must be developed in order to attain it.* It is quite different with the second triangle.

II.

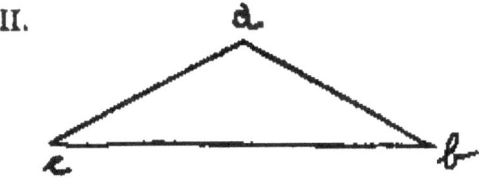

Again there is a certain striving, but here at the same time one feels checked by the bottom line, which has, as it were, been forced backwards: there is a wish to go further, but this line—the rod, that is to say—interferes; one must exercise restraint, discretion: the *Peace Dance*. This exercise has a 'calming effect upon quarrelsome children'; when carried out daily in a group the love of peace and harmony will gradually make its appearance.

* See Appendix.

The rhythm to which both these forms should be stepped is the Anapest; with the Energy Dance: two Anapests to each of the longer lines and one to the short line; with the Peace Dance: one Anapest to each of the short lines and two to the long line. (Where a text, as for instance, the one given by Dr. Steiner in the XII Eurythmy Lecture, is recited to this exercise, the number of Anapests can, of course, be altered.) The tempo varies. Either the two side lines may be moved quickly, again as indicated by Dr. Steiner in Lecture XII, or one may employ the method which he formerly recommended for most of these exercises—namely beginning with a slow tempo, getting faster and faster, finally returning again to the original tempo. Here, of course, it is the reciter who must determine this increase and decrease of speed; the pupil must follow exactly, his whole being must become ear so that he may instantaneously adjust himself to each variation. The habit is thus formed of following each sound or tone as it strikes the ear from outside, of being pliable and not obliged to remain egotistically bound to a rhythm entirely dependent on himself.

The educational exercises hitherto described, and also the following exercises, should be practiced in this living and mobile way. In the case of the Energy Dance the increased speed may well be combined with an increase in the size of the form, the two long lines being extended further and further until the step which falls on the accented beat passes over to a wide spring.

Now in addition this dance-like movement to the triangle must be given more definite shape and form by means of sounds, and here indeed the vowels in question must not be felt as arm movements merely, but the actual sides of the triangle must be experienced as sounds projected into space. The line with which one begins must be felt as *i;* it is the straight line, defining a *single direction* of space, stretched out just as in the ordinary way the arm is stretched out. The movement of the body must be laid right into this line of the form; as the line begins towards the left, the left shoulder must be pushed somewhat forwards, the arm slipping, as it were, into an invisible *i* drawn through space. The second line which is joined to the first line by an angle, coming as it does from a different direction, forms a cross, an *e,* which would be visible if the two lines were projected beyond the point where they meet. And the third line, which closes the form, must be understood as an *u* by making oneself realize how the holding-on-to-oneself, the withdrawing-into oneself, the stiffening-of-oneself of the *u* (See Lectures II and III) correspond to this leading-back-into-itself of the form.

These three vowels must be intoned by the reciter to a musical interval, *i* and *e* to the key-note, *u* to the minor third above it. Dr. Steiner stated further that these dances were practiced in the Greek Mystery Centers and that consequently we are here dealing with old temple dances. The dancers took up their position in a circle, each one planting his rod in the earth a certain distance in front of him, and with this as a goal the movement to the triangle form began. The reciter stood in the center (as with us when this exercise is being taught) calling out the three vowel sounds to the aforementioned interval in a loud, resonant voice, simultaneously marking the Anapestic rhythm by soft and loud blows with his rod on the ground.

At this point it may be well to mention the emphasis laid by Dr. Steiner upon the fact that (apart from certain exercises practiced to choral speaking with a view to strengthening the feeling of the community) wherever it is a question of giving artistic expression in eurythmy to the sounds of speech, the eurythmists as they move should never themselves recite. It is easy to see that it would then be impossible to attain to that which really gives eurythmy its essential character, namely the *repression* of the tone so that it may be metamorphosed in order to reappear as movement. Simultaneous movement and recitation would always be a sort of hybrid and the movements to the sounds of speech could never be carried out with the concentration and intensity necessary to artistic results.

The very next exercise to be described belongs to those few exercises where the pupils themselves speak the accompanying words in chorus. This is :

The exercise against jealousy and false ambition. Here it is not so much a question of letting the sound flow into the gesture, but rather of the moral effect of the group movement; and in order to strengthen this effect all those taking part together speak the words: 'I and you, you and I, I and you, you and I—are we.' The first position of the exercise is a circle, each person standing two or three paces away from the next;

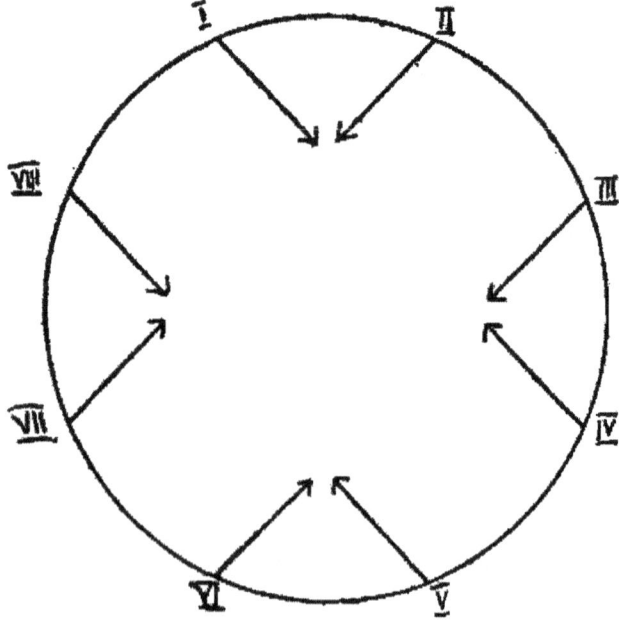

they are grouped in pairs, the two turned slightly towards each other and looking each other in the face. Now they begin to speak the words 'I and you', moving towards each other in a diagonal direction; with the third step, to the word 'you', they stand close together, shoulder to shoulder. (See diagram.)

They then retrace their steps, still looking at each other, with the words 'you and I'.

These two lines are repeated once more and then, with the words 'are we' they all—continuing their own direction and consequently crossing with their partners—run forwards and form a small central circle, where they either take hands or all together make the sound *i*. Retracing the line (with the words 'I and you, you and I') at the same spot as in the forward form but now walking backwards, they cross once more and when each one has regained his original position the exercise begins anew. (See diagram.)

Each individual, each 'I' has approached the other, the same spot as in 'you', then withdrawn from him, again approached, and finally been caught up into the circle which unites them all. This exercise, during which attention is so strongly directed to one's fellow men, to the community, has as its aim the eradication of everything of the nature of 'envy', 'egotism' or 'false ambition'—the very qualities that engender antipathy.

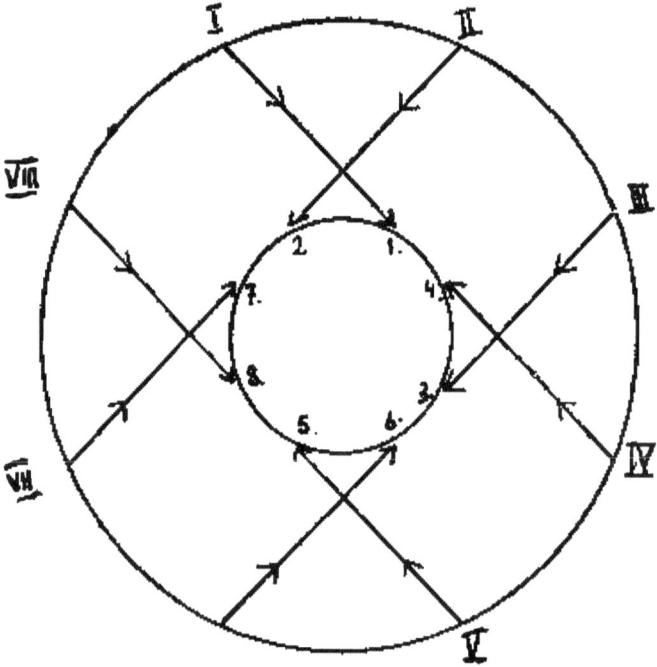

The arms either make the movements for the vowel - sounds contained in the words: *ei u, ei u* and so on; or they may be held in a gesture expressing the mood of *lightness*—a gesture which will be described later together with other eurythmy movements.

We now come to certain 'space-forms' and exercises, all of which spring from the same origin as the three last described: they were Greek temple dances, choral-forms, practiced in the mystery centers and revealed to public gaze at the religious festivals. The presence of the God Dionysos was felt as a direct experience when the groups formed themselves into the circle.

These space-forms have been awakened to new life by Dr. Steiner in the eurythmy exercises and explained to us in their deepest significance. In this connection be spoke of certain lines in space which accurately portray what is experienced by man as the *realization of his own being* and his *relationship with others*. It is just these experiences which find expression in the use of the personal pronouns:

'Thou, he, we, you and they'; and for each of these words Dr. Steiner gave a corresponding form in space.

'I'—a straight line forwards and backwards. We shall understand that this line is the expression in movement for 'I 'when we consider how closely this going somewhere and turning-back-into-oneself corresponds to the conception of 'I'. When we accurately observe this inner experience of 'I' and then compare it with a line which turns back on to itself we shall comprehend the words The line which on its backward journey touches every point of its forward journey is the expression for *I.*'

'A line which on its backward journey only touches itself at one point is the expression for *Thou.*' This is the lemniscate with all its variations.

This form, which does not retrace its original path but seeks another, which goes away from itself and only suggests a transient coming-back-to-itself at one point, the point where it crosses—this form by its very nature represents what takes place in the soul in the experience of 'Thou'.

When such a form is carried out by several people at the

same time an impression is created of 'Thou' in the plural, of 'You'.

This can be developed into a kind of round dance, which, strengthened by certain words spoken in chorus by all those taking part, calls forth the *realization of mankind, as a whole,* the experience of 'You'. *Inner harmony* and *healthy merriment* are developed by these exercises in the lemniscate form.

They can be carried out in many ways. The pupils first place themselves in a circle and each one describes such a 'thou-form' to the center. Here again, as with the triangle exercises the movement is anapestic, each quarter of the form consisting of one Anapest.

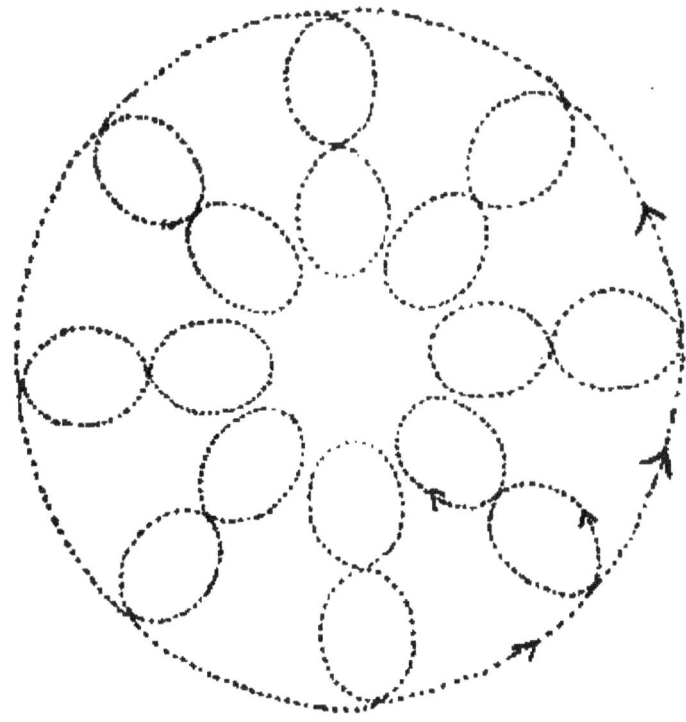

BASIC PRINCIPLES OF EURYTHMY

When each individual has described his form in four Anapests, he passes along the periphery of the circle in two Anapests to the next place, where he begins anew; thus the movement continues unbroken. (During the whole exercise the faces should remain turned towards the center.)

One can also begin the lemniscate in the middle, that is to say, where the line crosses, and complete it at the same point, which is also the starting-point for the transition to the next form.

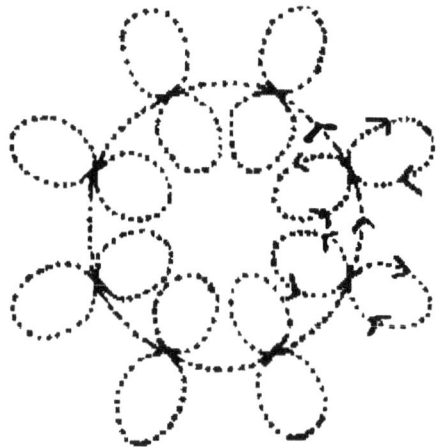

Or a third possibility is that each one moves the lemniscate backwards, beginning at the top, thus laying the entire form behind and making the transition along the inner circle.

In this exercise the arms are held in one of the gestures still to be described—gestures expressing various moods of soul---or else the movements for the vowel-sounds are used. Poems in anapestic rhythm dealing with subjects of *general*

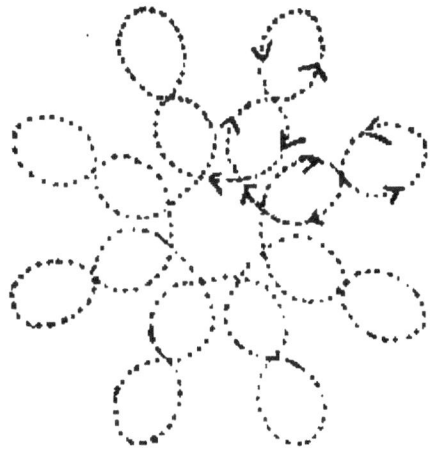

human interest will best strengthen the mood and feeling this exercise is intended to call forth. For instance:

> 'Saget an, saget an, was ihr treibt,
> Dass ihr heiter und strahlend verbleibt?
> Habt den Jungborn im Tann ihr erschaut?
> Hat ein Weiser euch Tränke gebraut?'
>
> 'Wohl, so wisst, ja, ein Spruch ward uns kund,
> Aus der Weisheit entsiegeltem Mund.
> Und wir halten Und üben ihn ganz:
> Jede Zeit hat im Jahr ihren Tanz!'
>
> *O. Fränkl*

These verses on account of their joyous character are also well adapted to the form of lemniscate known as 'merry'.

Here there is a certain divergence from the original form. Each loop is carried out in two Anapests. The body must rapidly follow the changing directions of the form, and in order that the circle formed by the outer loops may not spread too widely the pupils are made to join hands.

A further metamorphosis is the *harmonious* lemniscate. This arises when one pictures the original form pulled downwards, as it were, at either end.

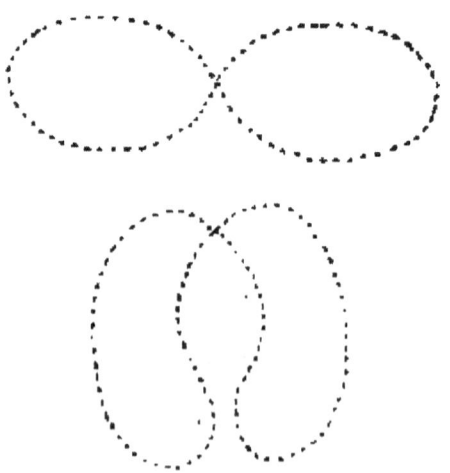

When carrying out this form special care must be taken that the curve of the two inner lines is well brought out. Both the outer and inner lines of the form are moved in three Anapests. Beginning at point A, for instance, (walking backwards), in

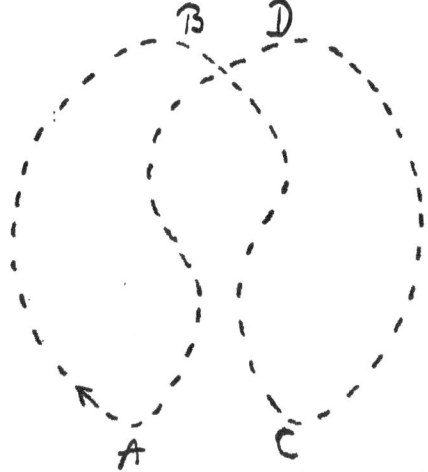

three Anapests one will have arrived at B; and now, taking the inner line to point C the first Anapest (the steps of which must naturally be somewhat smaller than on the outer line) is in this direction :

the second in this :

and the third once more in this direction :

thus bringing about the following wave-like form:

Then, again moving backwards, there follows the outer curve between C and D; and the final inner line back to the starting point is taken in the way described for the line B-C.

This 'harmonious lemniscate' must be moved very freely and rhythmically, and here perhaps the first attempt may be made—though only after much repetition and when the exercise has become quite fluent—towards following all the curves of the form with the movements of the upper part of the body. One will most easily succeed in this if the arms are held in the position for *merry**; for in this supple bending in the form practically everything depends upon the harmonious movement of the shoulders, and this natural balance is best attained when the arms are held upwards, freely and lightly, as in the movement for *Merriment*.

If this exercise is carried out by two people, one of them starts at point A, moving backwards in the direction of B; the other, beginning at point C, moves towards D. If two more are added to the form, the third takes the direction B—C, the fourth D—A. This exercise can, however, be done in such a way that number two, who begins at point C, first takes the

---

* See chapter: Eurythmy Soul-Gestures

inner line, also in the direction of B ; they then pass each other at the point where the lines cross, and C who now has to move the bigger curve *(B A)*, gives way and passes behind the same thing occurring when they meet at this point for the second time.

If four pupils move the harmonious lemniscate in this way, one must imagine for the two newcomers a second form lying in the reversed direction, with the point where the lines cross in front. The second pair, moving forwards, begin their lemniscate at points a and *c,* a on the outer and *c* on the inner curve.

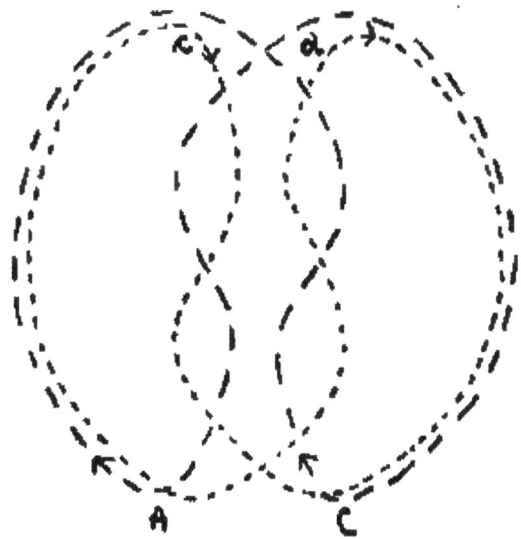

A beautiful group movement results when lemniscates in a sideways direction are laid into these two forms (one from right to left, the other from left to right). In this way eight pupils can participate in the exercise (those moving sideways employing the crossing-over step).

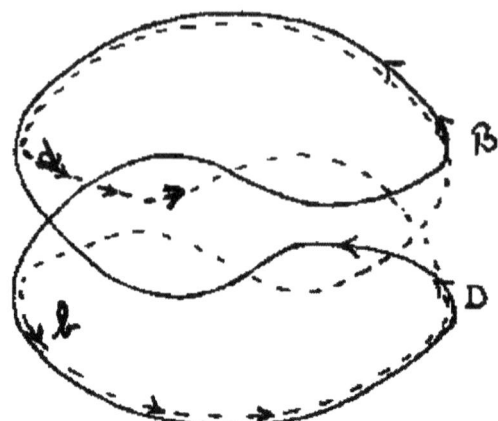

The harmonious mood engendered by this exercise or round dance is embodied in a poem by Franz Bühler, where this brotherly feeling of the 'you' is extended to the elements. (The four lines lacking for the completion of the lemniscate can be substituted by music, a number of chords in Anapestic rhythm.)

Überspringet ihr Wasser den Stein
Über schwinget ihr Wolken den Fels
Und verlachet sein starres Gebein.

Überklinget ihr Lüfte das Meer,
Übersinget das Wandelgewölk,
Wehet lachend sie unter euch her.

Doch ihr strahlen, ihr lichten, der Sonne,
Glühet hebend euch aus in die Welt,
Ziehet aus von dem goldenen Thron:

Dass ihr adelt der Felsen Gestalt,
Dass es adelt der Lüfte Getön,
Dass ihr adelt der Wasser Gewalt.

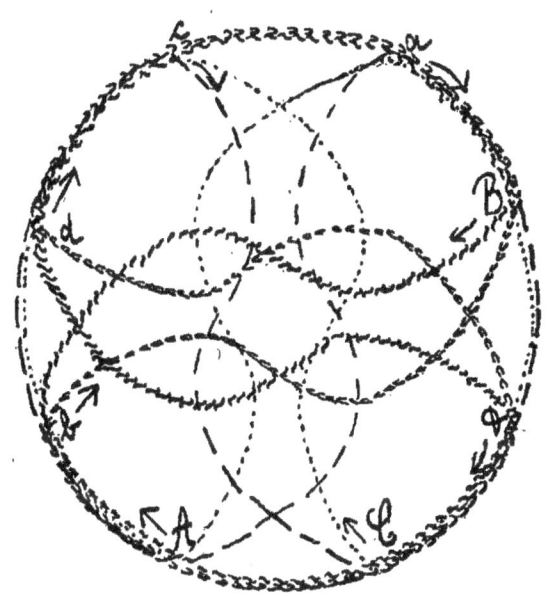

Just as one can pass over from 'thou' to 'you', one can also pass from 'I' to 'we', by letting the 'I'-line be simultaneously carried out by a number of people, all striving towards a common center and again returning to their starting-points.

Standing in the outer circle they all join hands; then, on the way to the center, accompanied by the word 'we' spoken in chorus, they all carry out the eurythmy movement for *i*. If one divides the line forwards and backwards into four steps each way, the exercise should be begun with the third step; thus the original position is not the outermost circle but somewhat narrower. Everyone now takes two steps towards the center and four steps back, twice intoning the word 'we', and so on, always forwards and backwards, the final position again being half-way up the form.

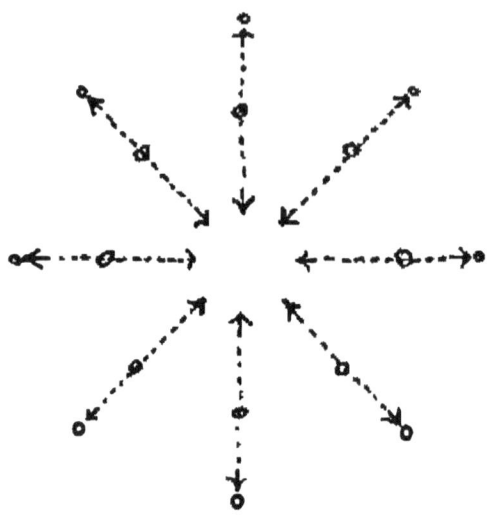

Joy in communal existence, delight in being together finds outlet in this exercise. Oneself, the *realization of oneself* is the experience of the 'I' or 'ich' form when carried out alone. When the sounds as well as the form are to be expressed, the forward journey, which need not consist of more than two steps, is accompanied by *i*, the backward journey by the consonant *ch : ich**.

In this *ch* there is a breathing-in of that spiritual element which is wafted towards man on the air. The experience inherent in the *ich* of the German language is twofold: firstly the strong emphasis on the personality, the feeling of the individual self, and then the opening-of-oneself to the higher being, the divine, which approaches man on the element of air. That we might feel the deep content of this word, Dr.

---

* In response to inquiry Rudolf Steiner recommended for English speaking pupils the vowel-sounds *i, o,* which sounds, *h* said, bring about a correct balance between *beig-within* and *going-out-of-oneself.* (Translator's note.)

Steiner gave for the practice of the sound *ch* the wonderful words: 'Ich—ein Hauch des Höchsten.' The movement consists of a gentle fan-like gesture of the hands from outside, from the circumference, towards oneself. When making this indrawing movement the hands can remain for a moment in front of the face, as if to waft the stream of the air towards the mouth.

Thus in these forms and gestures for the personal pronouns the relationships of soul and spirit expressed in these little words are made consciously and visibly manifest.

'He'—behind this word, when grasped in its innermost nature, there lies a feeling of veneration, a reverent yielding-oneself-up to something other than oneself, more particularly to some being of a super-human, divine nature. The form expressing this consists of a line which goes quite outside itself, which finds no point of contact with itself—it is the circular line. In the center of the circle one must imagine the being to whom this devotion is directed, the God in whose praise the

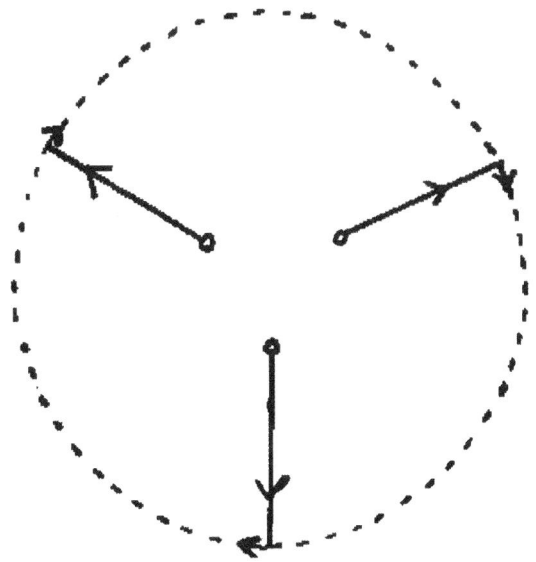

dance—for here again we have what was originally one of the temple dances dedicated to Dionysos—is carried out.

On one occasion—the first time that this circular form was demonstrated by a number of pupils—Rudolf Steiner, out of direct, creative intuition, spoke these magnificent words:

> Der Wolkendurchleuchter—
> Er durchleuchte,
> Er durchsonne,
> Er durchglühe,
> Er durchwärme
> Auch mich.

> (He who illuminates the clouds,
> May he illuminate,
> May he irradiate,
> May he inspire
> And fill with warmth and light,
> Even me.)

This hymn or prayer, adapted as it is to present-day human consciousness, is so built up that each of the four main lines begins with' Er (He)* and this imparts to the whole movement of the form that mood of sanctity upon which everything depends: *Reverence,* and the *tranquillity which is gained through reverence.*

The vowel-sounds are carried out with a feeling of solemnity, the gestures being directed towards the center, while the form is moved to the rhythm of the words, one step to each accented syllable. During the whole form the eyes re-

---

* In translating this verse it proved impossible to begin each line with the actual word 'he', as is the case in the original German.

main turned towards the center. To begin with— whether the exercise is carried out by one individual or a group—the first position is on the periphery of a small inner circle; with the opening words 'He who illuminates the clouds' everyone takes three steps[†] backwards so that the circle widens out; then, with the four middle lines, there follows the movement round the circumference; and with 'even me' (us) one again takes three steps towards the center (see drawing).

Now in order to express 'they' (third person plural) a number of these circular forms must be moved by several people simultaneously.

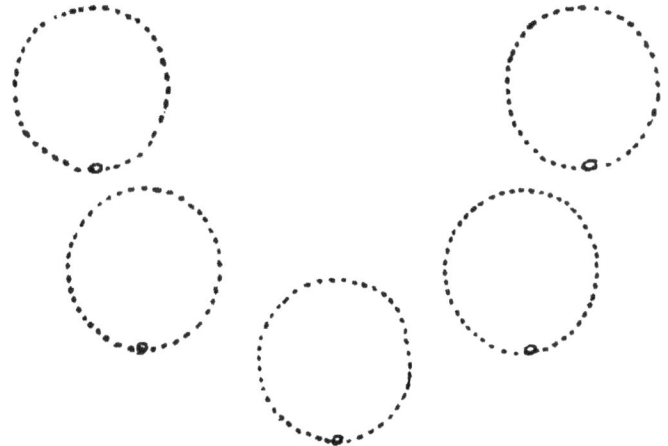

In the VIII Eurythmy Lecture Dr. Steiner designated further variations and metamorphoses of these forms for the personal pronouns, showing us how this I-, thou-, he-, we-, you-, they- character may be sought for in the lines or verses of poetry and how the corresponding forms may be applied. At this juncture, however, we will only describe the simplest

---

[†] When this exercise is practiced to the German text the accented beats require two steps instead of three throughout. (Translator's note.)

way in which these forms may be practiced.

Now we have yet another exercise, also falling into the Dionysian category, which expresses a quite definite aspect of the life of soul and spirit—the exercise known in eurythmy as *Question* and *Answer*. What speaks thus from soul to soul finds expression in eurythmy movement in spiral forms; the involving form, contracting and condensing from out-side inwards, represents the *Question,* the *Answer* being given by the spiral which begins in the center and winds outwards.

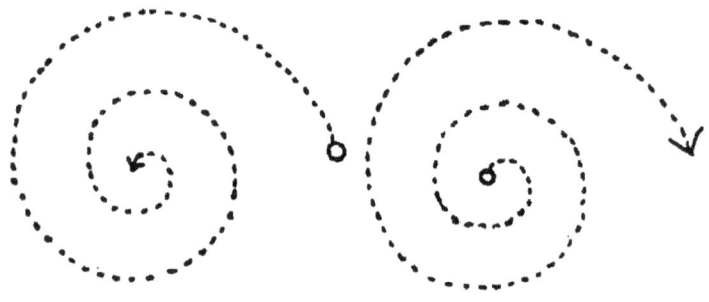

This dialogue, this interplay between question and answer, can be manifested in space by the movements either of two individuals or two groups (see diagram, next page). The one who first begins, taking half the space (to the left side as seen from the audience) describes a spiral by moving to the central point in six Anapests (the face always directed towards the front). While at the circumference of the circle the arms are held out widely (or else crossed at the back) then as the center is approached they are gradually drawn inwards till finally both hands lie over the heart. This gesture of the hands from the outside inwards approximates to a certain gesture of yearning, to an *u,* which is formed in such a way that the hands, starting from the position for a, are gradually bent inwards and drawn together till they reach the heart—the backs of the hands laid parallel one against the other forming the *u*. This gesture may, however, also be regarded as *Eu* (as the Greek *Eu)* the 'pointing towards the heart'.

When this first spiral, the question, has run its course, the answer begins from the opposite side. This answering form starts from the centre-point, the hands being laid over the

heart in the position just described, and the spiral winds its way outwards to the rhythm ∪ ∪ – ∪ ∪ —∪ ∪ – ∪ ∪ — (to the so-called 'second Ionicus'), ending with the arms opened out widely or else crossed over the back. The exercise can now be carried further, number one again beginning with the question, then the answer, and soon. If the eurythmists are placed in a semicircle the following figure will result:

This form can be accompanied by gestures for the sounds carried out in the appropriate mood. Later this basic form developed into a group exercise for which a definite sequence of consonants was chosen, so that, in the sounds also, there might be an indication of the question and answer. If this form is accompanied by a text in the correct rhythm the vowel-sounds can be carried out in such a way that the arm movements are directed as much as possible from outside inwards and *vice versa*. If, for instance, one takes the accented vowels from the following text, which is in question and answer form :

∪ ∪ − ∪ ∪ −∪ ∪ −
'Wie bewahr ich im Leben das Mass,
∪ ∪ −∪ ∪ −∪ ∪ −
Dass der Alltag die Seele nicht bricht ?

∪ ∪−∪ ∪ − −
'Lass umrahmen dein Tagwerk
∪ ∪ − ∪ − −
Von Erleben des Geistworts.'

(How preserve a true balance in life,
That the daily round crush not the soul?
Let the course of thy day's work
Be impregnate with God's word.)

O. FRÄNKL.

The gestures for the *a e a* of the first line must be formed with large and wide gestures, the a and e of the second line becoming smaller until the last *i* is formed low down and close to the body. The first vowels of the answer *a a e*, must as it were, issue from the heart, the arms being led outwards and upwards with the *e ei o*.

The following text, though not definitely built up of question and answer, does yet express in Anapestic rhythm something of this form—the darkening of the mood, the self-contraction, and then the tranquilized yielding-up-of-oneself :

Wie das braust! Über's himmlische Meer
Jagen wolkige Wogen daher;
Spritzt die Gischt urn mein irdisches Schiff,
Droht schon Not, droht der Tod mir am Riff.

Aber wenn die besänftige Flut
Nachtlich blau über'm Haupte mir ruht,
Winkt die Fülle. Dann angle ich gern
Einen Fisch, einen goldenen Stern.

O. FRÄNKL.

In this case we have twelve Anapests for each form, and consequently the spiral must be amplified by one or two additional whorls.

That one need not invariably hold to the rhythm originally given is shown by the fact that Dr. Steiner, in the Speech Eurythmy Course, indicates six Anapests for the answering spiral, just as for the spiral that asks the question.

If we now pass over from the study of the artistic aspect of this spiral-exercise to its curative-educational aspect, it must be said that the effects of this form extend as far as the ego-being of man and the constitution of the *blood* connected with it. Now it is a fact that this exercise works in a definitely opposite direction according to whether one winds from outside inwards, or, beginning at the center, from within outwards. In the latter case it works as a counteraction to *overdeveloped egoism*. *Full-blooded* children easily become egoistic, *anemic* children lack the feeling of self. If, in the latter case, the involving spiral is moved—the form which winds from outside towards the center, condensing itself and drawing itself together—the result is a confirmation of the ego, a gradual *strengthening of the feeling of self,* and this even works curatively upon the physiological defect, the *anemia*.

If, on the other hand, one gets children who are all too conscious of themselves, who cannot find sufficient outlet for their forces and who tend towards an egotistical self-assertion, to run the spiral which begins at the center and goes outwards (this can very well be applied to little children, without definite rhythm, simply making them run the form), such children will with time absorb into their very disposition of soul the going-out-of-themselves, the yielding-themselves-up to what is outside them which is inherent in this form; and here also an influence will make itself felt which will penetrate right down into the condition of the blood.

All these exercises are directed towards harmonizing the whole soul-life, towards balancing one-sided development and strengthening and ennobling the moral impulses. We have here described the basic forms originally given by Dr. Steiner; certain variations have already been incorporated into the system of eurythmy teaching and further developments will doubtless arise out of the living work of the future.

VI

EURYTHMY SOUL-GESTURES

In the V and VI Lectures of the Speech Eurythmy Course, Dr. Steiner spoke about these gestures which bring to expression certain moods and tendencies of soul. Previous to this, however, he had already given detailed indications about these postures; and, as we have seen that they may be introduced into the exercises described in the last chapter, we will now mention those which were originally given.

In the exercise *I and You,* for instance, and also in the lemniscates which are laid into the circle, the posture which expresses *Lightness* is used : the hands lie one over the other somewhat below breast-level (the left over the right), the palms of the hands turned upwards and the fingers slightly parted.

The same posture, but with the difference that the fingers lie close together and are held more tensely, is made use of when one wishes to give visible expression to an *earnest* mood of soul.

All the eurythmy exercises can be enriched by means of these soul-gestures. For instance, in all such exercises as depend upon an artistic style of walking, it is very usual to retain these gestures while moving the form. In the case of such words, for example, as :

> 'Holdes Bitten, mild Verlangen,
> wie es süss zum Herzen spricht.
>
> (Mild supplication, gentle request,
> how sweet is their language to the heart.)

the inwardness of feeling which one must endeavor to bring

into every step becomes clearly visible when the arms are at the same time held in the gesture corresponding to *Inwardness:* lightly stretched forward, the palms of the hands opened upwards, with the thumb touching the index-finger. Such positions can be retained for a long time, especially when walking is being practiced; or they can be introduced when expressing the vowel-sounds of a poem, either at an especially significant moment or as introductory and closing gestures. It is also possible, however, to let the posture merge into the sounds, to fit, as it were, each vowel-sound into the soul-gesture, so that the latter plays into every combination of sound.

If the left arm is raised, not forwards but so that it is bent over the head from the left side, and if the right arm makes a corresponding movement which is, however, directed downwards, there arises the gestures for *Lovableness* or, as Dr. Steiner also called it *Charm.* Here the heels are slightly raised from the ground; if the posture is practiced to walking, the steps must be taken on the toes, with a light undulating movement.

Now if the right arm also is raised and the curve of the arms opened out so that a wide half circle is formed over the head, the fingers being spread out and the body poised high on the tips of the toes, there arises the expression of *Merriment.*

Grief, Sadness is expressed when the right arm hangs down slackly, slightly bent inwards, the left being crossed over the middle of the body, with the hand, limp and passive, laid against it. (A more intense movement for the expression of grief is given in Lecture V.)

It may also happen, in poems for example which are mainly contemplative, where the element of reflection plays the chief part, that *Cleverness* is felt as the dominant mood;

here the left arm hangs down (also somewhat bent), the right hand being laid against the breast, with the fingers pointing upwards.

In the gesture for *Solemnity* the left arm is bent at right angles, the upper arm, when the position is looked at from the front, being turned towards the right, the forearm directed outwards, and the hand turned slightly inwards with the fingers pointing up. The right arm is held in the same position as in *Earnestness*. If the posture for *Solemnity* is to be looked at in profile, the left arm is carried forwards, the right arm being brought into the same position, only somewhat higher.

The mood of *Devotion* is represented when the hands are joined as if in prayer with the head somewhat bent. When the finger-tips, which in this posture are only gently laid against each other, are allowed to cross, this indicates the attitude of soul: *Piety*.

Resignation or *Sacrifice* (Hingabe) is expressed when both hands are laid against the breast, the left crossed under the right ; and in *Hope* the arms are opened with a feeling of expectation into a downward tending a (which slightly approaches the *o*; the gaze of the eyes is straight outwards and the toes are slightly raised, so that the weight of the body rests on the heels.

Of all these possibilities of expression---even if certain of them were not mentioned in the lectures of 1924---not one should be left out of account; on the contrary, we should endeavor to make the utmost use, in every conceivable direction, of the wonderful diversity of the eurythmy movements.

VII

DIONYSIAN FORMS

When the pupil has reached the stage of working out poems in eurythmy, not merely expressing the vowels (or as the case may be the consonants which have yet to be described) simply standing still or walking—when the stage has been reached of evolving forms in space corresponding to the inner character of the poetry and combining these forms with the movements expressing the sounds, it is necessary, as the first step, to ascertain, quite apart from the actual content of a poem, the general mood of soul which underlies it.

One must distinguish three possibilities, three styles, any of which may have been employed by the poet. As a preliminary to working out any poem in eurythmy, one must always put the question: Was this poem born from that part of the soul which *thinks*, did it arise out of *feeling*, or was its source purely of the *nature of will?* In most cases these three aspects will interpenetrate, or differences of opinion as to which is dominant may well be possible, but some such distinction can invariably be made. Epic, as the narrative style of poetry, will always have the thinking, conceptual element as the dominant factor; in the lyric we have the element of feeling, and, where the character of a poem tends towards the dramatic, it enters the domain of will. In order to show how clearly a poem may bear one or another of these three characteristics a few examples are here given, illustrating, in the first place, the fundamental coloring of thought, the presentation of some idea, secondly of feeling, and finally of will.

DIONYSIAN FORMS

INSCHRIFT AUF EINE UHR MIT DEN DREI HOREN

Am langsamsten von allen Göttern wandeln wir,
mit Blätterkronen schön geschmückte, schweigsame.
Doch wer uns ehrt und wem wir selber günstig sind,
weil er die Anmut liebet und das heilige Mass,
vor dessen Augen schweben wir in ieichtem Tanz
und machen mannigfaltig ihm den langen Tag.
                                     MÖRIKE.

(We, slowest of all the Gods, our course pursue—
Decked forth with crowns of leaves—we silent ones.
Yet he who honors us, to whom we favors grant,
Because he loves charms sweet and moderate,
Before his eyes we sway in gentle dance
Varying for him the long hours of his day.)

Another example of thinking:

ANTEPIRREMA

So schauet mit bescheidnem Blick
der ewigen Weberin Meisterstück,
wie ein Tritt tausend Fäden regt,
die Schifflein hinüber, herüber schiessen,
die Fäden sich begegnend fliessen,
ein Schlag tausend Verbindungen schlägt ;
das hat sie nicht zusammengebettelt,
sie hat's von Ewigkeit angezettelt,
damit der ewige Meistermann
getrost den Einschlag werfen kann.
                                 GOETHE.

(See now with humble eye
The masterpiece of the eternal Weaveress :
One tread a thousand threads in motion sets,
The shuttle darts across and back again,
The threads in flying movement meet,
Thousand the influences of one batten-blow ;
No careful hand set up this loom.
From time primordial was its warp prepared,
That the eternal Master-Craftsman
Might trustily throw the weft.)

Now examples of lyrical poetry, wrought out of pure feeling :

> MIGNON
> Nur wer die Sehnsucht kennt,
> weiss, was ich leide!
> Allein und abgetrennt
> von aller Freude,
> seh ich an's Firmament
> nach jener Seite. Ach!
> der mich liebt und kennt,
> ist in der Weite.
> Es schwindelt mir, es brennt
> mein Eingeweide.
> Nur wer die Sehnsucht kennt,
> weiss, was ich leide.
> GOETHE.

(Ah! they alone who yearn
Suffer my pain!
Lone and forlorn I turn
Pleasure no gain.
Skywards I gaze and learn

Once and again
That he whose love I earn
Far is amain.
Dizzy and faint I burn
Him to attain.
Ah! they alone who yearn
Suffer my pain!)

GEBET

Herr! Schicke, was Du willt,
ein Liebes oder Leides ;
ich bin vergnugt, dass beides
aus Deinen Händen quillt.
Wollest mit Freuden
und wollest mit Leiden
mich nicht überschütten !
Doch in der Mitten
liegt holdes Bescheiden

MÖRIKE.

PRAYER

(Lord, send me what Thou wilt,
Pleasure or pain;
Enough that flowing from Thy hand
Each to me is gain.
Neither 'neath pain and grief
Nor yet 'neath pleasure
Shall I o'er-whelmed be !
Yet sweetly between them
Lieth fair measure.)

In this last sentence a bridge passage leading over to

thinking may be discerned; there is a delicate impression of knowledge, which yet, at the same time, is bathed in a tender atmosphere of feeling. And now the character of will :

DER RITT IN DEN TOD

Greif aus, du mein junges, mein feuriges Tier,
Noch einmal verwachs ich centaurisch mit dir !
Umschmettert mich Tuben ! Erhebet den Ton !

Den Latiner besiegte des Manlius Sohn !
Voran die Trophä'n ! Der latinische Speer !
Der eroberte Helm ! Die erbeutete Wehr !

Duell ist bei Strafe des Beiles verpönt....
Doch er liegt, der die römische Wölfin gehöhnt !

Lictoren, erfüllet des Vaters Gebot !
Ich besitze den Kranz und verdiene den Tod—
Bevor es sich rollend im Sande bestaubt,
Erheb' ich in ewigen Jubel das Haupt!

C. F. MEYER.

THE RIDE TO DEATH

(Forth, forth, O my youthful, my spirited steed,
Once again, like a centaur, I, one with you, speed !

The trumpet is sounding ! Yet louder the tone !
The Latin is conquered by Manlius' son !

Lead on with the trophies ! The Latin's bright spear !
The helm that is vanquished ! The sword once held dear!

Unlawful a duel! The axe is the price.
He scorned Rome's she-wolf and now lifeless he lies.

Fulfil now, Lictoren, thy father's command !
The crown I have won and my death is at hand.

Before, dust-besmirched, in the sand my head fall,
I lift it in triumph, in victory's call.)

With spiritual knowledge of these three members of the soul—thinking, feeling and willing—as a basis, Dr. Steiner gave the laws underlying the artistic production of forms :

The expression of *will* demands *curved lines* 'whether of

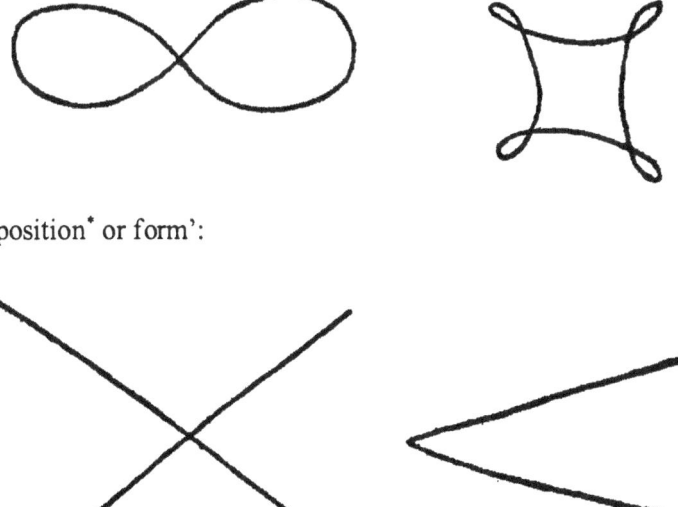

position* or form':

---

* This refers to the arrangement of the grouping.

The expression of thinking—*angular forms, straight lines*:

The expression of feeling—the combination of straight lines and curves:

Thus in feeling the two principles are united—the direct, sharp lines of thought with the circular lines of will, leading as these do in an undefined direction (see Speech Eurythmy Course, Lecture VI).

The following examples may serve to illustrate this method of interpreting poems.

For reflective, descriptive poetry :

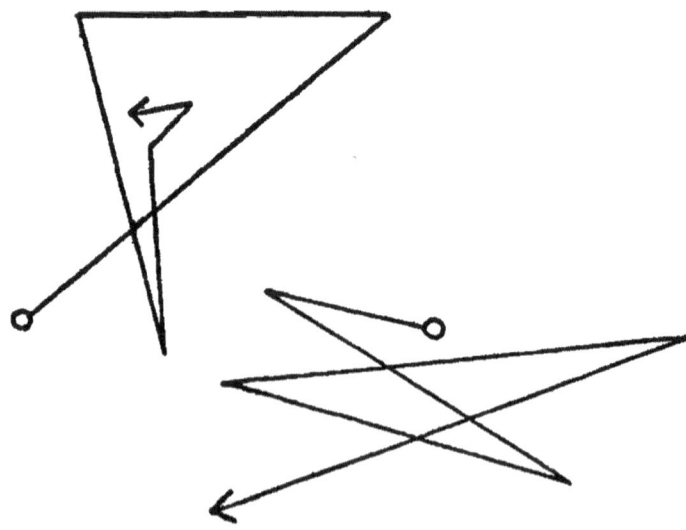

For poetry of a will character :

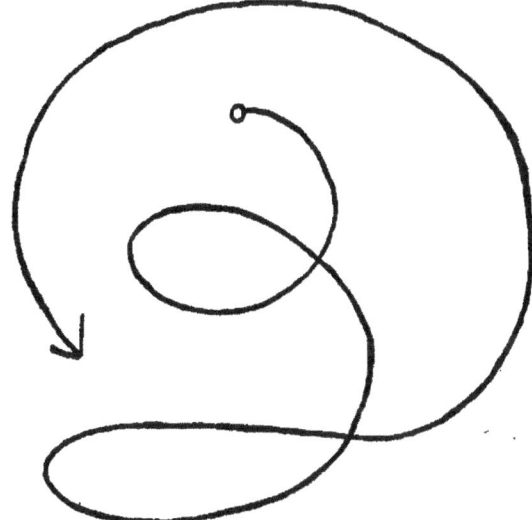

For lyric poems, which are the expression of feeling:

Now when these three moods of soul follow each other in a single poem, the character of the form must also vary. As an example clearly illustrating the transition of one state of soul to the other, let us take one of Nietzsche's early poems:

DEM UNBEKANNTEN GOTT

Noch einmal, eh ich weiterziehe
Und meine Blicke vorwärts sende,
heb' ich vereinsamt meine Hände
zu dir empor, zu dem ich fliehe,
dem ich in tiefster Herzenstiefe
Altäre feierlich geweiht,
dass allezeit
mich deine Stimme wider riefe.

Darauf erglüht tief eingeschrieben
das Wort: dem unbekannten Gotte.
Sein bin ich, ob ich in der Frevler Rotte
auch bis zur Stunde bin geblieben:
sein bin ich—und ich fühl' die Schlingen,
die mich im Kampf darniederziehn
und, mag ich fliehn,
mich doch zu seinem Dienste zwingen.

Ich will dich kennen, Unbekannter,
du tief in meine Seele Greifender,
mein Leben wie ein Sturm Durchschweifender,
Du Unfassbarer, mir Verwandter !
Ich will dich kennen, selbst dir dienen.

TO THE UNKNOWN GOD

(Once more, before the onward path I take,
And forwards send my gaze,
In solitude my hands I raise
To thee to whom I supplication make:
Deep in my deepest heart, to thee
Are altars dedicate,
Lest early or yet late
Again thy voice might summon me.
Thereon in glowing characters is burned:
'To thee, the God Unknown —His am I, though I own
That light companionship I have not spurned:
His am I—and I feel the spell
Destined to conquer me,
And, though I flee,
Me to his service yet compel.

Know thee I will, O God Unknown,
So deep my soul indwelling,
Yea, like a storm onswelling,
Incomprehensible, yet with me one—
Know thee I will: thy servant be.)

Here the poet takes his start from feeling veiled in an atmosphere of sadness ; with the second verse he passes over to clear contemplative thinking, concluding with a stormy outburst of will.

Thus, in making the form for the first verse, there must be a combination of straight and curved lines; the second verse must be expressed in direct, angular, sharply differentiated lines; and the ending—from 'Know thee I will' onwards in powerful curves.

It is of special interest to trace and inwardly experience the way these three moods can interplay. Dr. Steiner himself analysed a verse by Walther von der Vogelweide from this point of view, which, with the explanation also given by him, is here quoted:

The verse begins :

> 'Daran gedenket Ritter, es ist euer Ding,
> Ihr tragt die lichten Helme und manchen harten Ring,
> Dazu den festen Schild und das geweihte Schwert....'
>
> (Bear this in mind, O Knights, the cause is thine,
> By thee the gleaming helm and coat of mail are worn,
> The well-wrought shield and consecrated sword....)

This beginning is of the *nature of feeling;* the poet, that is to say, 'makes use of glowing words in order to stimulate the emotions'.

> Now there is an intensification of the impulse:
> 'Wollt Gott, ich war' für ihn zu streiten wert....'
> (Would God that I were worthy of this fight....)

This, then, is will. There follows thinking, 'genuine sober consideration':

> 'Nicht mein' ich Hufen Landes, noch der Fursten Gold,'
> (I do not mean a hide of land, nor yet the gold of Kings)

> 'Ich truge Krone selber in der Engel Heer,...'
> (I myself wore a crown amidst the angelic host....)

This last line is again *feeling;* then there is once more a transition to *thinking:*

> 'Die mag ein Söldner wohl erwerben mit dem Speer !'
> (This may a hireling well win with the spear !)

And now *willing*:

> 'Dürft ich die liebe Reise fahren über See,
> So wollt' ich ewig singen Heil
> Und nimmermehr : O weh !

> (Might I but take this joyful journey o'er the sea
> I would eternally sing songs of praise
> And nevermore lament !)

In order to show how a poem may be worked out from this point of view, an attempt shall here be made to evolve a form for the little Mörike poem which was quoted as an example of the principle of feeling:

> Herr, schicke was du willt,
> ein Liebes oder Leides,
> (Lord, send me what thou wilt,
> Pleasure or pain,)

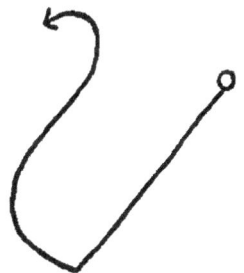

> ich bin vergnügt, dass beides
> aus deinen Händen quillt.
>
> (Enough that flowing from thy
> hand each to me is gain.)

Wollest mit Freuden
und wollest mit Leiden
mich nicht überschütten!

(Neither 'neath pain and grief
nor yet 'neath pleasure
Shall I o'erwhelmed be!)

Doch in der Mitten
liegt holdes Bescheiden.

(Yet sweetly between them
Lieth fair measure.)

The form as a whole appears thus:

Foreground

This form is intentionally worked out in such a way that where the *rhyming words* occur the line returns at least approximately to the *same spot*. Also, when a *vowel-sound re-*

peats itself, it should the second time be formed as nearly as possible like the first, that the *rhyme* may be clearly brought out. In the choice of the vowel-sounds the eurythmist is of course, quite free ; the unemphasized *e* of the final syllables may, for instance, be omitted as unessential. In such a lyrical, musical poem as this, one must be specially careful to carry out what has already been said about the vowel-sounds : the gestures must flow one into the other just as one note in music passes over to the next—even in the case of such a vowel-sound, for instance, as the *e* in *Herr,* which must be strongly marked and somewhat sustained.

While the vowel-sounds are being carried out in this way, the rhythm of the steps must be strictly adhered to. Variety may be introduced by sometimes taking the steps with the accented syllable only, sometimes drawing the foot up with the short beats, or, when the form permits, by swinging three or four steps with the long beat, and so on.

In the case of a poem such as 'Inschrift auf eine Uhr mit den drei Horen', one can arrange for the form to be carried out by three people. Grouped in a semi-circle or some similar form, each one of the three can either carry out his own little form—which may be identical with the others or independent ; or the forms can be arranged so as to cross and interpenetrate each other ; or else the three eurythmists may all move one and the same form, in which case they begin at a certain distance from each other and end in the same relationship. The aforementioned possibility of choral grouping, where a solo form is moved in the foreground, may also be made use of in similar poems.

At this stage, however, the pupil when moving should invariably remain facing the direction in which the audience is imagined to be. With the more undulating, swinging lines of the form, one naturally tries not to remain stiff, but to feel one's way into the form with the upper part of the body, with the shoulders, and, when moving backwards, also with the back; but if one already began to add all kinds of bending movements, half turning or entirely turning and thus over-emphasising the movement, the suppleness of the body—one would not sufficiently develop the necessary realisation of the independent existence of the form. (Dr. Steiner once mentioned that all turning round on oneself in a circle should only be regarded as 'padding'.)

All this must be looked upon as the rudiments, the introductory stages of that whole range of 'Forms' which was revealed to us by Rudolf Steiner—as the means of educating oneself up to some understanding of the *Standard Forms* which he himself later designed for innumerable poems—as a preparation for that lofty conception of art which was later brought into the development of eurythmy by Frau Marie Steiner.

These laws of movement, related as they are to thinking, feeling and willing, lie entirely in the sphere of the soul-life, which may itself be differentiated into thinking, feeling and willing. Thus here again we have a Dionysian principle, for the Greeks recognised in Dionysos the divine prototype of this very element of human soul. This is why the eurythmy forms built up in this way are called *Dionysian Forms*.

PART II
VIII

THE CONSONANTS

The vowel-sounds and their movements express what lives in the soul as feeling or perception. The movements for the consonants are related to the processes of the outer world; they imitate the forms of Nature, and, by means of movement, raise these naturalistic impressions into an imaginative picture-experience.

The tendencies of movement inherent in the larynx, or rather the etheric formative forces underlying the larynx and its neighboring organs—these movements-in-tendency, the investigation into which Rudolf Steiner took as the starting-point for the development of the laws of Eurythmy (see Preface)—had already, in much earlier epochs of time, made their appearance in gestures and postures of the whole human being. In the lecture (August 26th, 1923), already quoted in the Preface, Rudolf Steiner speaks as follows:

'Speech is essentially a universal means of expression for the human soul. And anyone able to look without prejudice into the earliest epochs of human development upon earth will perceive that in certain primeval languages a deeply artistic element held sway. But these primeval languages, far more than is the case with modern civilized languages, were drawn out from the entire human being. If, indeed, we follow this evolution back without prejudice we reach primeval languages which manifested almost as singing; but the human being livingly accompanied what he spoke with movements of the legs and arms. Thus, in the case of certain primeval languages, a sort of dancing was added to speech when anything exalted, anything in the nature of a definite ritual was to be brought to expression.'*

---

* This lecture is included in the book *Eurythmy as Visible Song* (the Tone-Eurythmy Course by Rudolf Steiner).

Further information about the primeval languages is to be found in the publication compiled from Rudolf Steiner's lectures on Spiritual Science under the title 'The Spiritual Guidance of Mankind'. Here, on page 63, we read : 'Now it is known through occult science that in ancient times, particularly in the Atlantean period[†], there existed a kind of primitive human language, a manner of speech which was similar all over the earth, because "speech" in those days came much more directly out of the depths of the soul than it does to-day. This may be gathered from the following. In Atlantean times people felt all outward impressions in such a way that, if the soul wished to express anything outward by a sound, it was constrained to use a consonant. What existed in space, therefore, demanded imitation in a consonant. The blowing of the wind, the murmur of the waves, the shelter given by a house, were experienced and then imitated by man in consonants. On the other hand, the sorrow or joy which was felt inwardly, or even what another being might be feeling, was imitated in a vowel. From this we can see that in speech the soul became one with outer events or beings....

....A man drew near a hut, which was arched in the ancient fashion and gave shelter and protection to a family. He noticed this, and expressed the protective arch by a consonant; and he expressed the fact which he was able to feel—that within the hut souls in bodies dwelt in comfort—by a vowel-sound. Thence arose the thought "shelter"; "there is shelter for me—shelter for human bodies." This thought was then poured forth into consonants and vowels, which could not be other than they were, because they were a direct impression of what had been experienced.'

It is to these original experiences when confronted with

[†] See Appendix

the outer world that we are led back by the structure of the Eurythmy movements for the consonants.

The very first form in which Dr. Steiner gave an explanation of these consonantal movements was in connection with a certain combination of consonants, so grouped together that the eurythmists doing the movement themselves experienced the effect of the sounds.

In each group five consonants are so combined that, when practiced in the order given, the first group has a calming the second a stimulating effect.

For the purpose of practicing these consonantal movements Dr. Steiner gave for each one a short sequence of words, wherein the sound in question plays a specially characteristic part, and which is of assistance in developing the fundamental mood and feeling.

First in this sequence of consonants stands *d*. It is the sound which portrays a reaction to the outer world in a state of rest.—Man looks about him, perceives around him the things of the world: 'Dies durch dich' is the answer made by his soul to that which he has perceived. Arms and hands indicate the objects which stand without, confronting the senses; they sink into their environment; they move with it. This indicating d-gesture can be carried out in all directions, sinking gently from above downwards or radiating out towards every side of the circumference. The foot also can play its part in the way it is set down—carefully, first indicating the spot where it is later to be placed.

Now one must imagine that the peaceful surroundings are suddenly changed, that a challenge approaches from outside —a call, a blow, lightning. This makes the resulting movement more energetic; the quiet sinking of the arms in *d* becomes the *f*—the sound which reacts to a challenge—firm and energetic, either thrust downwards, or elastically thrown off into the air, so that something like a light rebound occurs. 'Für frohe Feste'—these wordsdemonstrate the lively and energetic mood of *f*. (When one practices in this way it serves as a preparation for understanding what Rudolf Steiner said in the Speech Eurythmy Course about the deeper content of the sound *f*.)

Now when the outer world confronts man in such a way that he feels that he must resist it, defend himself from it, this occurs in the three sounds g, k, h. With g one is at the point of warding something off The approach of something unsympathetic is discerned and the hands make a warding-off movement, a slight movement of dismissal:

'genug gierig geniessen'.

As the attack becomes more vigorous, the reaction is intensified, the *g* becomes *k*. '*Kaum kräftig können*'—with these words the repulsion is already stronger. (The proportion of strength as between g and k is the same as between *d* and *f*.) And the *h* thrusts it aside—'hier heulen heute Hyänen'. Children make this liberating *h*-movement with special enjoyment and enthusiasm, for here, with clenched fists and taut muscles, they can thrust something away to their heart's content.

This first method of interpreting the sounds was, as already mentioned, more from the aspect of their effect upon the souls of the eurythmists themselves. What Dr. Steiner later brought forward in the Eurythmy lectures with regard to h as the Heranwehende (a wafting process) simply shows (as is also the case with his description of *e*, for example, and other sounds) another moment, a later phase of the same process. For, by freeing himself from every disturbance and hindrance, man makes himself receptive to the Spiritual which is wafted towards him on the breath of the air. He creates, as it were, space for himself by means of his repulsing movements; he brings this about by his own preparatory activity. The more one lives into these different aspects, so much the more real will the whole experience be at the moment of performance.

We have, then, this sequence of five tranquilizing sounds: *d, f, g, k, h*. They should be practiced both standing and walking. Just as the d, for example, can be emphasized by a gentle, careful placing of the foot, so with *f* the steps must be firmer and stronger. *G, k, h* can be carried out in any direction, turning aside, or moving hither and thither.

Now for the stimulating consonants: *l, m, n, p, q*. In *l* we have the sound which expresses a free inner unfolding. The arms are first brought downwards with a movement which intends, as it were, to create something out of the soil of the earth. This gesture, with the hands laid closely together, is then raised high upwards and there, as though at the point of blossoming, allowed to unfold to either side in a wide outstreaming movement, which then flows downwards again that the circle may begin anew. 'Leben lang lau' are the words which give the right atmosphere to the practice of the sound *l*. When speaking of this sound in the Eurythmy Lectures Dr. Steiner added to this description of the movement 'a flexibility and suppleness' of the arms, and also indicated for the feet a rocking-to-and-fro from toes to heels and back again. In m man penetrates right into the outer world; he feels himself in something, in some element, water, air, and so on. The hands push smoothly outwards, pressing themselves into whatever the surrounding matter may be; and there. wherever the movement ends, they must be bent somewhat downwards. When m is practiced walking in a backward direction, the arms and hands can, as it were, feel the way in advance, making the movement from the front backwards. 'Mit Mut machen'—here we have a courageous and intelligent penetration into what is outside ourselves. N, on the contrary, draws itself back; it touches something and hastily withdraws; it is the expression of a transient relationship. This negation, this withdrawal, is emphasized in the words 'nicht nur nein'. One can practice the sound n in a quite definite and tangible way by stretching out the hand and touching some object and then withdrawing it quickly, but as if one wanted to retain some part of that object. The finger-tips of both hands can also be made to touch each other and then hastily be drawn apart. The important point is the sharpness, lightness and transience of this with drawing movement, for this can lead over to what Dr. Steiner later termed a 'dismissal', an 'ironical understanding'.

In *p* we have the process already mentioned in the passage previously quoted from 'The Spiritual Guidance of Mankind'; it is the imitation of an enveloping process. In this movement there is indicated the taking hold of some object, a veil for instance, and the wrapping of it around oneself, the arms being drawn towards the body with elbows and wrists bent. This gesture is rapidly repeated three times or oftener. The first time it is carried out on a level with or above the head, then on a level with the shoulders, then still lower. When this drawing-towards-one of arms and veil is repeated very rapidly, so that the eye can scarcely keep pace with it, the impression of being wrapped around in a thick scarf or veil is actually created.

Q is the reaction to something painful—'a pressing of the limbs against the body'. It can be practiced to the words: 'stossen quer, arbeiten quirlig'. A thwarted, harassed, inharmonious condition must be brought to expression. Dr. Steiner also gave the word 'Qual' (affliction) for the practice of the sound q, and here the hands, which are pressed against the breast must, as though in an excess of suffering, once more be thrust outwards.

Both these groups of consonants can be intensified in their effect by appending to them another consonant, which, though neutral in itself, works equally stimulatingly in both cases. This is the sound *r*—'Richtung rechter Rand.' Here, walking is led over into running, as if 'one were carried by the wind in a definite direction'. The tempo must be varied, now quicker, now slower; but always one must be carried away by the movement, which must never be allowed to come to a standstill. The arms imitate a rolling movement, as if they were turning round on a wheel; this also can be carried out from the front backwards. If the *r* is practiced standing still one feels oneself really as a part of Nature, as a tree, for instance, or a bush, blown to and fro by the wind. The arms can be imagined as branches, blown hither and thither, up and down.

The consonants *v, b, s, t,* which occur in neither group, have one aspect in common, that is to say, they are formed with the aid of a foreign object, whether this object is actually grasped, or the act only accomplished in imagination.

V*— when not simply carried out in the same way as *f*— can be experienced as if one' had something in one's hand'. Thus the hand is stretched out in order to show that something is being touched.

B is the protective gesture. It expresses a seeking for protection and at the same time an enveloping-process. For instance, one might take a veil and wrap oneself in it, or one may indicate this process in the way in which the arms are held in relation to the body. Everything which works protectively upon the body forms a *b*. The shield with which the Greek hero protected his breast was the expression of *b*. So

---

* In the German language this sound is pronounced *f,* but Dr. Steiner gave it a movement for itself. (Translator's Note.)

indeed is everything which works reflexively. If, for example, by gazing at a curved movement of the hand one thereby emphasizes the relationship of hand to head, this already is enough to indicate a *b*.

An *s* arises immediately the human being grasps some external object—a rod, a blossoming branch, a veil, an instrument—and therewith makes a form. A man leaning on his staff is the prototype of *s*. In the case of a veil, one must move it in such a way that (in relation to the body) a definite form is built in the air. The hand can also be regarded as a 'foreign object', and something similar to an *s* described with it in the air. Carried out with both hands, approximately this from would arise:

or this form, which recalls the symbol of the staff of mercury:

All the sibilants, or hissing-sounds, are formed in this way, but differentiated in the movement according to their variations of sound. *Z* (*tz*) moves in jagged, sharp lines:

Sch* revolves in spirals; here one can picture forms such as are created by hissing steam in a cold atmosphere.

In the Fourth Eurythmy Lecture Dr. Steiner caused the *sch* to be carried out similarly to *ch* (see page 58), at the same time recalling the fact that the 'Hebraic Man of ancient times' perceived the 'wafting and weaving of Jehovah in the wind'.

Speaking of *s*, which he characterized in the Fourth Lecture as the sound which 'puts something out of its way with a sense of mastery', Dr. Steiner also emphasized, in the same passage, the importance of the relationship arising between the movements of one arm and the other.

T is a solemn gesture expressing a radiating inwards, an instreaming from above downwards. This impression is called forth when, descending from above, both hands touch the head. One can also touch something else, any foreign object; the important thing is the sinking down from above.

There remains the *w* (English *v*). This sound is represented by a movement of the hands imitating wave-like forms. The hands glide, as it were, over undulating water— up, down, again up, again down—and so on, further and further. In cases where the w can be regarded almost as a vowel-sound, in words expressing something of a soul-nature,

---

* This brings us to the English consonant *th*. It is expressed by a thick, downward movement, especially of the right hand. The hands must pass from side to side as if following the strata of the earth. This sound can also be expressed by a descending spiral-movement, which is in fact the *Sch* in a reversed direction.

sound, in words expressing something of a soul-nature, not anything naturalistic Now that we know the movements for the single consonants, we can pass on and consider a larger group of sounds, a sequence of twelve consonants, which, in this special order, bring to expression everything manifested in [as, for instance, in Wunder (marvel), Wonne (bliss), in contradistinction to Wind (wind), Welle (wave), warm (warm)]—in such cases its relationship with u must be indicated. The arms, held narrowly together, are raised upwards, while at the same time one must show that the hands are being experienced as heavy weights.* Now that we know the movements for the single consonants, we can pass on and consider a larger group of sounds, a sequence of twelve consonants, which, in this special order, bring to expression everything manifested in the evolution of mankind as a whole. The following diagram gives them in their order :

```
B ⎫
M ⎬   Man as he seeks for protection,
D ⎭
N ⎫
R ⎬   for stimulation to activity
L ⎭   and for tranquillity once more.
G
CH
F
S
—
H
T
```

Infinitely deep connections may be discovered in this sequence of sounds; from whichever standpoint they are studied fresh correspondences may continually be found. Bearing in

* This is also the movement given by Dr. Steiner for the English sound w.

mind what Rudolf Steiner said in this connection about the individual sounds, an attempt will here be made to give some sort of sketch of one way in which they may be conceived.

B—the giving of protection: enveloped, concealed as though in a mantle, man rests in the bosom of divinity—while at the same time he becomes aware of 'the other'; this may well be conceived as the moment of awakening to consciousness, the process of differentiation. From unconsciousness, from a tranquil concealment in the unity of the divine-spiritual, perception makes its appearance for the first time, the perception of something which has released itself, which has become 'the other' Now comes the attempt to enter into 'the other'—into earthly evolution, that is to say, into matter as such. This occurs in the *m*. Through this—through the effort of penetration, of uniting oneself with matter—'man becomes strong, he gains the mastery and finds himself'. *D*— 'Ich muss durch'—or, 'bei ihm da bin ich'—this is the secret of these first three sounds.

Now the stimulation to activity. When we consider that n was described as a 'transient relationship', we may well say : Man first lost the possibility of feeling himself one with the Divinity surrounding him. Imprisoned in his own bodily nature, as though blinded by the wall of the body, he becomes restless and gropes about him, but achieves as yet only a superficial understanding, a transient experience of things, in the short rapid movement of the *n*. Now the unrest increases. To a certain extent man allows himself to be 'carried away' by what is outside—*r*. The elements seize upon him, catastrophes assail him—and these may also be of a soul-nature if they are imagined as overwhelming him from without; desire, pain, dread, rapture drive him into intense agitation, an agitation which is suddenly tranquilized by the sound *l*. 'Man pulls himself together', he turns inwards. The unfolding, the faculty of development inherent in the *l* is realized by the soul; 'man calms himself' by entering into his inner being, by conquering matter.

Now we come to the second phase. This sequence of sounds can only really be understood in the light of what Dr. Steiner said later in the Eurythmy Lectures, when discussing each one of these consonants separately. A few of these descriptions will here be brought forward to show how the light given in 1924 throws its rays upon the description of this sequence of sounds given so many years previously.

In Lecture XV, *g* is described as 'an inner confirmation of self'; and this implies that putting aside of what is harmful, which we already knew. This inner confirmation makes its appearance after the tranquillity achieved in the *l*. *Ch*—taking up into oneself, filling oneself with the spirituality which is wafted towards one on the breath of the air. *F*—, as already pointed out, Dr. Steiner described this sound (Lectures II and III) as the sound which indicates the fact that the highest wisdom is contained in man. It was taught in the ancient Mystery Centers that the Isis-Wisdom surging in the human breathstream was exhaled in the sound *f*, which process is imitated in the elastic off-thrust of the Eurythmy movement. 'Wisse dass ich weiss' (Know thou that I know). And the sound *s*, related as it is to the symbol of the serpent, also played an important part in the ancient Mysteries; this sound, the knowledge of which penetrates with its enlightening, tranquilizing power into hidden, secret depths · Thus the second half of evolution is to be understood as a progression to ever higher stages of knowledge. The two final sounds, *h* and *t*, stand independently. One can imagine that in them there is a retracing of the way; evolution again enters into the realm of the purely spiritual. *H*— a wafting towards one: the approach, the annunciation of the spirit in whose image everything earthly is cast. And *t* establishes one in the spiritual world. Mankind has again attained to the Spiritual. Evolution, with all its results, has become experience. A new evolutionary circle, starting from a more advanced point of departure, can begin. (Attention must be paid to the transition from *t* to the next *b*. The gesture itself will reveal how what is final becomes a new beginning.)

Now we must come to the point of practicing the consonants in the combinations in which they occur in language. The best way, at first, is to select single words, which give one the opportunity of repeating again and again the movements for certain combinations of sounds and the transitions between them. Fluency in a given sequence of gestures is thus acquired, and this must gradually be increased to the point where the limbs carry out the eurythmy movements with the same certainty and rapidity as the sounds are produced by the larynx. Just as, when speaking, there is no need to think about the separate sounds, so the eurythmist must not have to think about the movements when speaking with the arms, with the whole body. The important thing is the flowing of one movement into another; and this is why it is the transitions from one sound to another which must especially be practiced. It is possible to find certain combinations of sounds, short syllables perhaps, which appear again and again in the German language,* with which we are here mainly dealing. For instance, *nd, schi, schw, men, den, gen*, and so on. One must now practice, one after the other, such words as *Wind, lind, Hand, wund, branden*, etc. Thus there will gradually

---

* A translation of the German words is useless here, as they are chosen from the point of view of sound only. English words equally suited to the purpose can easily be selected. (Translator's Note.)

105

arise out of the words themselves the realization as to how this combination of sounds *nd* must be formed into a unity—how the transience and withdrawal of the n may be combined with the tranquillity of the succeeding *d*.

Where two consonants appear side by side, so that to the ear the two sounds are practically merged into one, as is the case, for instance, with *bi, br, dr, ki, pf*, and so on—they must be so carried out that the movement for the second sound is begun almost simultaneously with the movement for the first, and the resulting gesture allowed to flow over into the subsequent vowel. Here again attention must especially be directed to the transitions, to this 'picking out', as it were, of the vowel-sounds from the surrounding consonants. Let us study, for example, how the movements for the different vowels can grow out of the sound *l*. Here one would select such words as: *Blume, Luft, Labsal, Blatt, Blüte*, etc., and practice the Eurythmy movements just from this point of view; and again, when practicing the transition from *m* into the vowel-sounds: *Mut, Muhe, Mond, Moos, Muse, malen*, and so on. Thus one tries to experience, in so far as this is possible, each separate sound in the most varied combinations. After such exercises as these one can also practice the alliterations already mentioned in Part I in such a way that one makes the movement for the alliterative consonant at the moment of stepping, allowing it to pass over into the adjoining vowel. For example:

> An silberner Leine gelenkte Luchse
> in leichtem Lauf durch die Lüfte ziehn.

These lines would now be carried out thus: taking the first word—silberner—(which does not begin with the alliterative sound) the *i* must be done standing still, then with each step an *l*, passing over into whatever may be the following vowel, again standing still with the *i* of the last word.

When selecting poems to be expressed by the movements for the consonants, one should choose those wherein the mood and content are suited to the essential nature of the consonants—descriptions, that is to say, of Nature-processes, the portrayal in poetry of the weaving, living processes of Nature; and especially contemplative poems, in contradistinction to lyrical, musical poems, which should be expressed in vowel-sounds—and also strongly dramatic outbreaks of passion, for these can only be adequately interpreted by the plastic movements for the consonants.

Wonderful combinations of sound—words which reproduce in form and picture the inner being of what they are meant to express and wherein the spiritual weaving of the sounds may still livingly be traced—are especially to be found in Goethe's descriptions of Nature:

> Segel schwellen
> Grüne Wellen,
> Weisse Schäume—
> Seht! die Weiten,
> Grünen Räume
> Von Delphinen
> Rasch durchschwommen!
>
> (Chorus from Rinaldo.)

Mai.

Leichte silber Wolken schweben
Durch die erst erwärmten Lüfte,
Mild, von Schimmer sanft umgeben,
Blickt die Sonne durch die Düfte.
Leise wallt und drängt die Welle
Sich am reichen Ufer hin;
Und wie reingewaschen helle,
Schwankend hin und her und hin,
Spiegelt sich das junge Grün...

It is possible to take almost any word from such poems and to enter deeply into the fundamental experience of each sound therein contained, vowel and consonant, slowly at first, then gradually increasing the fluency of the movements. This creation out of sounds and their combinations has reached to even higher levels in Rudolf Steiner's poems, which are drawn out of Eurythmy itself, out of the very realm of movement. In the Preface with which Marie Steiner introduced the collection of Rudolf Steiner's poems Wahrspruchworte,[*] we read a sentence which shows the direction in which the ideal poetry of the future must be sought, the direction in which we must turn in order to find a language, which, descending as it does from the spiritual home of Eurythmy, is also capable of being translated in the most perfect way into the movements of Eurythmy. The passage reads: 'The inner rhythm of the sounds, which in the poetry of the future will take the place of the rhyme, has been solved by Rudolf Steiner, and the forming and shaping of sounds as the highest principle of art disclosed to our souls. The law of movement in the element of

---

[*] Published by the Philosophisch-Anthroposophischer Verlag at the Goetheanum, Dornach, 1925.

sound, which makes language independent of what is purely musical, pictorial or plastic, which discloses, in spite of the connection of language with all the other elements of art, a domain of its own, all-inclusive yet complete in itself—this he brought down to us from the realm of spiritual dynamics.' *(Wahrspruchworte,* Preface, Page IX.) There follows a detailed elucidation of the laws of sound whereon the poem 'Weltenseelengeister' is built. In all the poems which Dr. Steiner created for Eurythmy, and also in certain parts of the Mystery Plays—such as *The Story of the Fountain,* the words which resound from the spirit-world or which are spoken by the elemental beings, sylphs and gnomes—everywhere we find this living movement of sound and therewith the possibility of a complete experience in the movements of Eurythmy of each single sound exactly where it occurs.

...'But it is only when reproduced by the word, artistically formed and shaped in the freely flowing breath, that one can have a complete realization of the resounding life of feeling, the scintillating vibrations of light, the plastically formed consciousness contained in this language.' *(Wahrspruchworte,* Preface, Page X.)

This art of the word, this truly spiritual treatment of language, which Marie Steiner herself has mastered and teaches in so wonderful a way, is absolutely necessary to the eurythmist, the moment he endeavors to realize movement in a truly artistic way, for it is the force which carries and sustains, the force which releases one from physical weight.

The eurythmist will not, it is true, always feel the necessity of doing every sound in a word. In poems where the language is not perfected it is possible to omit the unessential; words or syllables which are not of vital import may be left out to avoid weightiness or confusion. Also, when endeavoring to emphasize some specially definite mood or feeling, it is possible to select from the sounds those which are most typical. In a poem, for instance, which portrays the tranquillity of Nature, one would make a point of bringing out all the *d*-sounds, indeed any consonant which works with a quietening effect; while, where activity makes itself felt, the stimulating sounds would be chosen, and so on.

Now the sounds can also be practiced in the following way: two people stand facing each other, one of whom undertakes the vowels of a text, the other the consonants, and each of them tries clearly to bring out the essential character of his part; in the vowels the musical line of the melody, while the plastic, living, moving consonants play around the quiet gestures of the vowels. An exact interplay between the movements is most important; neither eurythmist must start his sound before the other has finished. The movements must grow out of each other, as if they were being carried out by one person. If this condition is strictly observed there arises a living impression of the essential impersonality of the movements of Eurythmy; one feels how a word in Eurythmy lives in the movements passing between the two people. (This method of practicing forms a good preparation to the 'Presentation of a Poem on three different Levels', to be described in Part III.)

The single eurythmist also must realize the importance of what may be called the structure of the movement. Just as, in the spoken word, there are emphasized and unemphasized syllables, so in Eurythmy also these must be borne in mind. To acquire this element of rhythm, this faculty of distributing lightness and weight, the consonants may be practiced in three different ways. In the first place one can take the gestures from the shoulder joint, thus using the whole arm for each sound; large, weighty, emphasized movements are the result. The same sounds are then carried out from the elbow joint, and here we must strictly observe that the upper arm really does take no part; and finally the hands only are brought into movement, each consonant arising from the joint at the wrist. This results in delicate, intimate movements, which may, as it were, just be slipped in between the movements bearing greater emphasis.

A further attribute which must be striven for is the conscious distribution of the sounds in space. Here, in the first place, we must consider *three zones*. The 'upper' comprises everything which lies above shoulder-level. (Also, for instance, that part of space which lies behind the head.)

Then comes the 'middle zone', which comprises all movements at breast-level (both in front and behind), and finally the 'lower zone' which must not reach higher than the middle region of the body.

This division of the sounds into three zones may be applied as soon as the opportunity arises of bringing out in some definite way the three aspects of *thinking, feeling,* and *willing.*

The *upper* region of space is regarded as the sphere of movement as long as *feeling* is predominant. If one is active in the element of thought, all sounds are distributed in the *middle* zone, and in *will* the movements are directed *downwards,* in the third zone.

These same laws of movement indicate that in the case of *feeling* the face is directed upwards in *thinking* the face is directed downwards', and in *willing* the 'face is directed straight forwards'. These last directions can, naturally, only be indicated by the *gaze of the eyes.*

This division of space is specially important when portraying the three spirit-beings, who reveal themselves in Rudolf Steiner's Mystery Plays as the prototypes of the Human soul-forces: Philia, Astrid, Luna. Here the sphere of the movements is strictly defined: Philia in the *feeling-,* Astrid in the *thought-,* and Luna in the *will-zone.*

IX

APOLLONIAN FORMS

In order to gain an understanding for the Apollonian and Dionysian element in eurhytbmy, we will here quote certain passages from *Nietzsche's Birth of Tragedy*—a work to which Dr. Steiner made reference in this connection :

'We shall have gained much for the science of aesthetics if we approach it, not from the aspect of logic only, but from the direct reaiisation that the development of art is bound up with the duality of the *Apollonian and Dionysian*—just as procreation is dependent upon the duality of the sexes, upon a perpetual struggle and only occasional reconciliation. These names are borrowed from the Greeks, who made the profound mystery-teaching on their conception of art intelligible to the discerning, not by means of concepts, but by the forceful significance of the figures peopling their world of the Gods. We know that in the art of the Greeks there exists an antithesis of style, which may be traced directly back to their two divinities of art, Apollo and Dionysus. Two different impulses flow along side by side, generally in mutual dissention and stimulating each other to new forces of production in order to perpetuate the struggle: till finally, at the zenith of the Hellenic "will", they appear fused together as the common progenitors of that artistic creation, the Attic Tragedy.

In order to make these two impulses more comprehensible, let us first think of them as the two distinct realms of art *dreaming* and *rapid motion* (Rauschen); for between these physiological phenomena we may draw a contrast similar to the Apollonian and Dionysian.'

It was to these contrasts of style, the Apollonian and Dionysian, that Dr. Steiner linked his division of the Eurythmy forms into the Dionysian (with which we have already dealt) and the Apollonian, which we are about to discuss. For him, however, these two divinities did not represent *dreaming* and *rapid motion,* but be described Dionysos as *fire,* Apollo as *form.*

The picture of Apollo sketched by Nietzsche in the *Birth of Tragedy* appears to be in agreement with this comparison:

'Apollo, as the God of dream-concepts, is at the same time the prophetic and artistic God. This divinity, who sends his roots down into the world of phenomena, is the God of Light and Lord also of the beautiful illusion of the world of dreams. The realisation of the higher truth, the perfection of this dream-state, in contradistinction to the only partially comprehensible state of waking-reality, as also the realisation of the helpful and healing processes of Nature in sleep and dream—these lead us to Apollo, as the symbolic analogy of the prophetic faculty and of art as a whole, through which life is made worth living and the future brought into the present. But that delicate border-line, which the dream-picture must not overstep—if the result is not to be pathological, fraught with deluding and deceitful appearances—must also not be omitted from the picture of Apollo, the Sculptor-God, with his strength-giving limitations, his freedom from unrestrained motion, his wisdom-filled tranquillity. His eye must be sunlike, to conform with his origin: even when its gaze is full of anger, the consecration of glory is upon it.' *(Birth of Tragedy.)* As Nietzsche here sees him and conjures him up before our eyes—'the sculptor-God'—so must we picture Apollo, that divine being who works inspiringly into the domain of Eurythmy forms, bringing into a performance the structural element, the power of harmonious moderation.

The part which logic plays in language—the introduction of order, limitation, individuation (in Nietzsche's sense)—must also have its place in Eurythmy, forming as it does the inner framework, the living structure of the movement.

'Intellectual Forms' (*Sinn-Formen*) was the name given by Dr. Steiner to these strictly ordered movements in space. 'Up to this point we have, as it were, learned our letters; now we must go deeper and pass over from the presentation of words to the presentation of their meaning and content',— thus run the words which he spoke to his pupils when introducing the following system of analysis, which depends upon the sense of each single word and gives to each single word its definite form in space.

We must differentiate:

I. The *adjectival* element;
II. The element of *activity,* which finds expression in verbs;
III. The *objective* element—nouns, which may be classified as concrete, abstract, conditional, of a soul- or divine-spiritual nature;
V. *Prepositions*;
V. *Conjunctions*;
VI. *Interjections.*

In eurythmy everything of an adjectival nature—we include in this connection adjectives, adverbs, numerals and articles—is shown by bringing the movement to rest, so that, as a general rule at least, such words are carried out standing still. Only in exceptional cases can a word of the adjectival class be included in the form of the word which it qualifies,'

Verbs are divided in Eurythmy into different categories, firstly: those expressing a *passive* condition; here the form moves in a straight line forwards.

APOLLONIAN FORMS

In the sentence 'the sun shines', for instance, the movements for the sounds of the word shines should be accompanied by this line forwards. Wherever a feeling of endurance is inherent in the verb itself, indeed wherever there is the implication that something is already done, where something effortless, something which happens of itself, is to be expressed, as in *to have, to be able, to find—one* must move the line of this passive form.

Secondly, the *active* verbs, as, for instance, *to will, to seek, to seize* and so on. These are expressed by a line moving backwards, at the same time trying to feel how in this movement backwards, in contradistinction to the movement forwards to which we are usually accustomed, there lies a definite element of activity.

The auxiliary verb to have is regarded as *passive*; 'to become' is expressed by the *active* line. Dr. Steiner gave as an example of an active verb the sentence: 'The lion bites.'

'The lion roars', on the other hand, implies an activity which is extended over a certain period of time. The same may be said, for instance, of 'to take pains', 'to practise', 'to develop', and so on. Such verbs (as also the auxiliary verb 'to be') are regarded as expressing *duration* and are shown by moving to and fro along a horizontal line.

The observation of these delicate sub-divisions should in no way lead to pedantry; on the contrary, it sharpens one's perceptions and keeps them mobile. The same verb may be regarded as active in one connection, in another as expressing the mood of duration. Or the tending of one characteristic in the direction of the other may be noted and indicated in the form. For instance, verbs which are felt as active and which yet give an impression of continuing over a certain period of time, as 'to strive', 'to struggle', can be so expressed that the original direction of the active verb is modified by moving, not directly backwards, but backwards and somewhat sideways, thus approaching the line of duration.

In the same way a verb of duration can tend in either an active or passive direction, or a passive line may be protracted into a line of duration, according to how the word is experienced in the individual cases.

Now the objective element. In this category are reckoned, in the first place, all nouns designating something *concrete,* something accessible to the senses. Such words are expressed in space by describing an angle with its apex in the background.*

---

* See Appendix.

APOLLONIAN FORMS

One will gradually learn to feel when the angle should be made *obtuse* and when *acute*. Let us take the words: Rock, crag, lightning—with these words one would make the angle narrower than with sea, goblet, willow, and so on. These things are gradually determined by the experience of the sounds and also by the feeling for darkness and light. Forms which are sharp and narrow in character call forth a darker

As the opposite of the *concrete,* we have the second group: *abstract nouns*—nouns, that is to say, which express the conceptual element, indications of space and time, generalisations and so on. Here again one person will feel one thing, another something else. A fairly reliable guide (in the German language) as to whether words are to be conceived as 'abstract' may be found in the terminal syllables: *ung, heit, keit, nis,* etc., which as a general rule indicate generalisations and abstractions. Thus: *Betrachtung* (reflection), *Verirrung*

(aberration), *Gepflogenheit* (habit), *Versäumnis* (negligence), and so on. Such words are expressed by a semi-circle forwards, or by an incomplete circle which begins in the forward direction.

The empty 'hollowness' of the abstract (as Dr. Steiner once described it) must be felt in this form as it arches forwards, leaving what lies in the background incomplete.

The case is similar with *nouns of condition;* these are also expressed in the forward direction, but now in the form

117

of angles.

Among words which express condition may be counted those nouns which are directly derived from verbs, with the article merely added, for here there is the indication that an activity has passed over into a condition: das Lachen (laughter), das Weinen (weeping), das Larmen (uproar), das Treiben (activity), etc. ; also indications of conditions, as sleep, darkness, suffering, joy, dreaming, magic, and soon. From these conditions which are determined by man's relationships and surroundings, we must clearly differentiate *what is of a soul-*

nature—everything located within the soul itself, as: love, hate, musing, faith, sincerity, and so on. Nouns designating a soul-quality are expressed in space by means of a wave-like line.

This form permits of much variation; it can be deeply indentated or merely a delicate suggestion. It can also be laid in such a way that a lemniscate arises.

Yet another gradation of feeling can be introduced when, in the case of some painful experience, the first curve is made

to sink into the background, while, when the soul-experience is joyful, the first curve is begun forwards.

In cases where the soul element is very dominant in a verb, as in: yearning, hoping, enduring, and so on, it is possible to combine the soul- with the verb-form, thus making the soul-line in the active or passive direction.

The same thing can be done when it is a question of expressing some being, some reality, which yet has its existence in the world of soul (demons, furies, etc.). These lines, which sink down into, or rise up out of the depths, create a much more vigorous and living impression than do the sideways movements, which give the impression of a flat surface.

The *nouns of spiritual reality,* which designate everything related to what is divine, to what is super-earthly, have as their form the semi-circle, or any more or less completed circle which begins in a backward direction. The names of the

Gods, for instance, would be shown in eurythmy in this way; and also such words as: God, eternity, angels, and certain words which, in their context, lose their own abstract character and give the impression of a spiritual noun. For instance:

> Was ist nun noch mein Sinn,
> Als dass für eine Pause
> Ich einzig deine Klause
> Mein *Grund* und *Ursprung* bin ?
> (CHRISTIAN MORGENSTERN.)

All these determining factors must not be conceived in a narrow way, but with fantasy and delicate perception; there will then develop a feeling for the beauty and harmonious restraint of these space-forms. And one will also experience, when these forms are rightly divided in space, how one form mutually balances the other. In order to achieve this, and also to bring rhythm and variation of tempo into the performance, the utmost freedom may be introduced into the way these forms are applied; so that in the one case, for instance, a whole sentence may be expressed in *one* duration-form, or again a number of words signifying a similar thing may be included in *one* soul-form. Let us suppose that different, yet similar conditions of soul are enumerated :
'trust, love, activity, strength'. Here, if it is the intention to bring a certain repose into the performance, one strongly-

marked soul-form would suffice; or should one desire to take the intensification of mood into account, one could include 'trust, love' in one soul-line and express 'activity and strength' by an angle of condition.

Interjections, prepositions and conjunctions find visible expression, not by means of forms, but by a bending and raising of the head and upper part of the body. In the case of interjections, according to whether a feeling of joy or sorrow finds outlet in the exclamation, one must make a little spring or a slight bending-movement. The prepositions (of, against, on this side of, on that side of, etc.), find expression in a sideways movement of the head and upper part of the body* and the conjunctions (and, or, yet, but) in a bending or raising of the head in a vertical direction.

These movements must be practiced until they become the absolutely natural expression for the words in question, until they stream out from the soul with a living force; by this means a special element of lightS and supple grace will be brought into the performance of Apollonian forms. The actual space-forms, also, should not simply be moved step by step; the body must always follow the tendency of the form, and this calls forth in the movement an impression of flexibility or strength. If the direction of an angle is backwards, one must emphasise this penetrating into the background by an energetic tension of the muscles of the shoulders and back; in the case of a passive form, the

---

* See Appendix.

body must not simply be carried forwards, but must, if one may put it so, merely be allowed to drift; the active line, on the other hand, must be accompanied by an exertion of all the muscles as if one were striving against some obstacle. The soul-form is the most mobile; here one must feel how the body absolutely gives itself, moulds itself to the double curve. A good preliminary exercise for the attainment of this suppleness, this interplay of the body with the form, is that of standing still and indicating the form with the upper part of the body—or even with the head alone.

These Apollonian forms, which are carried out by movements of the head only, may, for instance, be applied in an exercise for the *harmonizing of thinking, feeling and willing*—an exercise where one of those taking part carries out the intellectual forms, the forms corresponding to the meaning of each word, with the head only, at the same time moving a triangle—thus a thinking form—to the *dactyl* rhythm, but to a text where the recitation is Anapestic. The following translation from Antigone offers a good example:

'Am erspriesslichsten ist stets um glücklich zu sein,
　　　　　　　　　　　　　der besonnene Sinn ;
Und nie frevle darum an der Götter Gesetz !
Der Vermessene büsst das vermessene Wort stets
　　　　　　　　　　　　　mit schwerem Gericht !
Bis im Alter er dann noch lernt, weise zu sein.'

It is quite possible to accompany any rhythm one may choose by beating-in-time to another rhythm; one must simply transpose them both into a musical rhythm - in this case common time—by reckoning two unemphasized to the one emphasized syllable, thus forming bars containing four even beats. Now the dactyl can be shown by treating the first two short syllables as one long and the following long syllable as two short. The Amphibrachus—which in this exercise is beaten time to by a second eurythmist, to this same text—is achieved by the following division: the first short beat of the Anapest is coincident with the first short beat of the Amphibrachus; now the second short and the first half of the long syllable are conceived as one long beat, and the movement for the last short beat comes with the second, that is to say the silent halt of the long beat—seemingly during a pause:

∪ —— ∪ ∪ —— ∪∪ - ——∪∪ ——∪
Am erspriess | lichsten ist | stets um glück | lich zu sein,
∪ — ∪∪ — ∪
der beson | nene Sinn....

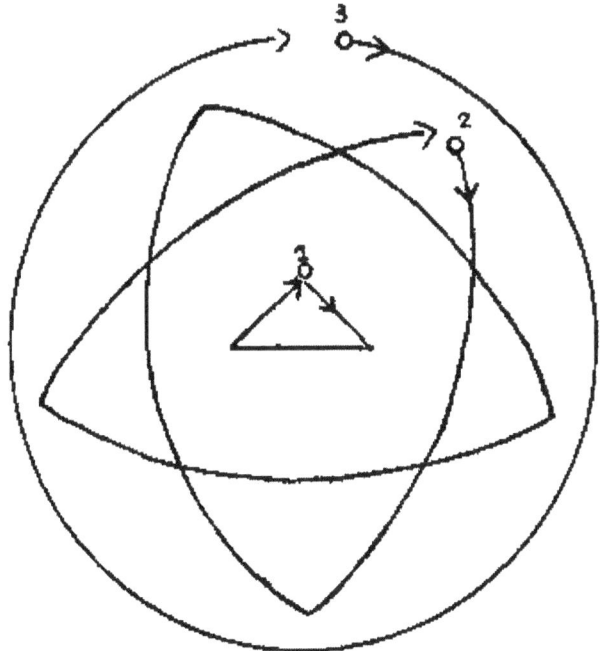

To this measure of the Amphibrachus (also beating time with

the arms) the second eurythmist moves a feeling-form. The third has to describe a will-form, a circle. This eurythmist steps to the *anapestic* rhythm and carries out all the *consonants* of the text: the one standing in the middle (see foregoing diagram), who moves the triangle—which represents thinking—must carry out the *vowel-sounds*. This one has the hardest task: the feet must step the dactyl, carrying out the Dionysian form, the arms must do the movements for the vowel-sounds and the Apollonian forms must be expressed by the head.

Returning to the purely Apollonian forms, one thing is of special importance, namely, the rhythmical and harmonious combination of the sounds with the form. Let us take the name Apollo; if we wish to carry this out to the semi-circle which expresses what is of a divine-spiritual nature we can, for instance, do the movements for the sounds *AP* to the first part of the form, lay the *O* into the middle—where the highest point of the form may be felt—immediately concluding it with the last sounds *LLO*. These things will, however, be differently experienced and expressed by each individual. The important thing is that every Apollonian form should, as it were, be felt as having its flow and ebb, and the sounds divided out accordingly. We will now give, just as an example, a poem—Schiller's 'Nenie'—with a diagrammatic analysis of an Apollonian form—first line by line with the corresponding individual forms and then welded together into a whole.

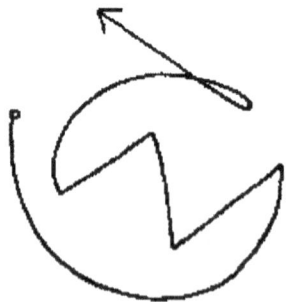

APOLLONIAN FORMS

'Auch das Schöne muss sterben! Das Menschen und Götter bezwinget....' Here a bending of the head with the word *auch* can make a very expressive beginning. *Das* must be treated as an adjective, so that here one remains standing. With *Schöne* we take the half-circle forwards; *muss sterben*— a passive line, laid somewhat slanting. *Das* is again adjectival; *Menschen:* the angle backwards (for a concrete noun); *und* could be accompanied by a raising of the head; *Gotter:* the half-circle backwards; *bezwinget:* an active form, tending towards the character of duration.

Nicht die eherne Brust rührt es des stygischen Zeus....' *Nicht die eherne* is entirely adjectival; one could, however, already begin the movement for the concrete angle for *Brust* with the last syllable of the word *eherne*. *Rührt* implies duration, tending, however, in an active direction; with *es des* one must again stand still for a moment, and for *stygischen Zeus* describe the spiritual curve.

'Einmal nur erweichte die Liebe den Schattenbeherrscher. . . .' *Einmal* nur—adjectival; erweichte—passive; *die Liebe,* a soul-form which moves from the back forwards; *den Schatten-beherrscher*—here, for *Schatten,* one could take an angle of condition, and with *Beherrscher* express the spiritual element.

125

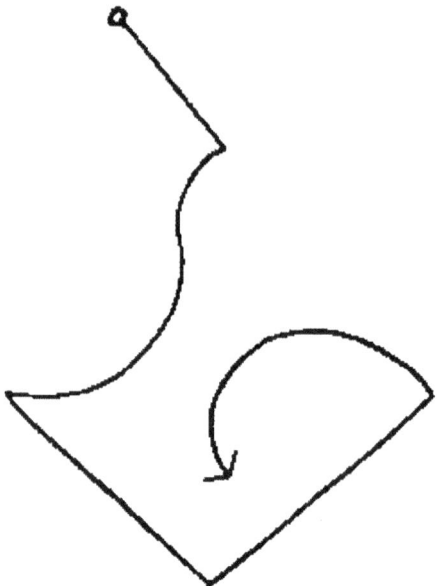

'Und an der Schwelle noch, streng, rief er zurück sein Geschenk...' *Und*—a bending of the head; *an*—a sideways movement of the head; *der Schwelle*—angle backwards; *noch streng,* standing still; *rief,* active; *er,* standing still; with *zurück* the spatial direction could be expressed by a movement of the head; *sein Geschenk*—the half-circle form forwards.

'Nicht stillt Aphrodite dem schönen Knaben die Wunde,' *Nicht*—adjectival; *stillt* implies duration (with short words, the moving to and fro which expresses duration, the retracing of the same line, may simply be indicated by a movement of

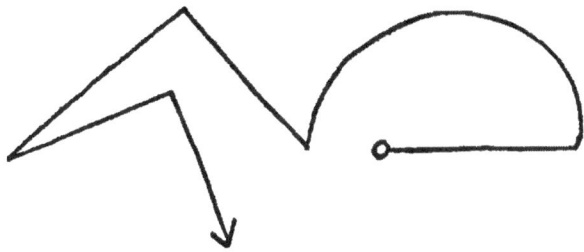

the body first in one, then in the other direction). *Aphrodite*—a spiritual form; *dem* schönen—adjectival; *Knaben* is concrete and *die Wunde* is also concrete. Here, immediately following, we again have two words which must be expressed by the concrete angle, and these, together with the two angles already described, bring about the following form.

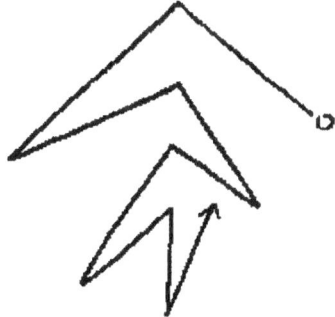

Die in den zierlichen Leib grausam der Eber geritzt.'

Thus one may take the opportunity of expressing the characteristics of this passage by means of a differentiation in the form of the angles.

The following lines can be understood by means of the diagrams:

'Nicht errettet den göttlichen Held die unsterbliche Mutter.'

'Wann er, am skäischen Tor, fallend, sein Schicksal erfüllt.'

'Aber sie steigt aus dem Meer, mit allen Töchtern des Nereus,'

'Und die Klage hebt an um den verherrlichten Sohn.'

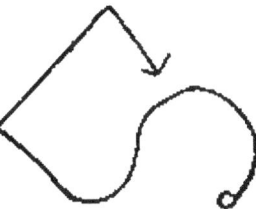

'Siehe, da weinen die Götter, es weinen die Göttinnen alie,'

'Dass das Schöne vergeht, dass das Vollkommene stirbt.'

'Auch ein Klaglied zu sein im Mund der Geliebten ist herrlich,'

(Klaglied zu sein is here included in one soul-form.)

'Denn das Gemeine geht klanglos zum Orkus hinab.'

APOLLONIAN FORMS

Nenie.

Auch das Schöne muss sterben! Das Menschen und Götter bezwinget,
Nicht die eheme Brust rührt es des stygischen Zeus.
Einmal nur erweichte die Liebe den Schattenbeherrscher,
Und an der Schwelle noch, streng, rief er zurück sein Geschenk.
Nicht stillt Aphrodite dem schönen Knaben die Wunde,
Die in den zierlichen Leib grausam der Eber geritzt.
Nicht errettet den göttlichen Held die unsterbliche Mutter,
Wann er, am skäischen Tor, fallend, sein Schicksal erfüllt.
Aber sie steigt aus dem Meer mit alien Töchtern des Nereus,

Und die Klage hebt an um den verherrlichten Sohn.
Siehe, da weinen die Götter, es weinen die Göttinnen alle,
Dass das Schöne vergeht, dass das Vollkommene stirbt.
Auch sein Klaglied zu sein im Mund der Geliebten is
herrlich, Denn das Gemeine geht klanglos zum Orkus hinab.
(SCHILLER.)

(The Beautiful too must die! This vanquishes Men and
  Immortals;
But of the Stygian God moves not the bosom of steel.
Once and once only could love prevail on the Ruler of
  Shadows,
And on the threshold e'en then, sternly his gift he recalled.
Never could Venus heal the wounds of the beauteous
  stripling,
That the terrible boar made in his delicate skin;
Nor could his mother immortal preserve the hero so godlike,
When at the West-Gate of Troy, falling, his fate he fulfilled,
But she arose from the ocean with all the daughters of
  Nereus,
And o'er her glorified son raised the loud accents of woe.
See! where all the Gods and Goddesses yonder are weeping,
That the Beauteous must fade and that the Perfect must die.
Even a woe-song to be in the mouth of the lov'd ones is
  glorious,
For what is vulgar descends mutely to Orcus' dull shades.)

Later on we shall also discover when and where forms must be made larger, when and where smaller; the first point to consider is the distribution of the forms in space, so that a harmonious sense of balance is created.

It will, of course, only in the rarest instances be possible

APOLLONIAN FORMS

to move an Apollonian form strictly to the rhythm of the words; but one must endeavour—in the whole way in which the movement of each form is begun, increased in intensity and again allowed to slacken—to retain an unbroken rhythmic line throughout an entire performance.

X

VARIOUS ASPECTS OF ARTISTIC EXPRESSION

With the movements for the sounds and the space-forms we have laid down the basic principles of Eurythmy as a means of artistic expression; but we have yet to consider certain points of view from which the content and structure of a poem can be regarded. In the first place we must return to that all-pervading trinity, the threefold impulse of *thought, feeling* and *will*. From this point of view—from this aspect of its soul-content—we must analyze every poem which is to be expressed in eurythmy, for this can determine the *size* and *direction* of the movements.

Taking the *thinking element,* with its different aspects and values, Dr. Steiner distinguishes three main categories:

I. *'Comprehensive or predominant thought* (die umfassenden oder übergeordneten Gedanken), which he also termed 'synecdoche'; for this mode of thought corresponds to the Synecdoche in poetry, in so far as this consists in employing the more comprehensive concept to express what is more circumscribed.

In the case of such *comprehensive* thoughts, the movements for the sounds must be made *large,* in order that, as the thoughts proceed to what is less comprehensive, the movements may become smaller. In the example of *comprehensive* thought selected by Dr. Steiner: 'All-beneficent Nature, direct what God has ordained for me...we have 'All-beneficent Nature' as the predominant concept, the thought which, as it were, encompasses the whole sentence and which must accordingly, be brought out by *large* movements for the sounds.*

In most cases the *comprehensive thought* can be recog-

---

* See Appendix.

nized in the structure of a sentence by the fact of its being separated off by a colon (:) or comma (,). For instance:

'*Alles geben die Götter, die unendlichen, ihren Lieblingen ganz*':
    Alle Freuden, die unendlichen,
    Alle Schmerzen, die unendlichen—ganz!'

(GOETHE.)

(*'All is given by the Gods, the infinite ones, to those whom they love—all*:
    All joy—joy infinite,
    All pain—pain infinite—all!')

'*Senke strahlender Gott*—die Fluren dürsten
    Nach erquickendem Tau, der Mensch verschmachtet,
    Matt ziehen die Rosse—
    Senke den Wagen hinab!'

(SCHILLER.)

(*Descend, radiant God*—the meadows pine
    For refreshing dew, men are athirst,
    Wearily pull the horses—
    Let thy chariot descend!)

II. *'Analogous or metaphorical thoughts'* (verwandte, metaphorische Gedanken)—the expression, that is to say, of identical or similar ideas in different imagery:

> Alles Vergängliche
> Ist nur ein Gleichnis;
> Das Unzulängliche,
> Hier wird's Ereignis;
> Das Unbeschreibliche,
> Hier ist's getan;
> Das ewig Weibliche
> Zieht uns hinan.
>
> (GOETHE, *Faust II.*)

> (All things corruptible
> Are but reflection;
> Earth's insufficiency
> Here finds perfection;
> Here the ineffable
> Wrought is with love;
> The Eternal-Feminine
> Draws us above.)

> Wie in hellem Sonnenblicke
> Sich ein Farbenteppich webt,
> Wie auf ihrer bunten Brücke
> Iris durch den Himmel schwebt,
> So ist jede schöne Gabe
> Flüchtig wie des Blitzes Schein;
> Schnell in ihrem düstern Grabe
> Schliesst die Nacht sie wieder ein.
>
> (SCHILLER, *Die Gunst des Augenblicks.*)

(As in the sun's bright rays a color-web is woven, as Iris
floats across the gay-hued bridge of heaven,
so, transient as the lightning's gleam, is
each fair gift, swift to be recalled into the somber grave of
night.)

In phrases such as these, which are separated from each other by a comma (,) or semi-colon (;)—it is the single train of thought underlying the analogies which must be brought out, and this can be done by making all the movements as similar in style as possible—letting the repeated sounds, for instance, imitate each other, and generally carrying out all the gestures in the same direction and approximately the same size.

III. *Contiguous thoughts* (Berührende Gedanken), which are also described as 'metonymous thoughts', for in their case, as in metonymy, the real meaning is not explicitly stated but rather conveyed by the introduction of another thought, which only refers to the former in the most distant way.

A verse from the *Hawamâl* of the *Edda* can serve as an example:

> 'Wie Körner im Sand, klein an Verstand
> Ist kleiner Seelen Sinn.
> Ungleich ist der Menschen Einsicht;
> Zwei Hälften hat die Welt.'

> (Like grains in the sand, barren of intelligence
> Are the ideas of the petty mind.
> How different the human concept;
> Two halves has the world.)

With thoughts of this type, which refer to each other only distantly—they may be recognized by the final full-stop (.), or semi-colon (;)—the movements for the sounds must be as diverse as possible. At one time vowels should be selected, at another consonants, and the size of the movements varied as well as their direction.

Now just in this sphere of the direction of the movements, we can be guided by certain differentiations of the *feeling element*. In this connection we must observe the emotions of *joy, sorrow, expectation, fulfillment, suspense, relief* and *yearning*. In order to bring these differentiations of feeling to expression, one must distinguish two zones, one *in the front,* the other *behind,* within which the movements for the sounds can be carried out. These two zones can be kept apart by imagining a dividing line, a plane, which does not cut the human body exactly in half, but is erected slightly to the front, making, as it were, a partition between *front* and *back.* Everything which takes place in front of this partition is active in the zone of *pain;* and all movements carried out behind it, behind the back and reaching right out into the background, express *joy.* This can be understood when one considers how, in the case of pain—as Spiritual Science teaches—there is a contraction of forces, a *turning inwards.* This is indicated in the movements by carrying out the sounds or combination of sounds in the direction from behind forwards, from without inwards, or else downwards. One can even make an intensification of the feeling of pain apparent by leading the movements from outside inwards by small stages, so that they become, as it were, more and more contracted. This is reversed when it is a question of reproducing feelings of joy. *Joy expands* the soul, leads it *outwards* into the environment. The Eurythmy movements must therefore be carried out in a backward direction, as though evaporating into the distance, and, within this backward zone, high up and narrow. This is also connected with the possibilities of expressing *light and darkness* already discussed in Part I. Pain is experienced as something dark, something bowed down; joy streams outwards, radiating light.

Expectation and *Suspense,* as feelings very closely related to each other, are also expressed in a somewhat similar way. During the mood of expectation all the movements for the sounds are carried out in the frontal zone, approximately at shoulder-level and radiating fairly widely to both sides. With the mood of suspense the arms are also stretched well forwards, but now their position is narrower and more contracted. When it is a question of expressing *Fulfillment* or *Relief* the gestures for the sounds are led over into the zone lying at the back—in the case of fulfillment to shoulder-level, and, in the case of relief, somewhat lower, letting the arms fall limp and relaxed. Taking the poem 'Alle' by Conrad Ferdinand Meyer, for instance, the whole last verse should be kept in this zone of fulfillment:

'Es sprach der Geist: Sieh auf! Die Luft umblaute
Ein unermesslich Mahl, soweit ich schaute,
Da sprangen reich die Brunnen auf des Lebens,
Da streckte keine Schale sich vergebens,
Da lag das ganze Volk auf vollen Garben,
Kein Platz war leer und keine durfte darben.'

(The spirit spoke: Look up! The azure air
Sheds sustenance immeasurable around,
Then gushed the fountains with life-giving streams,
None vainly stretched forth vessels to be filled,
The granaries were stocked with fruitful sheaves,
No place was bare, nor yet need any starve.)

A transition from marked suspense to the mood of fulfillment is to be found in the two final verses of another poem by C. F. Meyer:

'Ich sehe dich Jäger, ich seh dich genau,
Den Felsen umschleichest du grau auf dem Grau,
Jetzt richtest empor du das Rohr in das Blau—

Zu Tale zu steigen, das wäre mir Schmerz—
Entsende, du Schütze, entsende das Erz!
Jetzt bin ich ein Seliger! Triff mich ins Herz!'

(I see thee, O Hunter, thou art clear to mine eye
Round rocky crags creeping, grey against grey—
Now upward into the blue is thy musket-barrel pointing.

To descend to the valley, too cruel were the pain!
Discharge then O musket, let the shot fly—
Now bliss be my lot! Aim true at my heart!)

Here the sounds of the first three lines must be made quite narrow and well to the front; the sentence: ' zu Tale zu steigen, das wäre mir Schmerz,' as a thought which is only touched upon, must be carried out quite differently, merely inserted, as it were, while the two last lines must pass over from a strong impulse of will (which can be expressed by the gaze of the eyes, and also, as we shall learn later, by one of the foot-positions) to the mood of fulfillment, where with the words 'jetzt bin ich ein Seliger' the movements must be carried out in the zone at the back and in an upward direction. An example of *tension relaxed* is to be found in the poem: 'Der Tod und Frau Laura' by C. F. Meyer. The last verse runs:

'Der Lorbeer schwebt. Da raubt ihn eine Hand,
Frau Laura war es, die daneben stand,
Sie schmiegt ihn um die blonden Haare leicht,
Sie steht bekränzt. Sie schaudert. Sie erbleicht.'

(The laurel shakes, culled by a robbing hand.
Dame Laura was it, who beside it stood.
She bound it lightly round her flaxen hair.
She stands there crowned. She shudders. She turns pale.)

Here the movements must be led backwards, and a gradual sinking down of the arms must be added to express the passivity inherent in tension relaxed.

Yearning has a definite zone of its own—a narrow, contracted space immediately *in front of the breast*. One must imagine that, with each sound, there is a longing to get outside this zone and yet that one is unable to do so, being ever and again thrust back. This impression will be further intensified by contracting the muscles with a feeling of tenseness, of inner pain.

It holds good for all these aspects—as well as those which follow—that they can always be allowed to interpenetrate, to *play one into the other*. Indeed, it is the mingling and contrasting of these different possibilities which first make the movements interesting and expressive. It is not only the definite zone which is important, but the *direction from which the movement comes*; thus the *last,* the *preceding* gesture must always be taken into consideration. One can, for instance, indicate *fulfillment* or *relief* by a slight backward tendency in the movement, or express a passing feeling of *yearning*—right in the midst, perhaps, of some quite different mood—by a tension of the muscles so transient and slight that it practically remains inner feeling only.

Love and hate are counted as *impulses of will.* An impulse of love finds expression in gestures made from without inwards, as though gathering something together with a warm feeling of embrace. It is the movement which can most beautifully be combined with the sound *o,* the expression of loving wonder. With hate the direction is *outwards* and more especially *backwards.* Of course, with all these things the point is not only the zone or the direction, but the way they are carried out. The movements in the zone of fulfillment will be made wide and outgoing, as if dissolving in space, while everything connected with hate and antipathy will be carried out with abrupt and impetuous energy. Tenderness, abundance of warmth, must lie in the inward-tending movements of love, while pain contracts inwards, cramped and rigid. By means of this strict division into zones, the movements will reach a level above anything subjective, pantomimic or arbitrary.

Certain postures of the body can also be used to emphasize special points in a performance. In this connection we have to consider the Eurythmy expression for the *exclamation,* the *question,* and for those conditions of soul which may be described as *knowledge* and the *power to communicate something.* These four aspects are made use of to depict vivid accentuations of mood. In the case of the *exclamation,* wherever, that is to say, an exclamation mark occurs in the text, the upper part of the body and head are *bent somewhat backwards.* There must be the impression of very decided erectness. It must be borne in mind, however, that the arm movements should not follow this upward direction, but should remain in another zone, which can be determined by some other aspect of the text. An exclamation which contains much of the element of will—for instance, a command or order—could be very characteristically expressed if the backward-tending posture of the body were combined with sounds carried out in the will-zone, in a ownward direction, that is to say. Something dictatorial, something decisive, would then be brought to expression.

With the *question* one turns somewhat sideways towards the *right*. This questioning mood is best expressed, when, throughout the whole sentence containing the question, this posture is gradually taken up (the zone most frequently advisable for the arms is the zone of *expectation)* till—with the last word, where the question-mark actually occurs—the head and neck are stretched forwards in an attitude of listening. (This questioning attitude, which is expressed by the poise of the whole body and is bound up with the gradual trend of the sentence, must be distinguished from the arm-position given in the Speech Eurythmy Course as a definite posture, to be introduced just at the point where the question-mark or exclamation-mark *interrupts* the sentence, thus keeping the gesture entirely separate from the movements for the sounds. Either can be introduced according to the context—the latter where a definite posture would serve to call forth an expressive and strongly delineated impression, the former where one merely wishes to introduce a mood, something delicate and vague.)

If, in a text, a passage occurs which indicates the mood of *knowledge* this is expressed by holding the upper part of the body somewhat *bent over into itself.* Here one can feel how the forces of knowledge work contractingly upon the bodily nature. The process of mineralization, which, as Dr. Steiner taught us, is active in thinking, can be experienced in this—at most only slightly indicated—stooping or bending of the body.

When it is a question of *making a communication,* if anything is recounted or described, the upper part of the body must tend *slightly forwards.* This gesture also can be very convincing; one must, however, be careful that the gaze of the eyes is not turned downwards or inwards, but freely outwards, just as in ordinary life anyone making a communication looks straight in the face of his hearers.

Certain differentiations can also be made, according to whether what is to be expressed takes place in the *past, present* or *future*. If events from the past are to be portrayed, the posture of the eurythmist can be such that the body is, as it were, somewhat *pressed down into itself* (In the case of the primeval conditions of mythology, it is indeed possible to assume almost a *crouching posture.*) For everything to do with the present the *normal* posture of the body is retained; and, if it is a question of the future, one must, as it were, increase one's stature, reaching upwards until one is *standing on the toes*.

The size, not of the gestures only, but also of the form, can be determined from the following points of view. In the case of everything bound up with *hearing* the eurythmist introduces *large gestures and forms*. If it is a description of anything bound up with *sight, small forms* must be described, the gestures on the contrary remaining *large*. And with *feeling*, with the inner experience of the soul, both sounds and form must be of *medium size*.

Now as to *tempo* and *pauses*. With regard to tempo, we have three possibilities: the movement of the form can be *accelerated, retarded* or remain at the *same speed*.

Something active is always inherent in *acceleration;* it is the expression of opposing something, offering resistance, *warding something off*. This can also be used in suitable passages as a means of expression. *Retardation* of the movement of the form gives the impression of *passivity;* it is the expression of *pain, either of body or soul*. When, on the other hand, the tempo of the movement remains *unchanged,* this can show 'that one is in a state of contentment both of body and soul'; that one is 'holding one's own' in the most comprehensive sense of the term.

The *pauses,* the intervals occurring between the movements, are also very significant. If, in the case of a dialogue, for instance, the eurythmist makes longer pauses between the separate parts of speech, holding the gestures for quite a long while, this is a way of saying that one 'intends to retain the content of the conversation ', to make it part of oneself. If the opposite is the case, if one will have nothing to do with the matter in question, wishing to 'get rid' of the content of the conversation, this freeing oneself from the whole business is expressed by *short pauses only* between the movements, thus calling forth an impression of speed and haste.

These are the most general aspects from which one can study a text to be expressed in Eurythmy. In countless individual cases, however, Dr. Steiner gave in addition definite postures, gestures, positions of head, feet or of the whole body—indications drawn out from the spiritual origin of the poem in question and greatly enhancing the truth and vividness of the whole impression.

XI

CERTAIN CHARACTERISTIC EXERCISES

A profound effect on the soul is produced by an exercise, which, in simplified form, can be learned even in the first stages of eurythmy teaching. Such an exercise will, however, only be fully experienced when through frequent repetition, everything thus far described has become second nature, when the body has reached the point of instinctively following the fundamental laws of eurythmy.

This exercise consists in expressing in movement the Hebrew word *Hallelujah*—the meaning of which Rudolf Steiner rendered in the phrase: 'I purify myself from everything that hinders my looking upon God.' This conception will be understood in a living way, if, from the standpoint of eurythmy, one enters into the formation of each single sound contained in the word.

It begins with the sound *H,* and here we can already feel the wafting breath of the God Jehovah. This opens itself expectantly into an *a,* which passes over to *l* seven times repeated. The *l* begins tenderly, in an inward mood, and increases in size with a feeling of ever freer expansion. The succeeding *e* intensifies the mood of reverent expectation; the soul realizes: 'It is approaching'—the divinity, that is to say, for whose appearance the soul is preparing itself. Now an *l* is formed three times, with large, reposeful movements, and then comes the culmination: 'It is here'—with a feeling of awe the mystical union with the divinity is realized in the *u*. The final vowels *jah*—the initial letters of the name *Jahve*— are carried out, as though with re-echoing jubilation, in that part of space which forms the zone of fulfillment.

A still deeper insight into what occurs in the soul during

the utterance of these vowel-sounds *A E U I A* has been vouchsafed to us through words spoken by Rudolf Steiner, in another connection, about the nature of the vowels. In one of the wonderful forewords, which he made a point of giving before eurythmy performances, he said: 'When we utter an *a* we have the feeling that something spiritual enters into us, which becomes united with our soul-life, and which cleaves us, as it were, in two.' And in the previous sentence: 'When we utter an *e*, we feel as though this spiritual element (which, as he previously explained, makes itself known to us in the sound *o)*, penetrates into our own body and there holds sway.' And speaking of u: '...that the sound *u* springs unconsciously out of the human soul whenever this human soul comes into connection with what, as super-earthly occurrences, is outside itself. . . .' And 'When uttering an *i*, we only have a correct picture when we see in this *i* the confirmation of the spiritual within ourselves, the process, as it were, of increase brought about by what comes from ourselves.'

These words will be a revelation to the student, bringing to his consciousness the reality of the movements he is carrying out. When this sequence of sounds has been entered into thus deeply, the movements of the arms can be combined with a form ; at first in such a way that the eurythmist moves the lines of a pentagram, standing still at each point and there doing the whole word once through. The beginning is taken from the point of the pentagram lying in the background.

The transition from one point to another can be made with either five or seven steps, the arms retaining the last *h*-movement. The face—this also applies to the transitions—must be strictly directed towards the front.

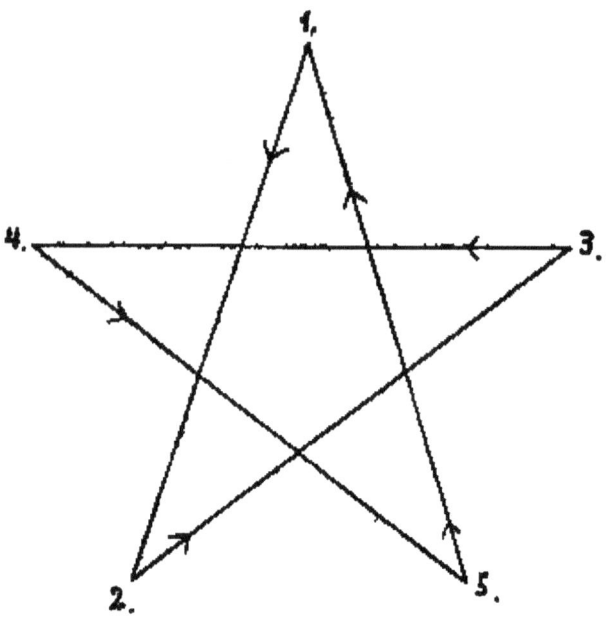

This exercise can, however, also be carried out in such a way that a person stands on each point of the pentagram; they do the sounds simultaneously and then, beginning to move the form, exchange places. When 1 has got to point 2, 2 to 3, 3 to 4, 4 to 5 and 5 to 1, the word is carried out a second time, the places are again exchanged, and so it goes on till everyone has moved a complete pentagram. Or again, the movements for the sounds can be carried out during the movement of the form in the way described in the Speech Eurythmy Course.

If seven people take part they are arranged as follows:

Here again the exercise is first done in such a way that all stand still and simultaneously carry out the eurythmy movements for the word Hallelujah, and then each one makes the transition to the next place with three, four or five steps—excepting the one standing at point 7, who runs in a half-circle, behind the places of those standing at the back, to the place of number 1. This is repeated until the original position is regained. (A freer way of carrying out this form also is found in the Speech Eurythmy Course.)

An equally profound and striking impression is created by the eurythmy interpretation of the greeting *Evoe:* 'We seek and have found one another.' If this is done by two people (any number of pairs can be arranged in the circle), each one, with the sound *E*, takes a step towards the person standing opposite, bends forward and lightly touches him—*v*—regains the upright position with *o* and steps one step back with the final *e.* Or, alternatively, all those who are standing in the circle take a step towards the center with the first *e,* then the gesture of greeting is directed towards an imaginary presence in the center, everybody bending low and lightly touching the ground ; with the *o* they raise themselves up and the final *e* once more brings them back to the circumference. A single person also can express the greeting in this way, by the deep bending movement that is to say, and the touching of the earth.

These movements, combined with a circular form and accompanied by the various soul-gestures—inwardness, *merriment, earnestness, solemnity* and so on—gave rise to the exercise *Evoe,* which, with suitable music, is specially adapted to precede and follow poems of earnest and solemn content.

'*I look up* '—it is in this mood of soul that one carries out another exercise in which the hands are placed together in the gesture for *devotion;* the arms are at first held high up, the gaze of the eyes is also directed upwards, the heels are raised from the ground and one stands poised on the toes. Now, quite gradually, as slowly as possible, one sinks downwards, with the knees bent. While making this downward movement, the arms are also drawn down. When this kneeling posture has been reached (always remaining balanced on the toes,) the hands will be close to the body at breast-level ; the gaze of the eyes is lowered. Now, equally slowly, without jerk or interruption, the body is again raised up and the arms also move in an upward direction until finally one is again standing in the original upward-tending posture.

This exercise can also be carried out somewhat differently, so that the arms move in an opposite direction to the body. As one sinks downwards, with the knees bent, the arms and hands are raised upwards in the gesture of devotion. It is as though the heavier part of man, the physical, were sinking downwards and the soul being gently raised up. With the final kneeling posture the arms are raised right up and the gaze is also directed upwards. Now, as one re-assumes the upright posture, the arms are gradually drawn downwards; the soul-element is once more drawn back into the body.

'The inner has conquered.'
'The outer has conquered.'

These two states of soul can be brought to expression in eurythmy by means of definite forms derived from variations of the circle.

In a lecture given in Dornach (July 28th, 1914), in which Dr. Steiner spoke from the point of view of architecture about certain forms and the soul-experiences bound up with them, he drew these two variations of the simple form of the circle:*
'These variations of the circular line express a conflict, a coming into action, as it were, with the outer world...'*

This can be experienced in a really living way when these forms are reproduced in eurythmy movement. With the small indentations of the first diagram, one can immediately feel how a force—a soul-force—presses from inside outwards conquering what is external: *'The inner has conquered.'* When, however, the circle is cut into with jagged indentations, one experiences a conquest over what is within:

'The outer has conquered.' In the case of poems which

---

* The reader should be reminded that, when looking at the diagrams, the book should be turned upside-down. Here, then, what at first appears to be diagram I is in reality diagram II.
* From *Ways to a New Style of Architecture*, five lectures by Rudolf Steiner, published both in German and in English translation.

express something similar these forms can also be applied. The curves or jagged points, as the case may be, can, of course, be varied in size and divided out as seems best.

This group of exercises also includes the following form, which is carried out to the words : *'We seek for the soul—we are illumined by the spirit'* (Wir suchen die Seele—uns strahlet der Geist):

'We seek for the soul.'

'We are illumined by the spirit.'

Here one can either do the eurythmy movements for the sounds or the arms can be held in certain gestures—with the first sentence *Inwardness*, for example, with the second *Merriment* or *Solemnity*.

The following spiral-form is somewhat similar in character.

The pupils stand in a circle, and, to the eurythmy movements for the vowels *I U A,* move the spiral-lines of the form; then, during a slight pause, they swing back to their places (short dotted line), and with the same vowel-sounds, begin the form anew. Practiced at the beginning and end of a eurythmy lesson this exercise develops in the class a feeling of harmonious unity.

XII

THE COLORS

That sounds can be either light or dark was already mentioned when the vowels were being discussed. How this light and darkness arises—that in every stretched movement light is sent outwards, that in every curved movement light is inwardly consumed—all this, at the stage the pupil has now reached, can become an inner artistic certainty. Apart from this, however, there is a quite definite means of expressing colors in eurythmy. This must, of course, be preceded by an inner understanding of the nature of color, not only where this is actually visible to the eye, but also where it can be perceived as a spiritual reality underlying certain soul-experiences. A preparation for this conception of the nature of color may be gained from studying the final section of Goethe's Color-Teaching: *Sinnlich-sittliche Wirkung der Farben.* (The sensible-moral Effect of the Colors.) There, from an aesthetic-moral aspect, we find the experience of color intensified and spiritualized. Rudolf Steiner, who deeply appreciated the fundamentals of the Goetheanistic color-teaching, himself carried this spiritual method of investigation further; and he brings forward his results in a lecture, for instance, of 1915, where he speaks of the experiences one can have if one concentrates intently on the single colors; he points out the possibility of 'so intensive a union' with the colors, that one does not reach to the external sense-impression only, but penetrates to what can be experienced behind the colors, to the living force which manifests itself through the colors.

That some dawning feeling for the spiritual depths contained in these reflections on the separate colors may be aroused, and in order to prepare the way for an understanding of what really is intended in the presentation of color in eurythmy, a few short passages from this lecture will here be quoted. Speaking of red, the passage runs: 'If one merges oneself into a world of red, becomes identified with the color red. . . one will not be able to experience anything in this red world, where man himself is red, except that this whole world of red is impregnated with the substance of divine anger, which streams towards us from all sides, directed against every possibility in us of evil and sin.' And as a reaction to this experience something comes to birth in the soul which Dr. Steiner describes in the words:

'One learns to pray.'

When we live thus intensively with color, we experience orange as 'endowing us with inner force'. We feel 'that we become stronger and stronger, that we are not merely shattered by just punishment, but that we are approached by something which does not chastize, but rather strengthens. Thus we live into the color orange and we then learn the longing to enter into the inmost being of things and to unite it with ourselves. Living in the color red, we learn to pray; living in the color orange, we learn the longing for knowledge of the inner nature of things.'

And if one identified oneself completely with the color blue one would go through the world experiencing the need of passing with the blue ever further and further outwards, of conquering one's own egoism, of becoming macrocosmic, of developing the power of sacrifice. And it would be a happy thing to be able to remain in this state of mind, through which divine compassion approaches us. Passing through the world in this way we should indeed feel ourselves favored with divine compassion.'

Dr. Steiner once summed up in short phrases the fundamental idea of the colors, as these should be experienced by the eurythmist with a view to reproducing them in eurythmy-movement. He described the active colors, those, that is to say which range from red to yellow, which contain the light, as the *angry-courageous colors*; the passive aspect, the blue-violet colors, which always contain something of darkness, he described as the *yearning colors*; and green, the *neutral-balancing color*, which gives a feeling of satisfaction, of strength, but which also stimulates the egoistic forces, he described as the *pedantic-Wagnerian color*. (Wagner in the first scene of *Faust.)*

Out of such an experience, even though it is only dim—the germ merely of a more profound artistic understanding—the eurythmist will now begin to realize the colors which underlie a poem, following the changing mood conjured up by its pictures and words. These furnish a real possibility of eurythmy-expression, for we have, as it were, a eurythmy color-circle expressed in movement—primarily in movements of the hand. When a *stretched* movement of the arm is continued on into the hand (preferably with the wrist slightly turned, so that the palm of the hand is not directed downwards, but inwards) we convey the impression of green, the color which, from the standpoint of soul-experience, stands midway between the active colors and the passive. Thus if the color-mood of green, the calming, neutralizing atmosphere, appears in a poem—and there, too, where the actual sense-impression is described and yet the spiritual reality stands in the background—this finds its Eurythmy-expression in the stretched movement of the arm, which is continued on into the hand.

A brightening towards yellow is conveyed by opening the hand *outwards,* so that an angle arises between hand and forearm; and indeed, the more the hand is bent backwards, the more forceful and energetic does the color become, passing from yellow to orange and from orange to red. An impression of purple-red would be conveyed if one could manage to bend the back of the hand until it came into contact with the forearm, thus exposing the palm of the hand to the light to the fullest imaginable extent.

The passive colors are expressed when one portrays the darkness of their nature by a bending of the hand *inwards*. Here the color becomes more and more densified in proportion to the narrowness of the *angle* formed by the hand and inner side of the forearm. A merely slight bending inwards indicates the transition from green to blue; then the bending is mae more pronounced and the color indigo is experienced, which finally passes over into violet.

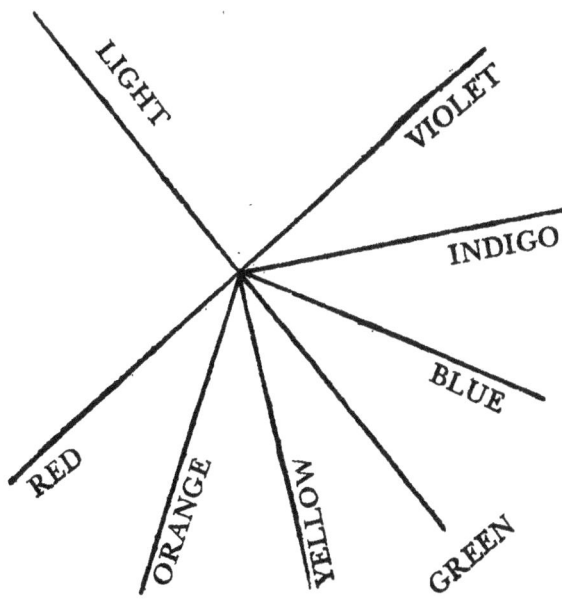

When the hand is *closed into a fist*, the impression of *black* arises; *white* is expressed when the fingers are spread out like rays, accompanied by a slight up-and-down movement of the hand (the palm being turned inward).

In this way, then, we have the possibility of coloring the sounds in accordance with the mood experienced. There are two ways in which the colors can be made clearly apparent. They may either be retained quite systematically through the entire sequence of the movements for the sounds—for instance, in a poem expressing a passive yearning each sound is formed with the hands bent inwards, so that the audience sees only the *back of the hands;* or—and this will be specially effective in the case of the active colors—the color is continually allowed to flash out from a neutral position of the hands. Thus an angry red can be introduced into a poem by forming certain sounds only with a pronounced jerk of the hand outwards, allowing it to fall back between whiles into its previous position.

These antitheses of movement—bending inwards and bending outwards—can, naturally, be carried over to the other limbs, to the elbow, shoulder-joint, and so on. One can, indeed, even feel the angle formed by the line of the back or nape of the neck as a possible means of expression for the active or passive colors, just as one does the angle at the wrist. That this freedom is permissible is clearly indicated by a remark of Dr. Steiner's about the portrayal of light and darkness in *form-running,* where, as he said, the movement of the form must either curve *sharply outwards* or else be *bent inwards.*

In a lecture of August 5th, 1922, Dr. Steiner spoke for the first time—with reference to the eurythmy-figures—about the definite relationships of color inherent in each individual sound. In the study of this very important aspect, we come, however, more into the sphere of inner feeling and conception and less into that of a definite method of presenting the colors.

XIII

POSITIONS OF THE HEAD

The positions and movements of the head express the relation of man to the spirit. Here again, when present at the working out of some artistic production, Dr. Steiner frequently gave individual indications—always original, characteristic and corresponding to the style and spirit of the poem in question—as to definite postures, sequences of head-movements or a special direction of the gaze of the eyes. There are certain simple, basic positions of the head which may be found more precisely analysed in the XV Eurythmy Lecture. As a general rule it may be stated that everything portraying a relationship to the spirit which is of the nature of will is expressed by a *turning* or *bending* of the head towards the *right side*. The way in which this is brought about—whether a greater or lesser tension of the muscles is exerted and where the inner impulse towards this tension is located —all this determines whether a positive or negative will-impulse is expressed; an: 'I will,' or 'I will not, that something occurs.' If, for instance, when bending the head, one feels a marked connection between chin and shoulder*, this gives a more affirmative impression: 'I will.' The same movement, made with less exertion of the muscles of the nape of the neck, merely allowing the head to sink (in the way demonstrated in the lectures), expresses:

'I will not'. This also holds good for the left side, where with the head correspondingly bent or turned—one can experience: *'I feel'* or *'I do not feel.'* It is much the same with the movement of the head in a vertical direction. If the head is lowered slowly, as though with thoughtful consideration, this portrays:

---

* See Appendix.

'I understand you.' If the head is allowed to fall with a jerk, the opposite impression arises:

'I do not understand you.' To quote the XV Eurythmy Lecture: 'One sinks into oneself when confronted with what one is unable to comprehend.' *'I understand myself'* is expressed by a slight upward-movement of the head; when the head is held in its normal, erect position, this signifies *'The utmost dependence upon universe and at the same time the utmost inner detachment.'*

When studying these positions of the head one must always bear in mind a remark once made by Dr. Steiner, that they do not bring the experience to *complete expression.* Just in this sphere of the head-positions, then, is it of special importance to approach each case with unbiased judgment and to allow the fullest freedom in the application of the movements.

XIV

POSITIONS OF THE FEET

The positions of the feet are introduced into dramatic texts when it is a question of intensifying certain effects or of laying special stress upon definite parts of speech. These foot-positions are best introduced when the sounds are carried out standing still; but they can also be introduced into the form-running, by means, for instance, of beginning or ending a form with a definite step.

These movements of the feet must be practiced for a long while and one must experiment with many examples before gaining a real feeling for them.

We must distinguish three ways of setting down the foot:

I. Placing the foot *straight* in front or behind; when carried out with the *right* foot, and in such a way that the whole foot is set down:
    in front = 'contentment', 'cheerfulness'.
    behind = 'discontent', 'earnestness'.
when carried out so that the *toe only* touches the ground,
    in front = 'sympathy'.
    behind = 'antipathy'.

II. When the foot is set down in a *diagonal* direction:
right, with the *whole* foot,
    in front = 'courage', 'activity';
with the *toe only,*
    in front = 'excitement'.
left, with the *whole* foot,
    in front = 'suffering', 'weakness '.
with the *toe only,*
    behind = 'a tranquilizing feeling'.

We must here make the following distinction: when this last position is reached with the left foot leading, one feels:

'I calm myself'; this final position can, however, also be reached by setting down the right foot somewhat to the side, leaving the left, which remains behind, quite free of weight; then the activity of this movement produces the feeling:

'I am calming you'.

III. One foot is carried in a slight curve (1/4 of a circle) and set down in front or behind the other:
right, behind,
    on the toes = 'suspense'.
    with the whole foot = 'aversion', 'I do not understand'.
    set down firmly = 'negation'.
left, in front,
    on the toes = 'a feeling of relief'.
    with the whole foot = 'I understand'.
    set down firmly = 'confirmation', 'affirmation'.

When both feet are set down firmly side by side, this creates an impression of 'persistent, calm strength'. A slight bending of the knees can be introduced when something relates to the past, when it is a question of 'memory'. When the feeling of courage and activity takes on the character of an 'order' or 'demand', the corresponding step can be strengthened by taking a preliminary step with the left foot and then the sideways foot-position with the right foot. This step can also express the 'bringing of a message'.

When applying the foot-positions—they are used most frequently in dramatic poems, also in monologues and dialogues—the impression of conviction which should be called up in the audience depends upon the intensity with which one is able to experience the special mood in which the foot is to be set down. Further, it is not the final position only which must be considered, but how one reaches it—with how much tension of the muscles the small curve backwards is described, how soothingly the foot can be set down with 'I am calming you', with how much energy the active, commanding step is made, and so on.

The foot-positions can be emphasized and made specially telling when, in a poem, the more descriptive or lyrical-musical parts are expressed in freely moved forms, and when, with the dramatic action—with dialogue, for instance—the actual space-forms are allowed to sink into the background, being supplemented as a means of expression by movements of the feet.

Two other forms shall here be sketched, as their dramatic effect is somewhat related to the foot-positions. They are used to express *'fear'* and *'alarm'*.

Fear.   Alarm.

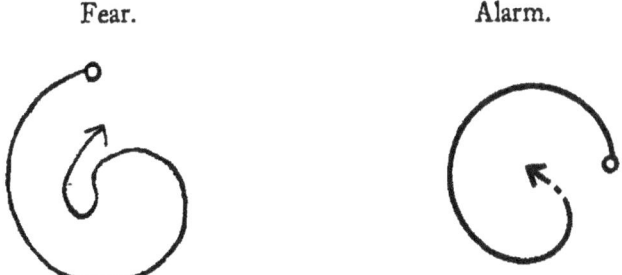

These forms are, fundamentally, spiral-forms. In the case of fear the line turns, as it were, slightly away from the middle, as though fleeing from the center-point; when alarm is to be expressed, the spiral-line is again moved inwards, but here the center-point is reached by means of a short spring.

The positions for 'irony' and 'roguery' can also be dealt with here, for both these moods often make their appearance where the foot-positions can be introduced. An ironic attitude is indicated by bringing the whole body into an s-like posture, this being brought about by raising the right shoulder, bringing the right hip somewhat forwards. the left knee also slightly forwards and touching the ground with the toe of the left foot. When irony passes over into 'roguery', the foot is set down firmly, the *s*- posture of the body being, however, retained, with the addition of a sharp sideways movement of eyes and chin.

These gestures and positions—taking into account all that Dr. Steiner said about them in the Speech-Eurythmy Course—may be called the *individual expression of the human spirit*. And indeed this whole domain will mainly be a question of individual study. The essential group-forms, the reciprocal interplay of several people in space—which are based upon definite laws of form and upon the structure of the various types of poetry—and finally the choral-forms, which are the reflection of cosmic events, all these will be described in the last part of this book.

Part III

XV

GROUP-EXPRESSION OF ALLITERATION AND ASSONANCE

Quite different is it, whether a single eurythmist makes use of his limbs as the instrument for visible speech (standing still), or whether a group of people are placed and move in mutual relation to each other. Dr. Steiner frequently mentioned this difference in his opening addresses. He spoke, for instance, as follows: ... 'Now when a number of people are formed into a group (or a single person moves *in space),* when the relationship of one person to another is expressed by means of groups, there enters into this speech made visible everything otherwise manifested in speech itself as warmth of soul, pleasure and pain, joy, sorrow and enthusiasm, as also rhythm, rhyme, beat and so on. All this is expressed by the movement of individuals *in space,* or by the movement of groups; whereas the word as such is expressed by the movement of a single person who remains quiescent ...(in space).

We must now make the acquaintance of a number of such group forms and exercises. In this connection we will first describe a development of the exercise in alliteration already mentioned in Parts I and II, in which what otherwise was carried out by one eurythmist alone is brought into a living relationship with the movements of others. In this case the pupils do not stand in a line as in the elementary exercise, but take up their places in a circle, composed, for instance, of six people; and now, from outside this circle—'from chaos'—there enters into this already existing formation a seventh eurythmist who, with the first alliterative word, stands behind the place of number I, making the movement for the first consonant of this word and letting it pass over into the succeeding vowel-sound.

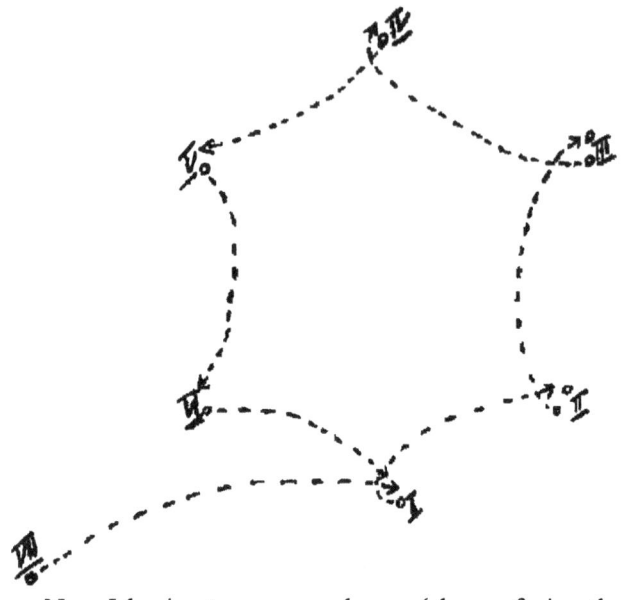

Now I begins to move and runs (always facing the front) behind the place of II, carrying out the alliterated consonant, while VII (who in between has taken a step forwards in order to take the place of I) repeats the sounds once more; then II runs behind III, and so on. Taking, for instance, the alliteration[*]: *Da wallen und wogen die Wipfel des Waldes, da brausen die Bäume und beugen sich bange*. With '*Da*' VII must enter, and with '*wallen*', already standing, do the eurythmy movements for *wa;* with '*und*' I runs to the next place, making the movement for *wo* behind II (VII at the same time repeating *wa*); then II goes behind III: *wi* (I repeating *wo),* and so on. When the new alliterative sound enters—*b* in this case—those already standing once

---

[*] This alliteration may be freely translated: 'Like a torrent it tears through the tops of the trees, with a battling of branches which bend in the blast,' and the form carried out exactly as with the German text. (Translator's Note.)

more show the previously alliterated *w*.

A beautiful interplay of the sounds is brought about when either one or several eurythmists stand in the middle of the circle doing the vowel-sounds, while those moving on the periphery express, not the first sound only, but every consonant of the alliterative word, at the same time adhering to the rhythm, in such a way that each time the one who is running is already standing behind the next place with his first sound.

Just as the basic principle in *alliteration* is the repetition of the initial sound, so *assonance* depends on the repetition of the vowel (or diphthong) which occurs in the accented syllable as medial sound. Assonance can occur either during a line or at its end, but where eurythmy is concerned it is the final assonance which mainly comes into consideration. As an example let us take the poem 'Nachtgeräusche', by C. F. Meyer.[*]

> Melde mir die Nachtgeräusche, Muse,
> Die an's Ohr des Schlummerlosen fluten.
> Erst das traute Wachtgebell der Hunde,
> Dann der abgezählte Schlag der Stunde,
> Dann ein Fischer-Zwiegespräch am Ufer,
> Dann? Nichts weiter als der ungewisse
> Geisterlaut der ungebrochnen Stille.
> Wie das Atmen eines jungen Busens,
> Wie das Murmeln eines tiefen Brunnens,
> Wie das Schlagen eines dumpfen Ruders,
> Dann—der ungehörte Tritt des Schlummers.

---

[*] In the third part of this book many German poems are quoted on account of their sound-content (assonance, rhythm and so on). In such cases translations are useless and have not been included.

When reproducing assonance in eurythmy those taking part—five in this case, but the number can vary according to the number of assonated words—place themselves in a straight line. As a general rule the one standing in the middle expresses the consonants of the text; but in this poem, which begins with five assonances, it would be better for this one to undertake the first line. Here, then, number I would carry out the vowel-sounds of the first line, retaining the *u* of the last word. Then II does the vowels of the second line, at the same time moving forwards (taking a step to each accented syllable) so that with the *u* of the word *fluten* he is standing in front of I. The third line is done by III, who moves from the opposite side and with the last *u* of this line also remains

standing in front of I and II; IV then carries out the fourth line in the same way, and V the fifth. All are now standing, one behind the other, in the posture for *u*. Now begins the new assonance on *i*. Before this is carried out the line previously formed must be dissolved, all returning simultaneously and with a rapid swing to their original places. (In this particular case the transition could be made with 'dann', because it is after this word that the longest pause occurs.) The next assonance can be formed in the same way, only in a backward direction. Thus with the line: *Nichts weiter als der ungewisse* II goes behind the place of I and remains there, standing in *i* (I could now do the consonants); and with the next line III, also making the movement for *i,* places himself behind II. Both then return to their places, and the last four lines are done in the same way as the first five lines, but here II can begin, while I does the consonant sounds the whole time. If the regular sequence of the terminal assonance is interrupted by the presence at the end of a line of a nonassonated vowel, this irregular vowel-sound can be carried out by two eurythmists standing on each side of the original line. It can also come about that the assonated vowels alternate as for instance:

>Als die neue Lehr' erblühte
>Hochrot wehten Christenfahnen,
>Kreuze drein die Krieger führten,
>Und die Heidengötter sanken.

In this case those representing the *ü* would place themselves in front, and those having the *a* behind.

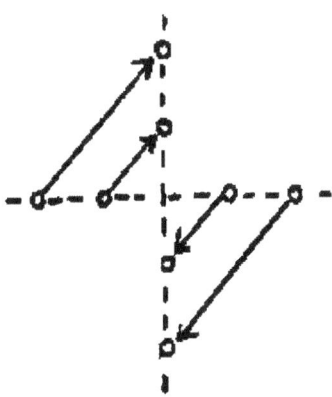

XVI

THE EXPRESSION OF RHYME IN EURYTHMY

The terminal rhyme, the usual feature of poetry in later times, is brought to expression in eurythmy by means of certain groupings and changing forms.

Rhyme in Couplets (a a b b).

> Nieder trägt der warme Föhn
> Der Lawine fern Getön,
> Hinter jenen hohen Föhren
> Kann den dumpfen Schlag ich hören...
> (C. F. MEYER.)

With the first line all carry out the movements for the sounds standing still; with the second line II does the sounds standing and I moves (in rhythm) across to II and stands behind him. Number III does the third line standing; with the fourth line the sounds are done by IV, while III moves across to IV and places himself behind him. (Whoever did the sounds for the first line of the couplet must repeat the rhyme-sound when the next rhyme-word occurs.) II and IV then move in a short silent pause to the previous places of I and III, and the latter take a step forward so that the original square is once more formed, although the people have changed places.

THE EXPRESSION OF RHYME IN EURYTHMY

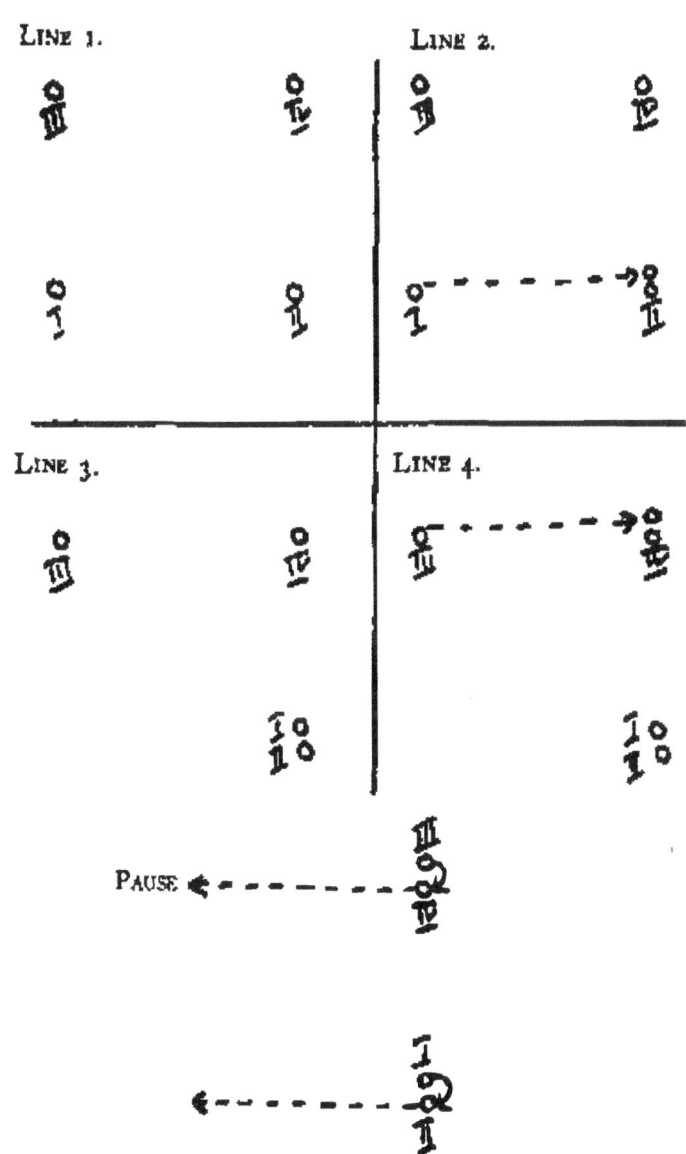

Another way of showing the rhymed couplet :

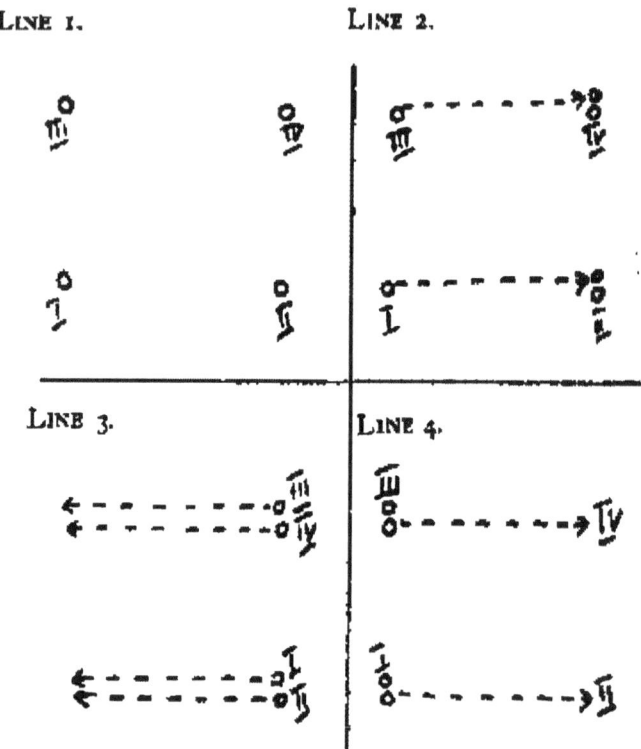

LINE 1: All do the sounds standing.
LINE 2: " " " " " while I and III move across and stand behind II and IV.
LINE 3: All do the sounds, at the same time moving across to the side from which I and III came.
LINE 4: All do the sounds, while II and IV return to their original places.

THE EXPRESSION OF RHYME IN EURYTHMY

Alternated Rhyme (a b a b).

Das ist ein eitles Wähnen!
Sei nicht so feig mein Herz!
Gib redlich Tränen um Tränen,
Nimm tapfer Schmerz um Schmerz
                      (HEBBEL, Scheidelieder II.)

First Way: **Text.**

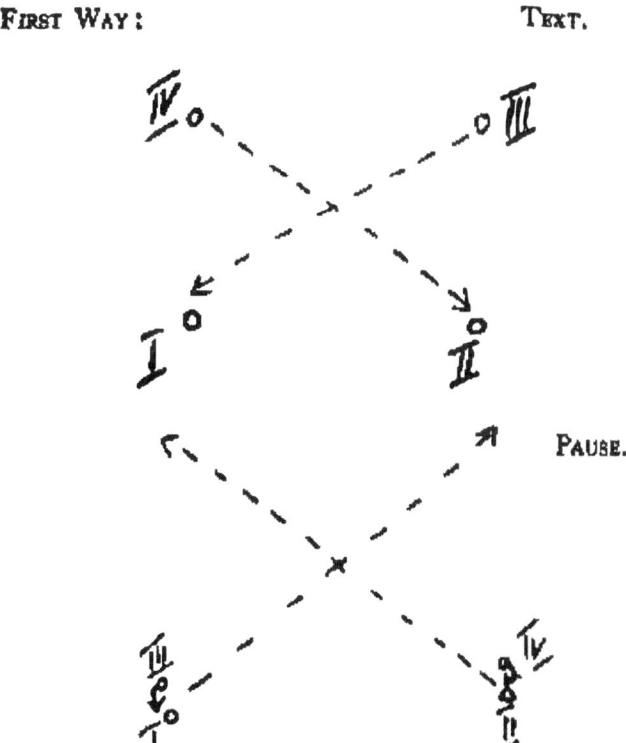

With the first line either all begin together, or else I begins alone; the sounds of the second line are done by II, of the third line by III, who at the same time moves behind the place of I (who repeats the rhyme); the fourth line is done by IV,

BASIC PRINCIPLES OF EURYTHMY

who goes behind the place of II (who likewise repeats the rhyme). Then (in a short pause before the second verse begins), I moves to the place of III and II to the place of IV.

SECOND WAY :　　　　　　　　　　　　　　TEXT.

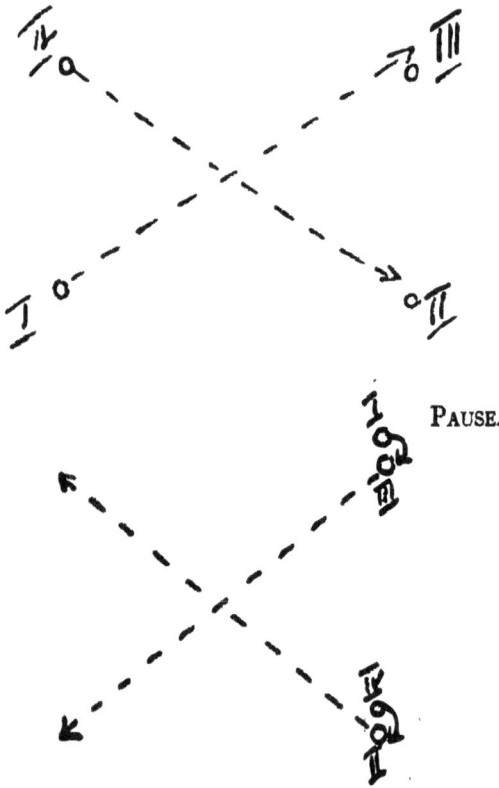

PAUSE.

The sounds of the first line are carried out by all together (or by I alone) standing still; the second line by IV, standing still; with the third line the sounds are done by III, while I moves backwards and stands behind III (repeating the rhyme); the sounds of the fourth line are done by II, IV passing across and standing behind II (likewise repeating the rhyme). And now II and III go to the previous places of IV and I.

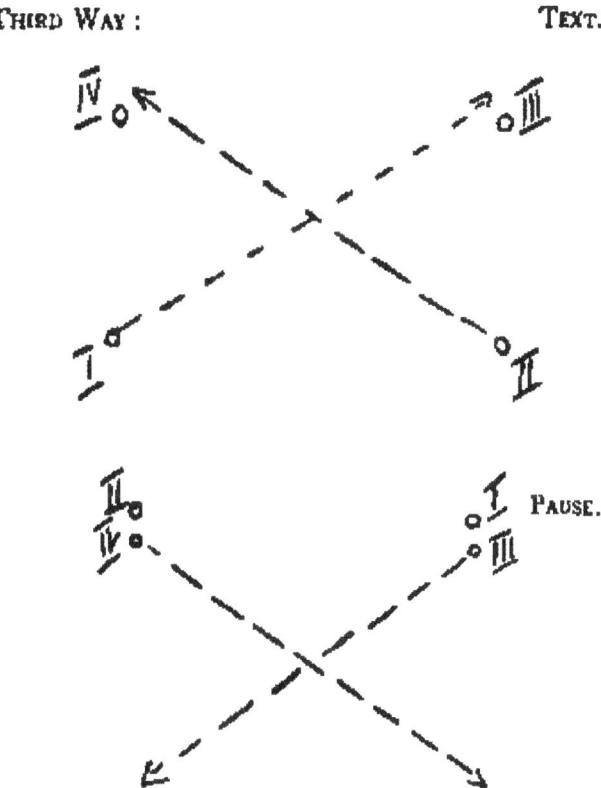

LINE 1. All (or I alone) do the sounds.
LINE 2. II does the sounds.
LINE 3. III does the sounds, I moves behind the place of III.
LINE 4. IV does the sounds, II moves behind the place of IV.
III then moves to the previous place of I, IV to the previous place of II.

FOURTH WAY:

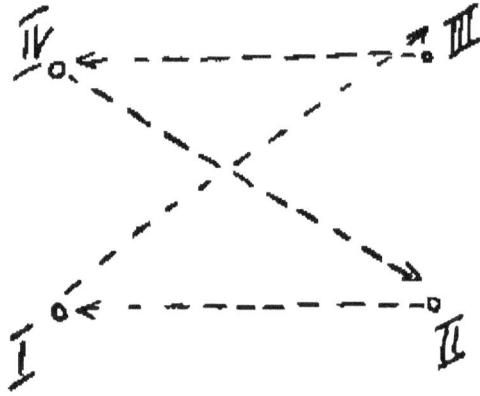

LINE 1. All do the sounds standing.
LINE 2. All do the sounds standing, IV moving to II;
LINE 3. All do the sounds standing, I moving to III.
LINE 4. All do the sounds standing, II and III moving to the previous places of IV and I.

Enclosed Rhyme (a b b a).

Quellende, schwellende Nacht,
voll von Lichtern und Sternen:
in den ewigen Fernen,
sage, was ist da erwacht....

(HEBBEL, *Nachtlied*)

TEXT:

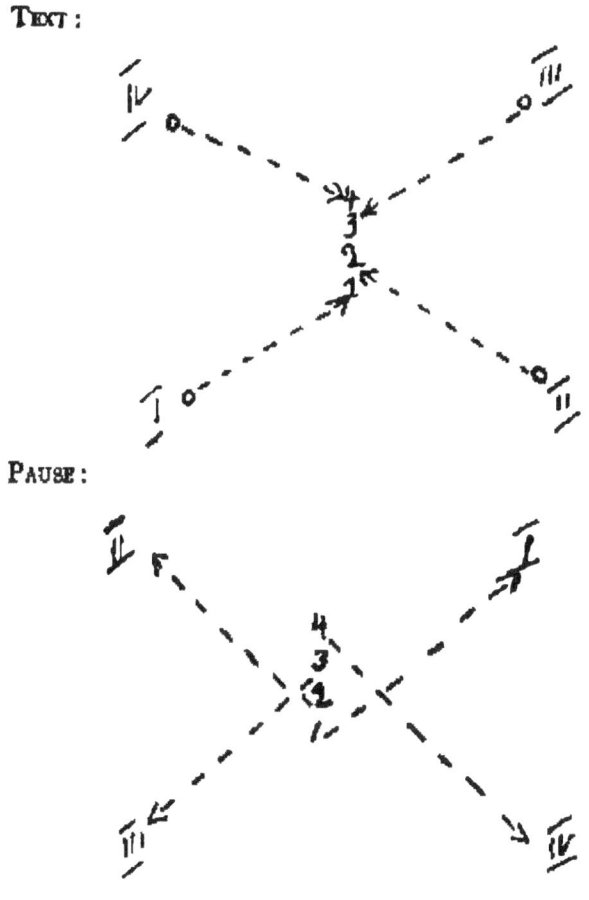

PAUSE:

LINE 1. The sounds are done by I standing.
LINE 2. The sounds are done by II, who at the same time moves to point 3.
LINE 3. III, who at the same time moves to point 3 where, together with **II**, he emphasizes the rhyme.
LINE 4. The sounds are done by IV, who at the same time

moves to point 4; simultaneously I, without doing the sounds, moves to point x, and there, together with IV, emphasizes the rhyme. A pause follows, during which I goes to the previous place of III, II to the previous place of IV, III to I, and IV to II.

A Rhymed Verse of Five Lines (a b c c b).

> Dort bläht ein Schiff die Segel,
> Frisch saust hinein der Wind;
> Der Anker wird gelichtet,
> Das Steuer flugs gerichtet,
> Nun fliegt's hinaus geschwind....
>
> (HEBBEL, Der junge Schiffer).

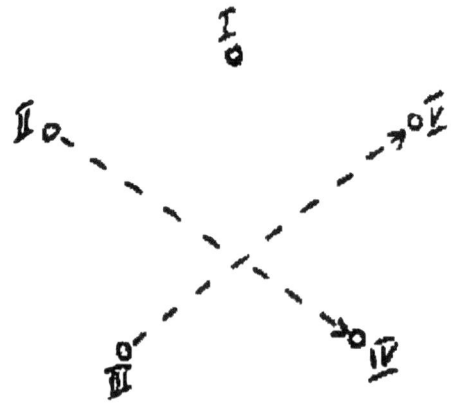

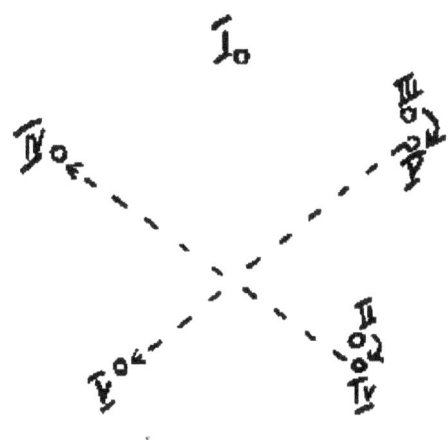

LINE 1. I does the sounds standing.
LINE 2. II does the sounds standing.
LINE 3. III does the sounds standing.
LINE 4. V does the sounds standing, while III moves in rhythmic step to V.
LINE 5. IV does the sounds standing, while II moves in rhythmic step to IV.
With the last word V swings rapidly to the former place of III, and IV to the former place of II. The second verse is then carried out in the same way as the first.

A Rhymed Verse of Six Lines (a b a b b a).

>Entsende deine Tauben
>An uns und alle Welt
>Dass wir der Bläue glauben
>In die du uns gestellt,
>Du hast sie erst erhellt
>Und wirst uns nicht berauben.
>(A. v. BERNUS, *Maria im Rosenhag.*)

BASIC PRINCIPLES OF EURYTHMY

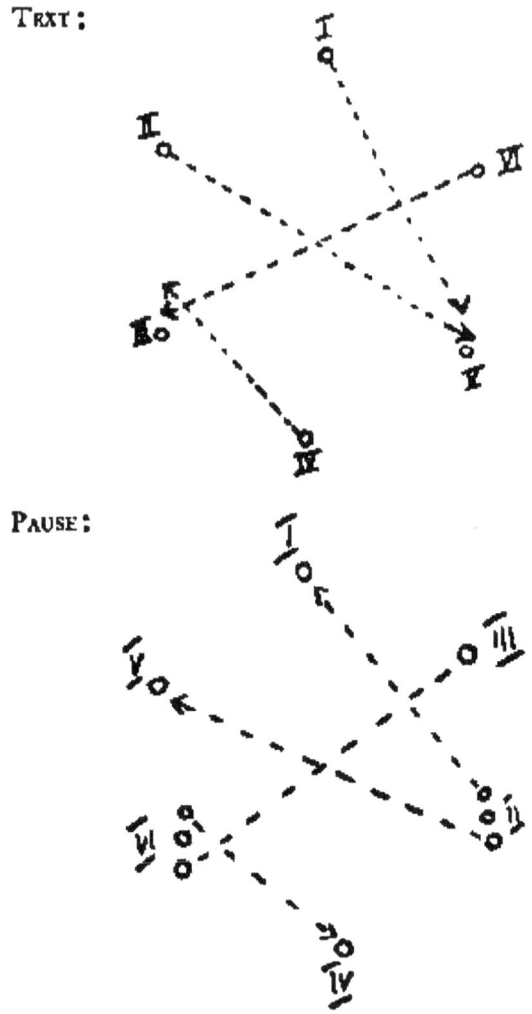

LINE 1. All do the sounds tanding.
LINE 2. I and V do the sounds standing.
LINE 3. III and IV do the sounds standing, VI, without doing the sounds, moves to III.
LINE 4. I and V do the sounds standing, II goes to V.
LINE 5. II and V do the sounds standing, I placing himself behind both II and V.

LINE 6. III and VI do the sounds standing, IV placing himself behind both III and VI.

III then moves to the former place of VI, V to the former place of II, I and IV returning to their original places.

A Rhymed Verse of Seven Lines (a a b c c c b).

    Als du frühmorgens gingst
    Und an der Sonne hingst,
    Pflücktest du dir,
    Die, von dir angeglüht,
    Still vor ihr aufgeblüht,
    Und nun den Duft versprüht,
      Rosen zur Zier....

                        (HEBBEL, *Die Rosen.*)

TEXT:

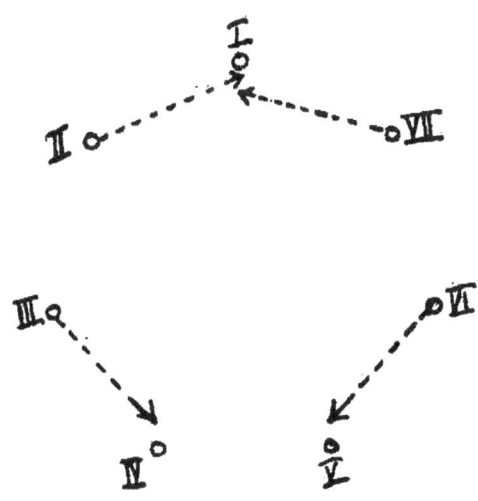

PAUSE:

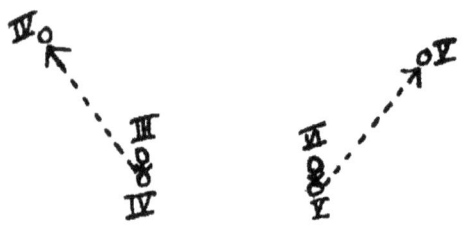

LINE 1. VI does the sounds standing.
LINE 2. V does the sounds standing, VI moves behind the place of V.
LINE 3. III does the sounds standing.
LINE 4. I does the sounds standing.
LINE 5. II does the sounds standing, arriving with the last word of the line in front of I.
LINE 6. VII does the sounds, arriving with the last word of this line in front of I and II.
LINE 7. IV does the sounds standing, III moves behind the place of IV.

In the pause   V moves to the place of VI.
               IV moves to the place of III.
               II moves to the place of VII.
               VII moves to the place of II.

A second way of presenting this is as follows:

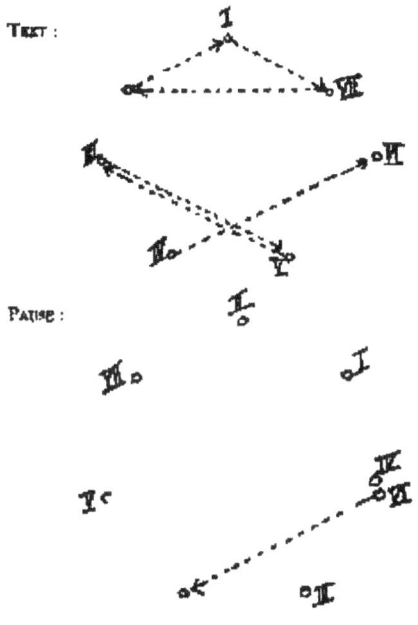

LINE 1. III does the sounds standing.
LINE 2. V does the sounds standing, III goes to V.
LINE 3. IV does the sounds standing, V goes to III.
LINE 4. II does the sounds standing, IV goes to VI.
LINE 5. I does the sounds standing, II goes to I.
LINE 6. VII does the sounds standing, I goes to VII.
LINE 7. VI does the sounds standing, VII goes to II.
Then, in a silent transition: VI to IV.

A Rhymed Verse of Eight Lines (a b a b a b c c).

Ihr naht euch wieder, schwankende Gestalten,
Die früh sich einst dem trüben Blick gezeigt.
Versuch ich wohl, euch diesmal festzuhalten?
Fühl ich mein Herz noch jenem Wahn geneigt?
Ihr drängt euch zu! Nun gut, so mögt ihr walten,
Wie ihr aus Dunst und Nebel um mich steigt;
Mein Busen fühlt sich jugendlich erschüttert
Vom Zauberhauch, der euren Zug umwittert.

GOETHE.

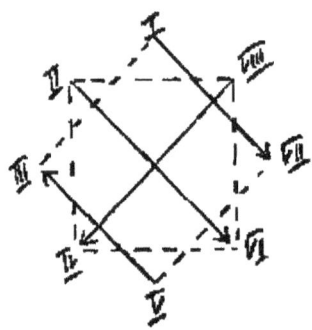

LINE 1. All do the sounds standing.
LINE 2. II, IV, VI, VIII do the sounds standing.
LINE 3. VI does the sounds standing, II goes to VI.
LINE 4. IV does the sounds standing, VIII goes IV.
LINE 5 and 6. I, III, V, VII do the sounds standing.
LINE 7. VII does the sounds standing, I goes to VII.
LINE 8 III does the sounds standing, V goes to III.

Then follows the silent transition :

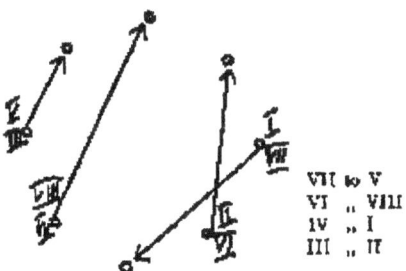

Here, as a beginning, all the transitional lines have been made straight. This can, however, be altered at will according to the mood of the poem in question. Where, for instance, the element of soul plays an important part, the transitions may be carried out in undulating lines (lines of a soul-nature), or one can begin the form with an outward swing, as though starting an evolving spiral, or can end the form with an involving spiral. In the case of rhymed couplets, for example, the form would look as follows:

BASIC PRINCIPLES OF EURYTHMY
or in spiral form :

With alternating rhymes :

In such cases the silent transitions would be carried out in a similar way.

The Ghazal.

The Ghazal—a form of verse borrowed from the Persian, and much used by Rückert und Platen—is a poem in which the lines are grouped in pairs. The first two lines rhyme, and then the same rhyme—or frequently instead of the rhyme a refrain—reappears in the second line of each couplet:

> Klage nicht, dass du in Fesseln seist geschlagen,
> Klage nicht, dass du der Erde Joch musst tragen,
> Klage nicht, die weite Welt sei ein Gefangnis. .
> Zum Gefängnis machen sie erst deine Klagen.
> Frage nicht, wie sich das Rätsel wird entfalten;
> Schon entfalten wird sich's ohne deine Fragen.
> Sage nicht, die Liebe habe dich verlassen;
> Wen hat Liebe je verlassen; kannst du's sagen?
> Zage nicht, wenn dich der grimme Tod will schrecken....
> Er erliegt dem, der ihn antritt ohne Zagen.
> Jage nicht das flücht'ge Reh des Weltgenusses,
> Denn es wird ein Leu und wird der Jäger jagen.
> Schlage nicht dich selbst in Fesseln, Herz, so wirst du
> Klagen nicht, dass du in Fesseln seist geschlagen.
>   (RÜCKERT.)

A short four-lined verse in Ghazal-form, in which the refrain occurs at the end of the rhyming couplets:

> Die Schöpfung ist zur Ruh gegangen, o wach in mir!
> Es will der Schlaf auch mich umfangen, o wach in mir!
> Auge, das am Himmel wachet mit Sternenblick,
> Wenn mir die Augen zugegangen, o wach in mir!
>   (RÜCKERT.)

Here the first position is as follows:

LINE 1. I does the sounds.
LINE 2. I and II do the sounds.
LINE 3. I, II and III do the sounds.
LINE 4. I, II, III and IV do the sounds.

The rhyme or the refrain is always carried out by everybody together.

The movements for the sounds can be accompanied by small forms in space—for instance, by Apollonian forms.

If the first, longer poem is to be expressed, I must begin again after every four lines.

The Sonnet.
(abba abba cde cde)

Als höchstes Wunder, das der Geist vollbrachte,
Preis ich die Sprache, die er, sonst verloren
In tiefster Einsamkeit, aus sich geboren,
Weil sie allein die andern möglich machte.

Ja, wenn ich sie in Grund und Zweck betrachte,
So hat nur sie den schweren Fluch beschworen,
Dem er, zum dumpfen Einzelsein erkoren,
Erlegen wäre, eh er noch erwachte.

Denn ist das unerforschte Eins und Alles
In nie begriffnem Selbstzersplittrungsdrange
Zu einer Welt von Punkten gleich zerstoben:

THE EXPRESSION OF RHYME IN EURYTHMY

So wird durch sie, die jedes Wesensballes
Geheimstes Sein erscheinen lässt im Klange,
Die Trennung völlig wieder aufgehoben.

(HEBBEL, Die Sprache.)

LINE 1. I does the sounds.
LINE 2. II do the sounds.
LINE 3. III do the sounds.
LINE 4. IV do the sounds.
The division of the second verse is similarly carried out. Then follows a silent transition on the part of I and II, and the two last verses are done in the following formation:

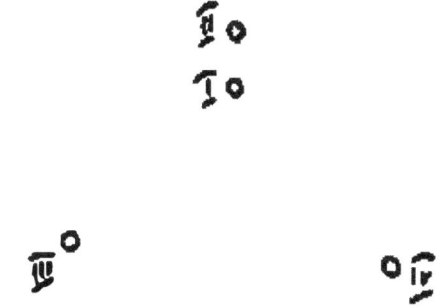

the first line of each verse being carried out by I and II together; III doing the second and IV the third lines. Here again it is possible to make use of Apollonian forms.

193

XVII

MUSICAL PRELUDES AND STUDIES

These musical eurythmy-preludes serve as an introduction, appropriate in style, to the poem which is to be presented, and suitable music can be used to enhance the mood of the poem in question.

'These forms may be introduced at the beginning of a piece of Eurythmy, at its end, or as interludes during its performance, and they must be carried out in conjunction with gestures suited equally to the musical accompaniment and to the subsequent or preceding recitation.' (From Rudolf Steiner's Foreword to the Edition of musical 'Auftakte zu eurhythmischen Darstellungen' by L. v. D. Pals.)

Some of these preludes or studies in form are mainly related to the mood of soul which should be conjured up in the audience and performers, others have a greater correspondence with the structure of the succeeding or preceding poem.

The poem which follows one of these musical preludes can be carried out in Apollonian or Dionysian forms, or else in one of those forms which serve to emphasize the rhyme; it is, however, also possible to carry over into the text itself the same basic form as was contained in the prelude.

During the musical accompaniment to these preludes, the movements in space—the form-running, the interplay of the ever-changing, constantly dissolving and rebuilding forms—are always combined with appropriate and expressive gestures of the *arms—delight, merriment, inwardness,* and so on. In the case of certain of these preludes, gestures for the vowel-sounds have been given, and further developments in this direction should certainly be attempted.

Studies in the different Verse-Forms.

I. POEMS WITH VERSES OF THREE LINES[*]

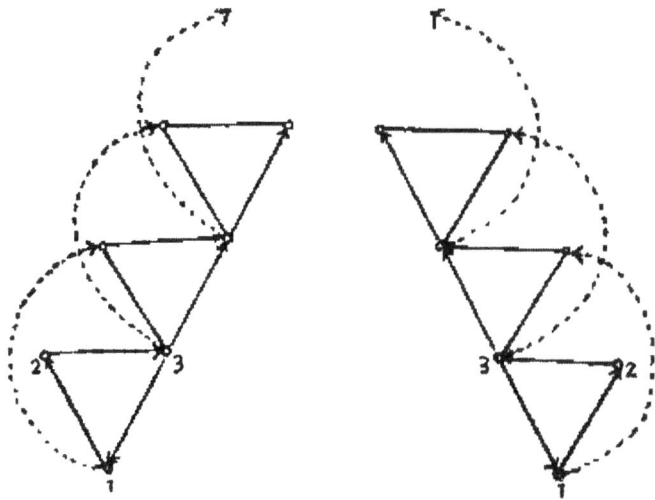

Foreground

Here two groups, each of three people, take up their position in the foreground in the form of two triangles. During the first bar of the music (or during line i, if the text is being expressed in this way), I moves rhythmically to the place of II, with the second bar II moves to III, and with the third bar III to the previous place of I. During the fourth bar (or, as the case may be, in a short pause in the recitation) the following transition is simultaneously carried out by everybody together: :

---

[*] Musical accompaniments to this and the following studies by L. V. D. Pals. (See Index at end of book.)

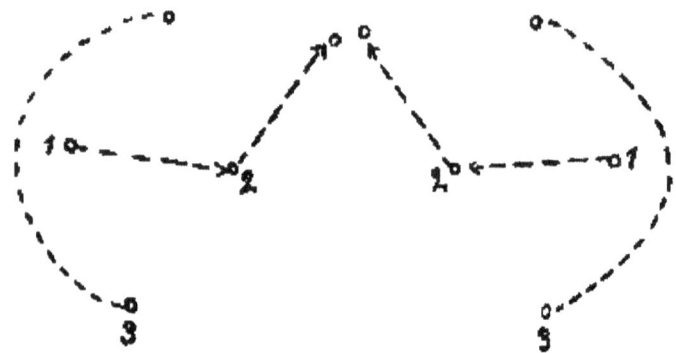

Then follows the second movement in the triangle, and the next transition to the new grouping.

This can be repeated as often as required, according to the available space and the accompanying music.

If one wishes to move both music and text (a poem of three verses, for instance) to this form, the direction can be reversed for the recitation; thus, when by the end of the prelude the back of the form has been reached, the movement of the triangles can be taken as follows:

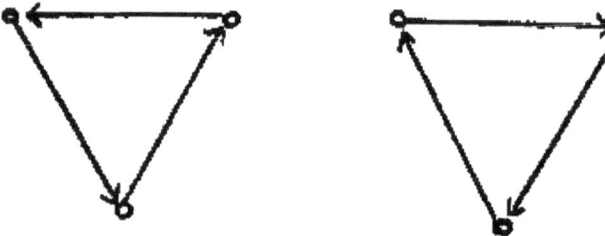

(The sounds of the line in question are always undertaken by the one who is moving, who then remains standing in the last gesture. This holds good for all subsequent forms of this type.) The transition to the next verse is then carried out as follows:

and finally the musical form is repeated in its original direction.

In a similar form for verses of three lines, three people only take part, moving in such a way that they change the grouping six consecutive times.

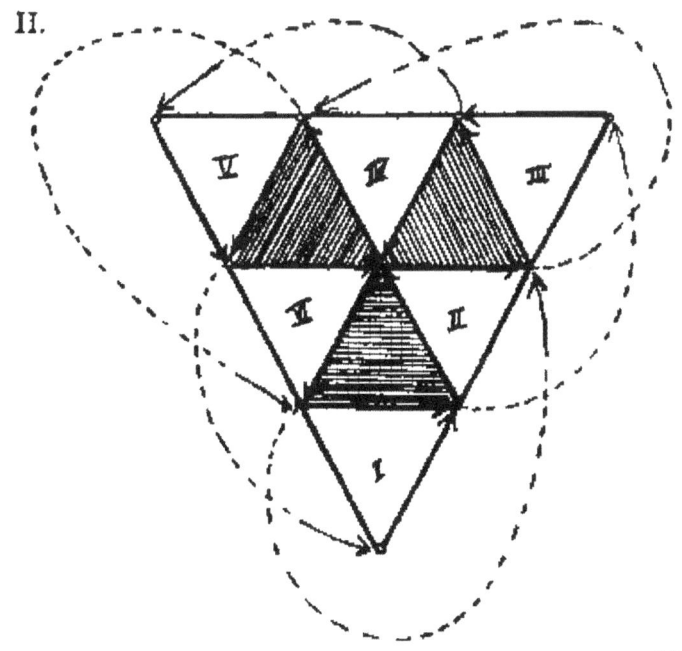

BASIC PRINCIPLES OF EURYTHMY

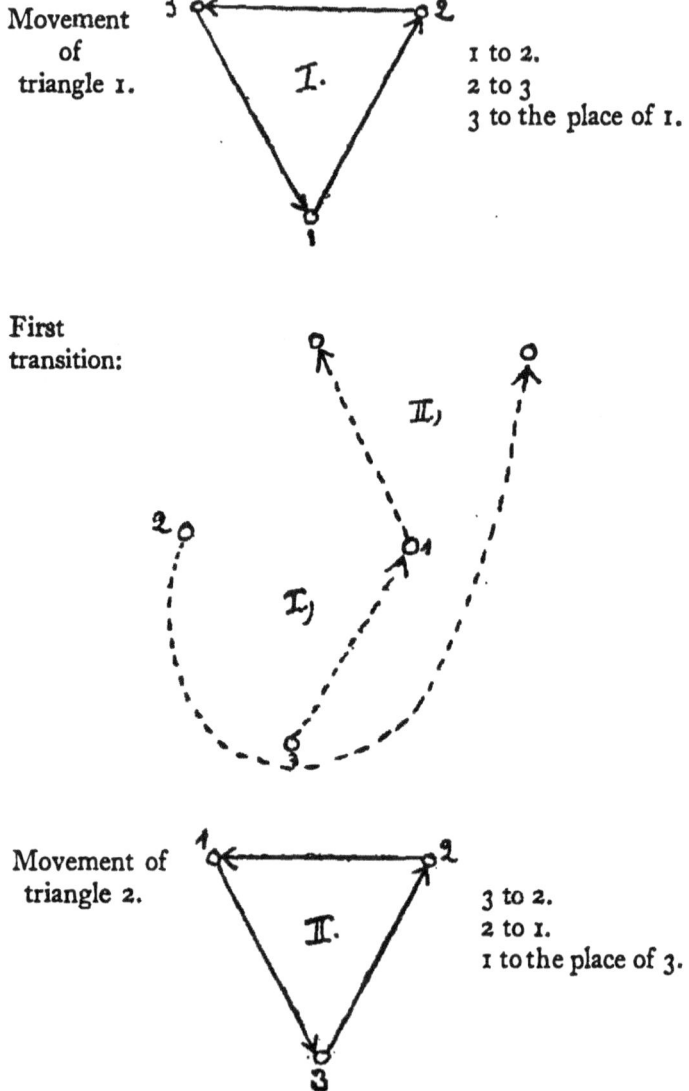

Movement of triangle 1.

1 to 2.
2 to 3
3 to the place of 1.

First transition:

Movement of triangle 2.

3 to 2.
2 to 1.
1 to the place of 3.

MUSICAL PRELUDES AND STUDIES

Second transition:

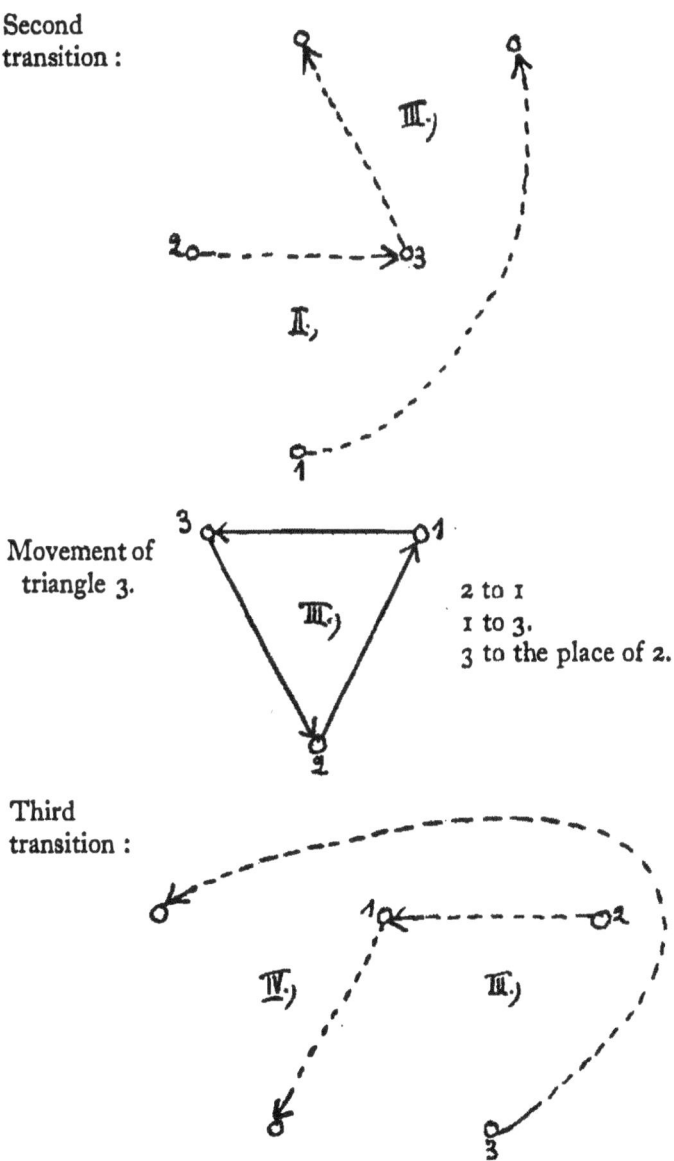

Movement of triangle 3.

2 to 1
1 to 3.
3 to the place of 2.

Third transition:

199

Movement of triangle 4:

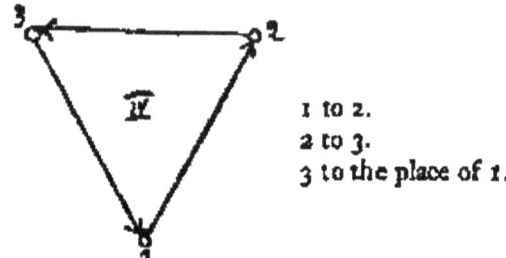

1 to 2.
2 to 3.
3 to the place of 1.

Fourth transition:

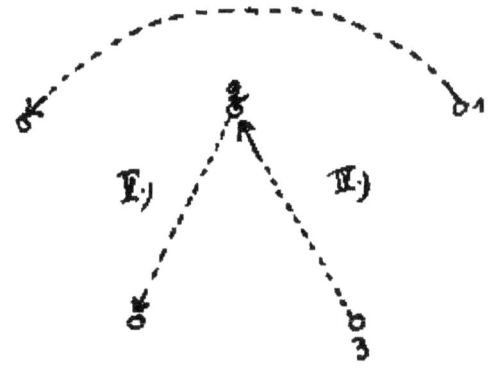

Movement of triangle 5:

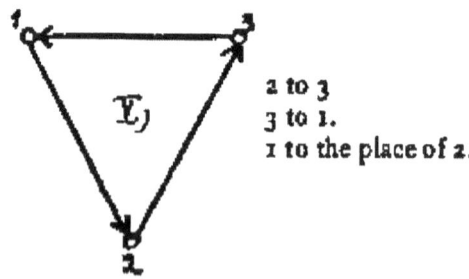

2 to 3
3 to 1.
1 to the place of 2.

Fifth transition:

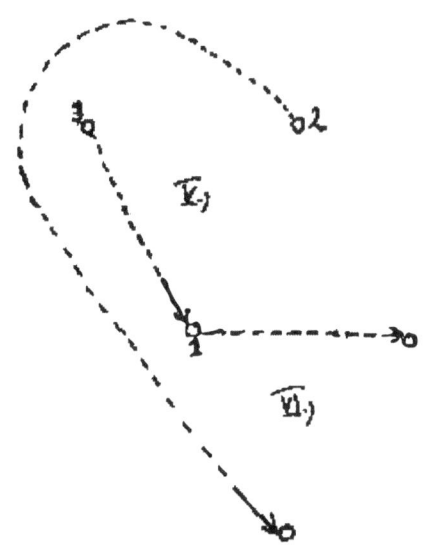

Movement of triangle 6:

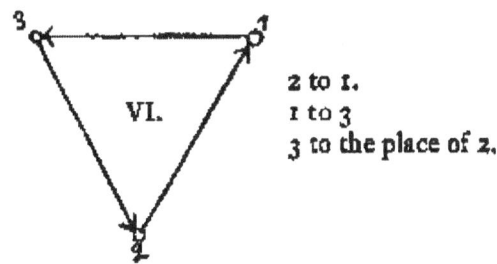

2 to 1.
1 to 3
3 to the place of 2.

Transition to the sixth and last position:

The same form can also be turned with its apex towards the back:

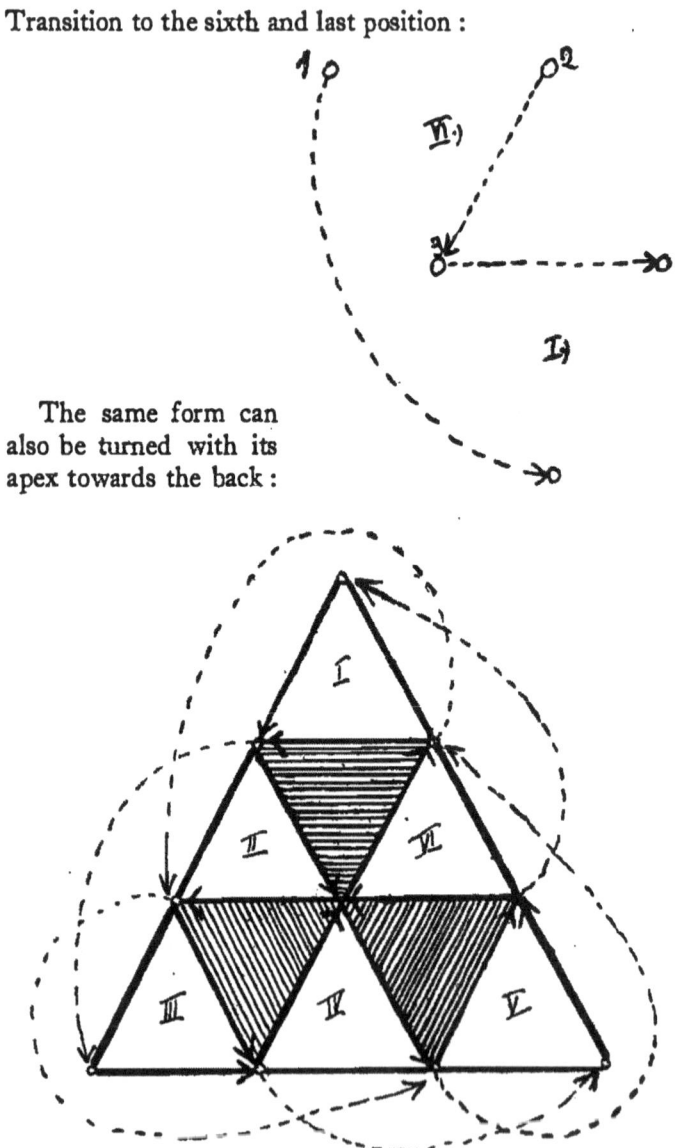

MUSICAL PRELUDES AND STUDIES

In the following diagram we have a form for verses of three lines based on a principle which always reappears when it is a question of expressing verses several lines in length. The space in which the form is to be run is divided into a large outer circle and one or more inner circles, into which the triangle (or square, pentagram, etc., as the case may be) is repeatedly placed until the circle is completed and the original position regained.

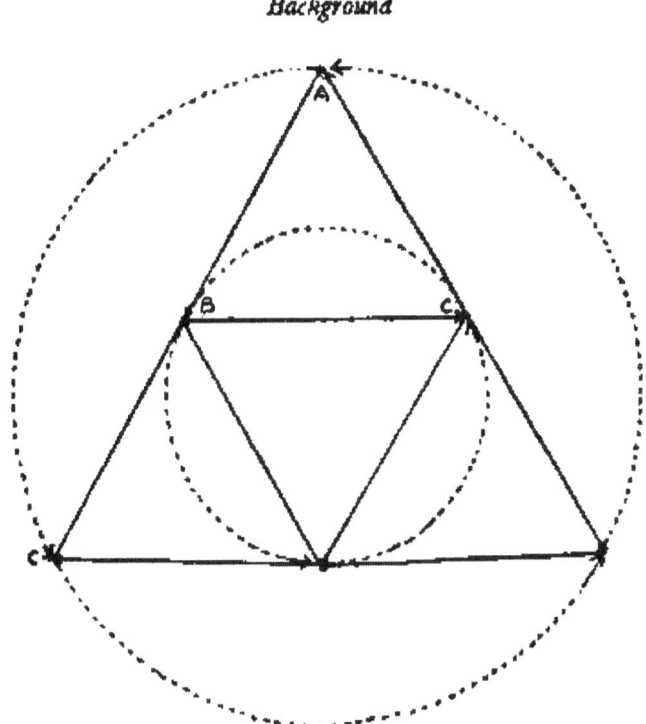

Background

A beginning is made by forming the first triangle in the background, one person standing on the outer circle and two on the inner. With bar **1** *A* takes three steps to *B*, then *B* takes

203

three steps to *C* then *C* to the place of *A*.* Now follows the transition: C has the big curve on the outer circle (in the direction from right to left, as seen from the audience), *A* and *B* go in the same direction on the line of the inner circle to their new places. The interchanging form is now begun by *C*, who forms the apex of this second triangle. After the interchange of places *B* is standing at the apex and has the line on the outer circle. The third form is done in a similar way, the whole thing concluding with the first position, *A* in the background, once more at the apex of the triangle.

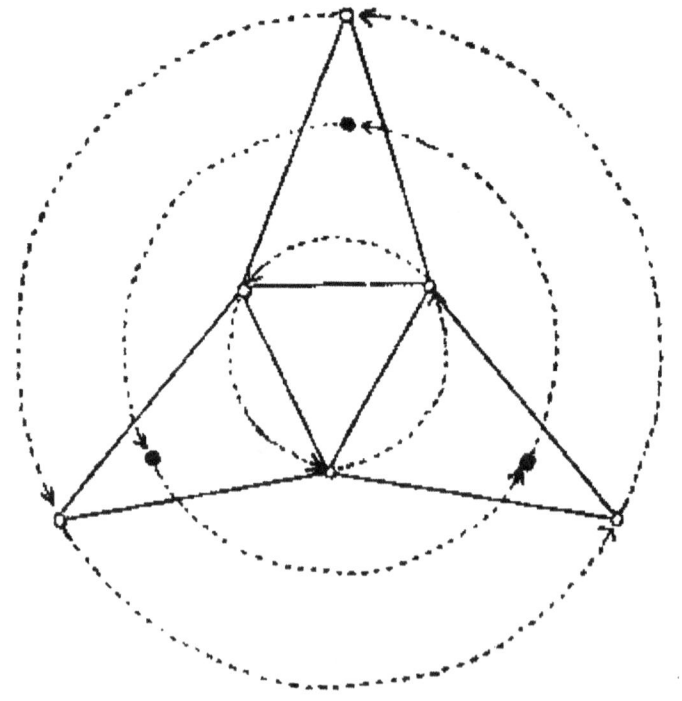

* See Appendix.

The same grouping and form, but with the addition of a fourth person, who stands in the middle of the triangle and moves along an intermediate circle, can be employed in poems where the fourth line constitutes a refrain ; the sounds of this line are then always carried out by this middle figure. (See diagram, page 204.)

When the content of a poem is solemn or earnest, the form of the prelude, as well as the transitions between the lines of the text, may be moved to the vowel-sounds *I A O; I* on the line **1** to **2** (with the gaze of the eyes directed upwards), *A* from **2** to 3 (with the eyes directed straight forwards), and *O* from 3 to **1** (eyes directed downwards). During the transitions all those taking part form the three vowel-sounds one after the other (with a similar direction of the gaze of the eyes).

POEMS WITH VERSES OF FOUR LINES

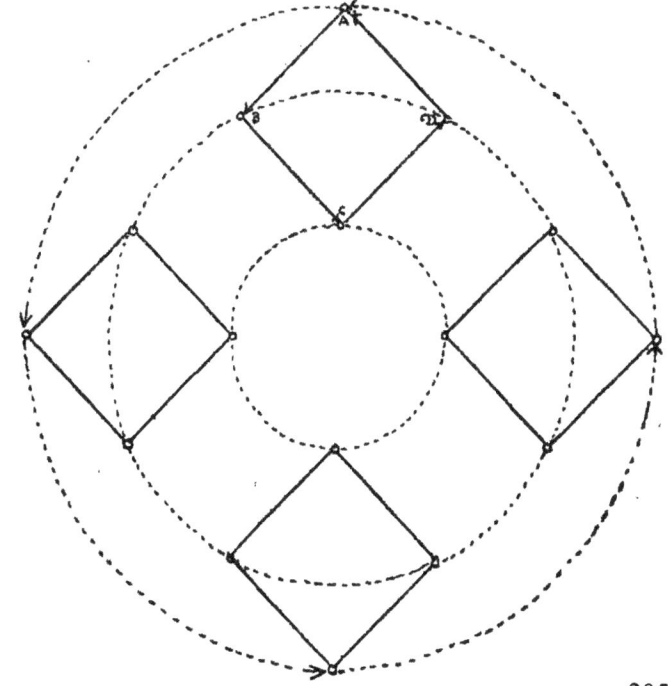

A as the apex of the first square, begins at the back and moves to *B*, *B* to *C*, *C* to *D*, and *D* to *A*'s former place. Now *D* has the transition along the outer circle, *A* moves in the same direction on the middle circle (but as this line is much shorter the tempo must be correspondingly retarded). *B* and *C* go in the opposite direction, *B* on the inner and *C* on the middle circle. Then *D*, as the outer point, begins the interior form. The apex is always regarded as being on the outer circle.

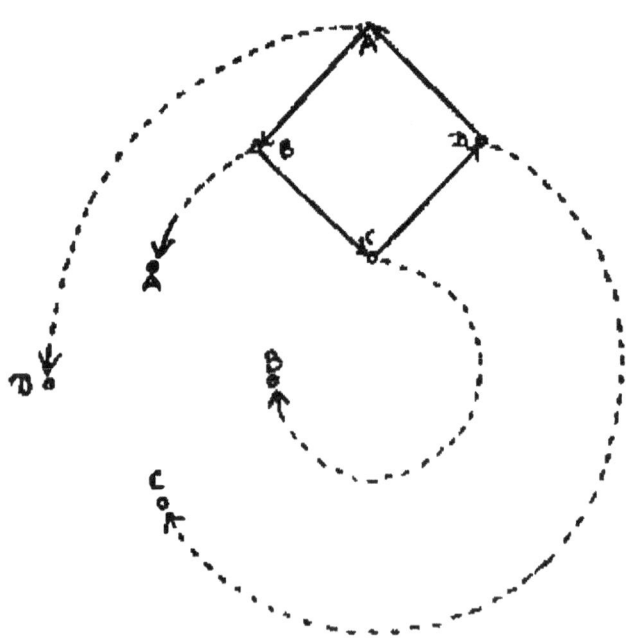

With the next transition *A* moves forwards on the outer and *D* on the middle circle, *B* and *C* again in the opposite direction, beginning their curve backwards, and so on.

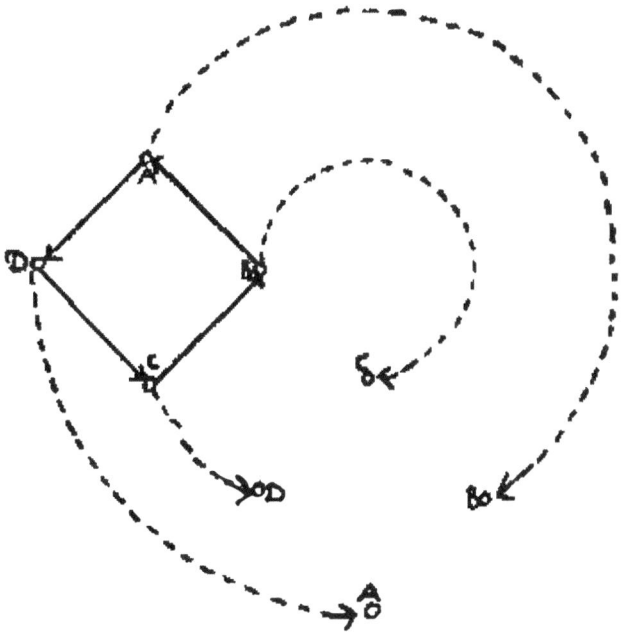

Both in this and the following forms one will never be at fault in the transitions if one always bears in mind that no person's line must ever cut either through the form already moved or through the form about to be created.

BASIC PRINCIPLES OF EURYTHMY

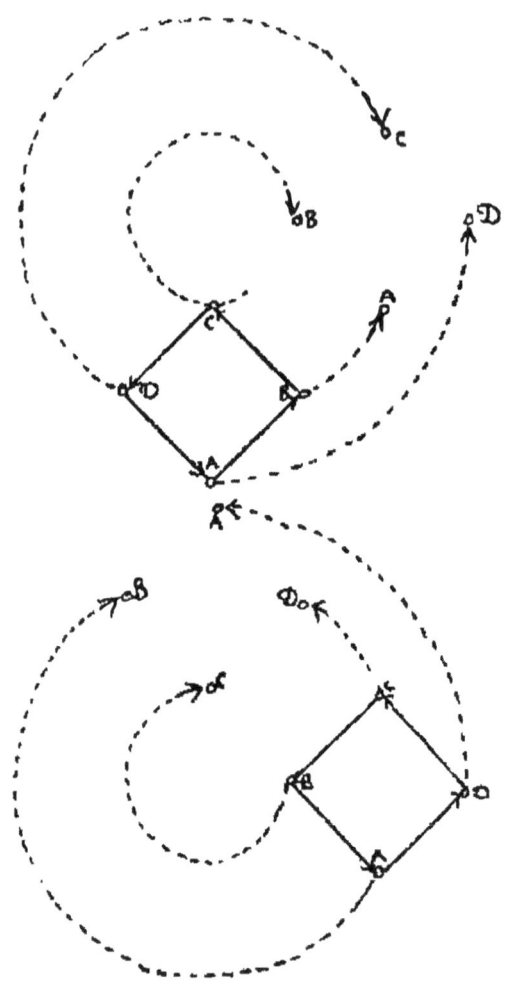

Here we have a somewhat freer arrangement of the square:

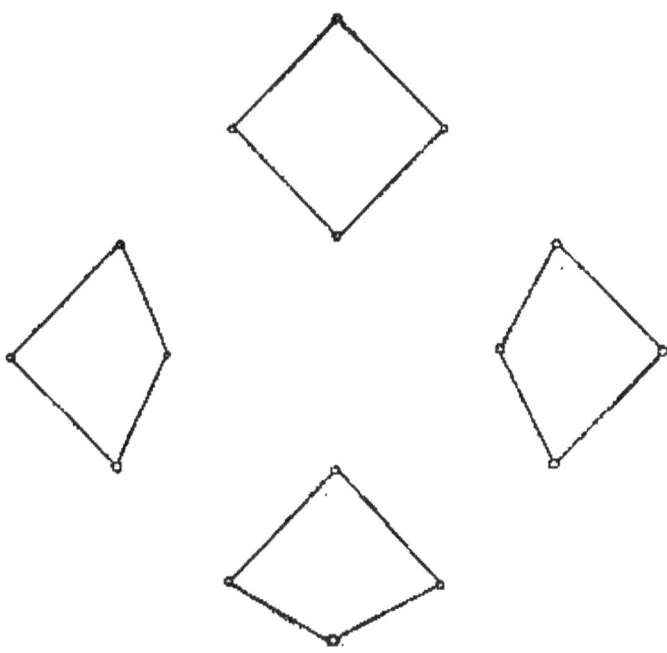

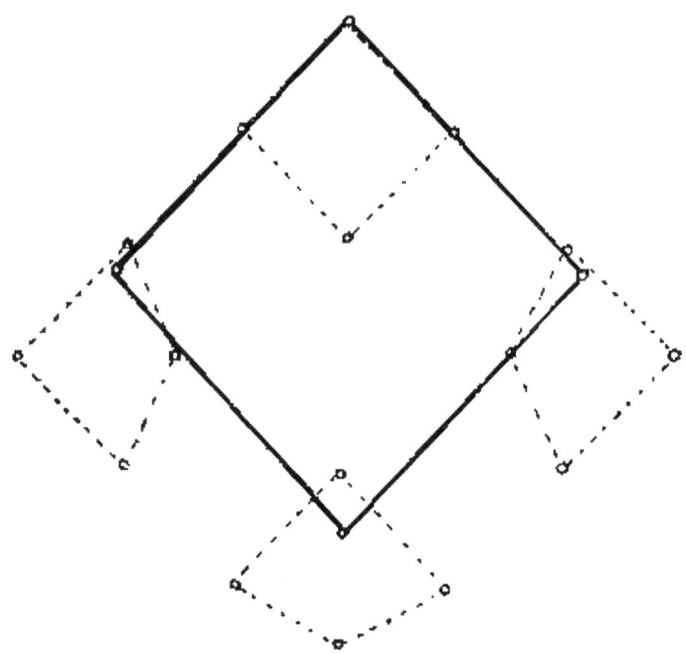

When the final position has been reached, *B* and *D* go outwards from each other to either side, while *C* moves forward to the front.

POEMS OF VERSES WITH FIVE LINES

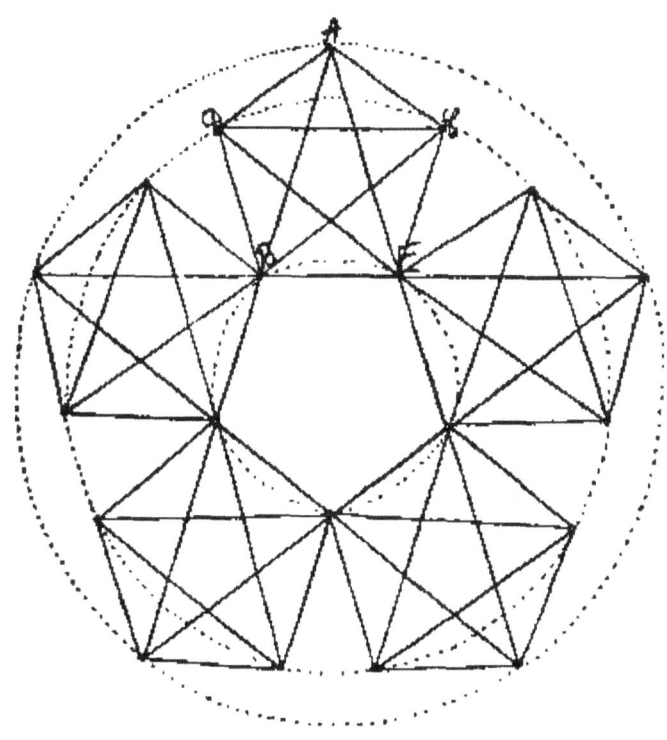

Interior movement: *A* goes to *B*, *B* to *C*, *C* to *A*'s former place; *D* to *E*, *E* to *F*, *F* to *D*'s former place.

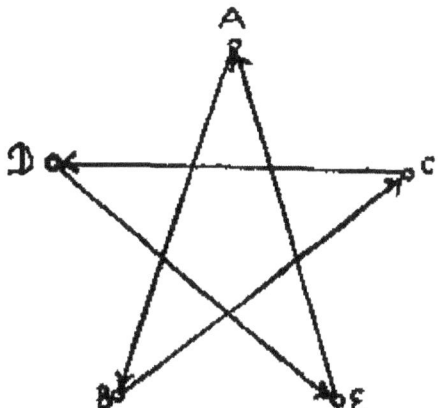

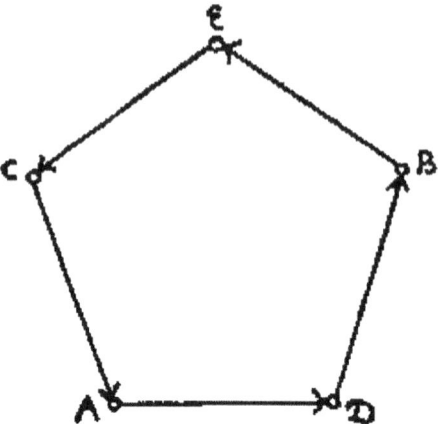

Then, before the transition to the next form ensues, the outer sides of the pentagram must first be transcribed : E places himself behind C, C behind A, A in front of D, D in front of B, B taking the apex. (When this form is used to express a poem, both the movement round the circumference and the transition are carried out during a pause in the recitation.)

With the transition B and E now move towards the left (as seen from the audience), B on the outer and E on the middle circle. A and D move towards the right, A on the inner and D on the middle circle. C remains stationary.

Then begins the movement of the new pentagram, starting from the apex—where E now is.* There follows the movement round the circumference, and, with the second transition, A and C move towards the left, B and D towards the right; E remains stationary. Thus (bearing in mind the fact that nobody's line must ever cut through the pentagram form) two people invariably go towards the left and two towards the right, while one holds the static point. The latter is only shifted when less than five pentagrams are laid into the circle.

* See Appendix.

POEMS WITH VERSES OF SIX LINES

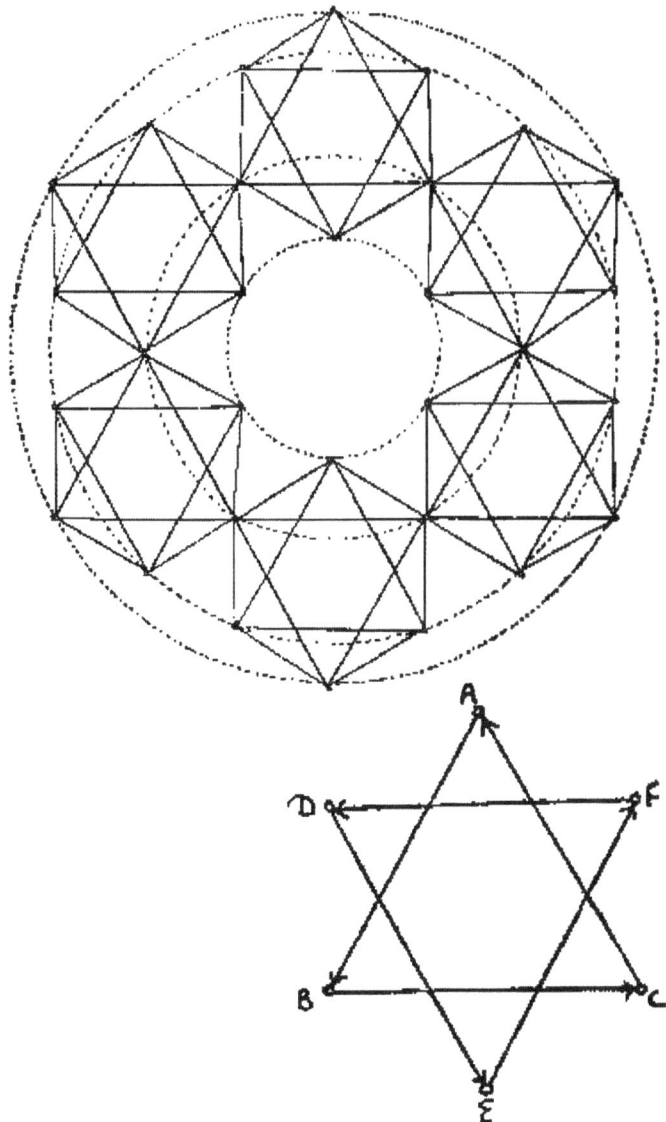

Interior movement: *A* goes to *B*, *B* to *C*, *C* to *A*'s former place; *D* to *E*, *E* to *F*, *F* to *D*'s former place.

Movement round the circumference: C to F, F to A, A to D, D to B, B to E, E to the apex.

With the transition to the next form, which takes place along four circles, E and C go towards the left, E on the first

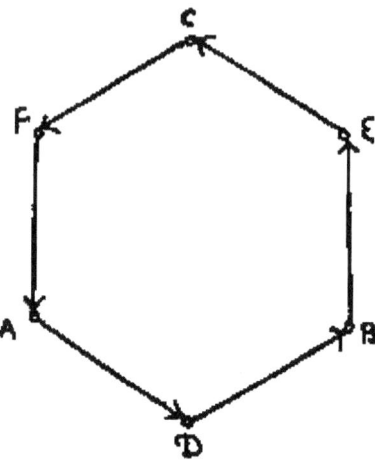

(the outermost), C on the second circle; B, D, A move towards the right, B on the second, D on the third, A on the fourth (the innermost) circle; F (on the third circle) remains stationary.

In the next form C is the apex. Interior movement:

C to B, B to A, A to Then the movement round the circumference; and with the next C's former place; E to D, D to F, F to E's former place. transition A and F move towards the left, B, D, E towards the right, C remains stationary.

The remaining transitions will become apparent when one holds firmly to the fact that whoever is standing on the outermost circle always describes this circle from left to right; likewise that whoever is standing on the second circle always has the shorter path to the next place. On the third circle one person always remains stationary (or shifts along, as shown in the following diagram), and the remaining three move on the second, third and fourth circles in the opposite direction to the two first mentioned.

THREE HEXAGONS IN A CIRCLE

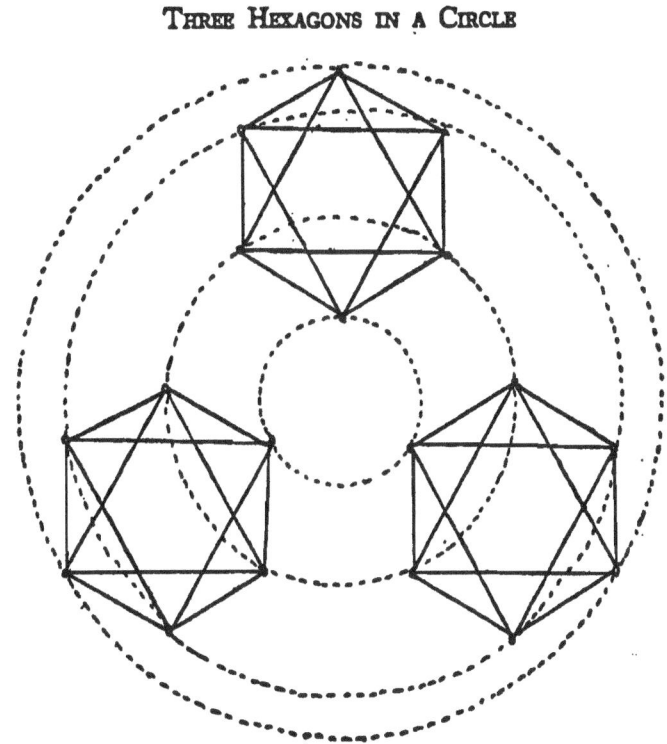

BASIC PRINCIPLES OF EURYTHMY

TRANSITIONS

1. Transition :

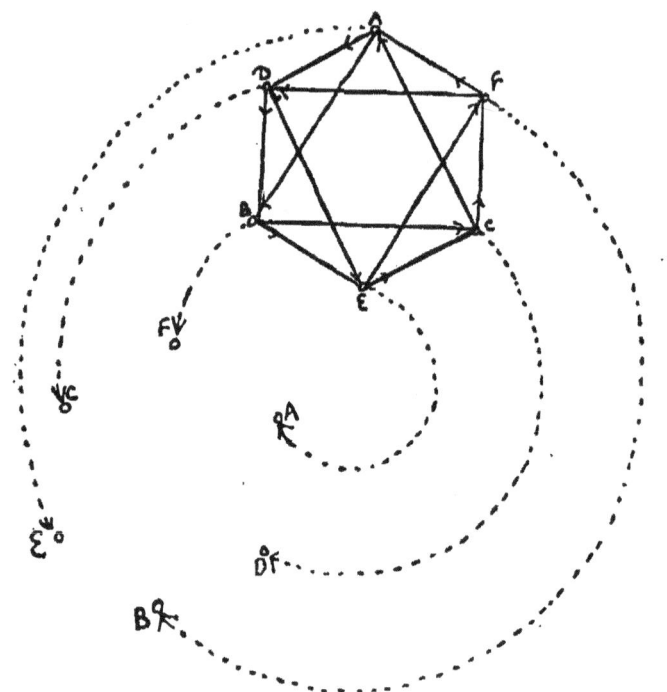

2. Transition :

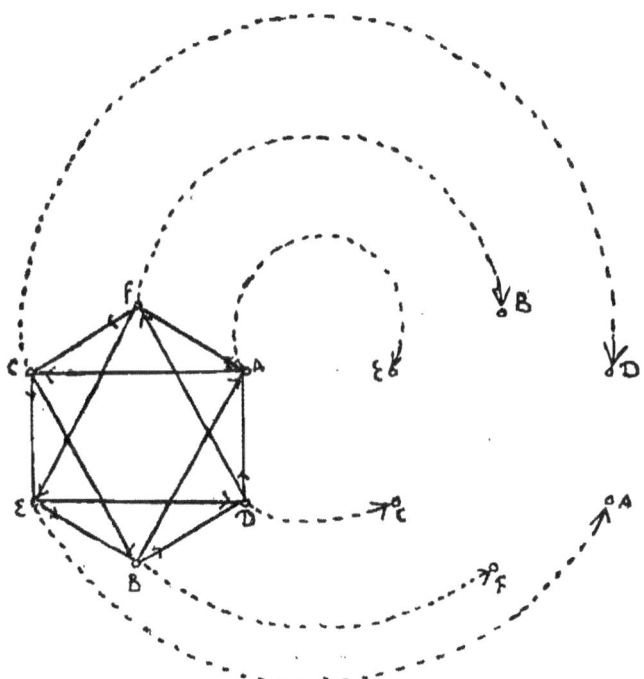

3. Transition :

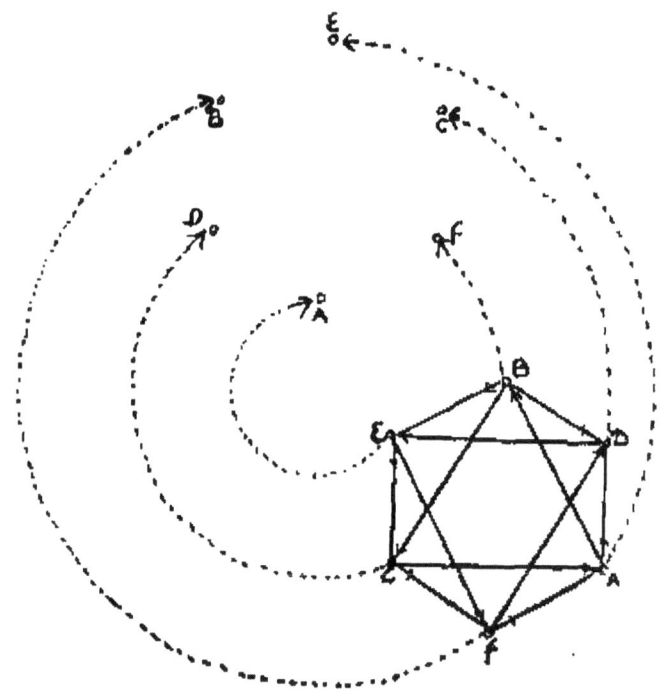

POEMS WITH VERSES OF SEVEN LINES

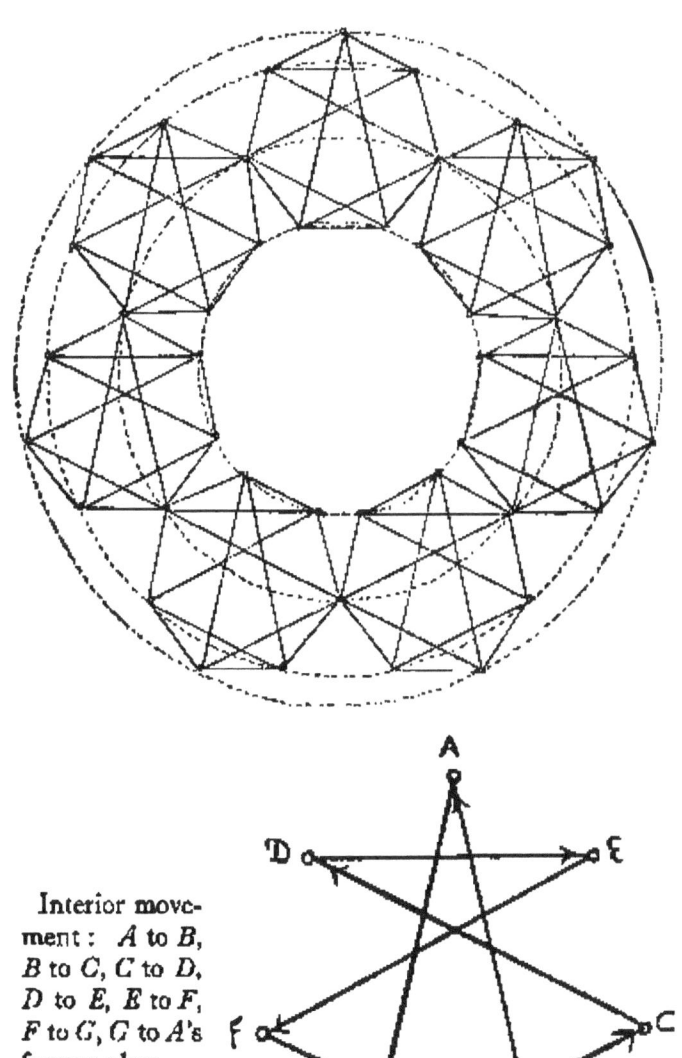

Interior movement: *A* to *B*, *B* to *C*, *C* to *D*, *D* to *E*, *E* to *F*, *F* to *G*, *G* to *A*'s former place.

Movement round circumference: G to C, C to E, E to A, A to F, F to B, B to D, D to G's former place.

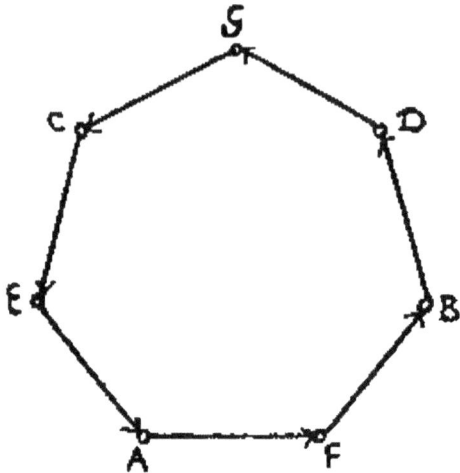

Transition: D, G, E move towards the left, D on the outermost, G on the second, E on the innermost circle; B, F, A move towards the right; B on the second, F on the third, A on the innermost circle; C remains stationary.

Thus three always move towards the left, three towards the right, while the one whose place coincides with one of the points of the neighboring heptagon remains stationary.

THREE HEPTAGONS IN A CIRCLE

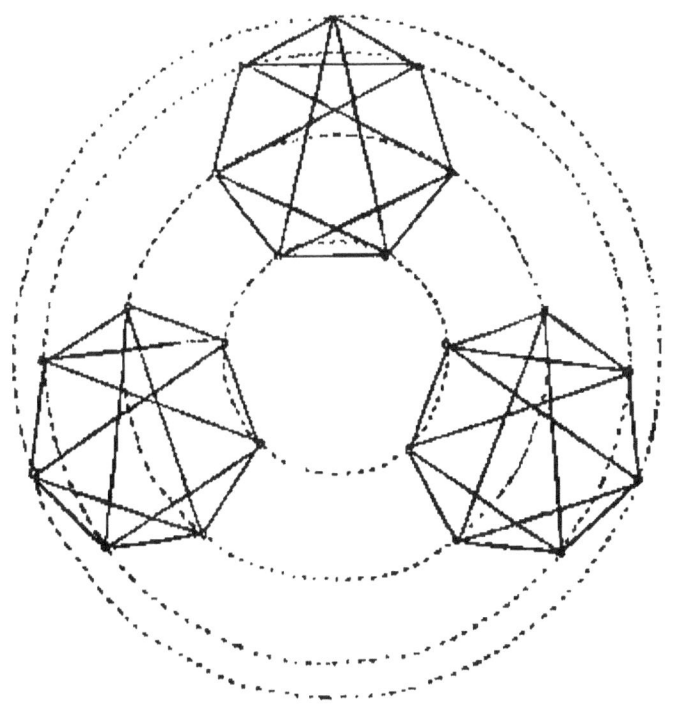

TRANSITIONS

1. Transition :

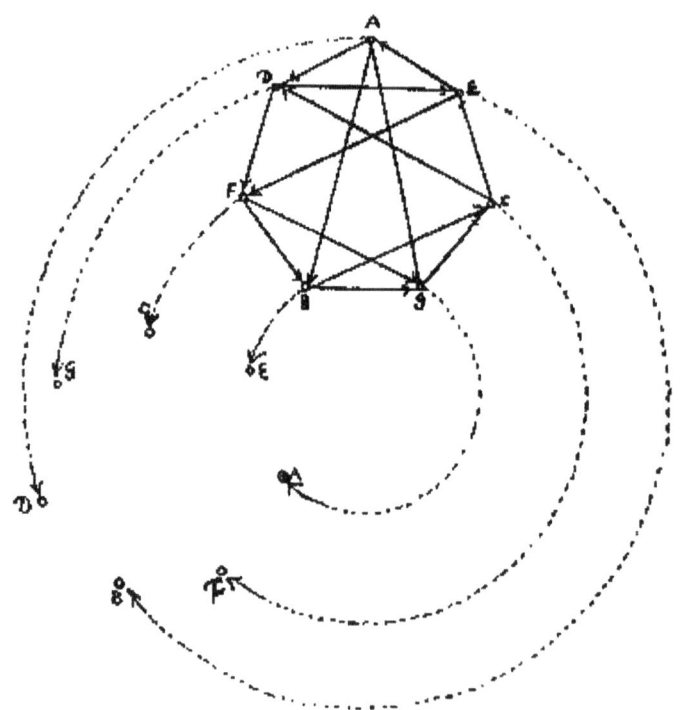

2. Transition :

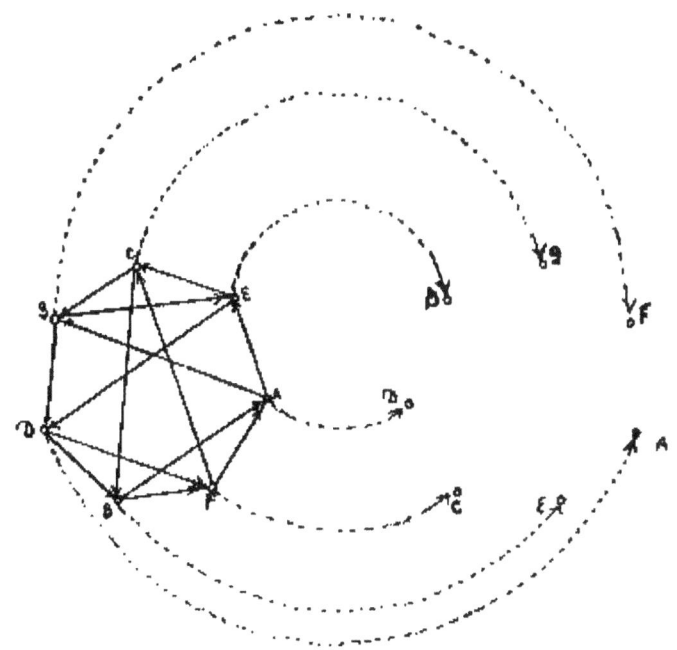

3. Transition:

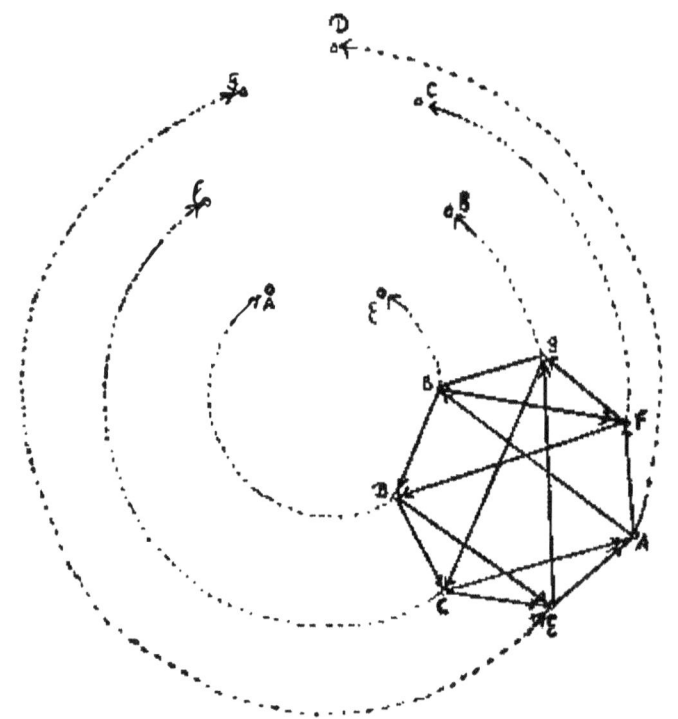

POEMS WITH VERSES OF EIGHT LINES

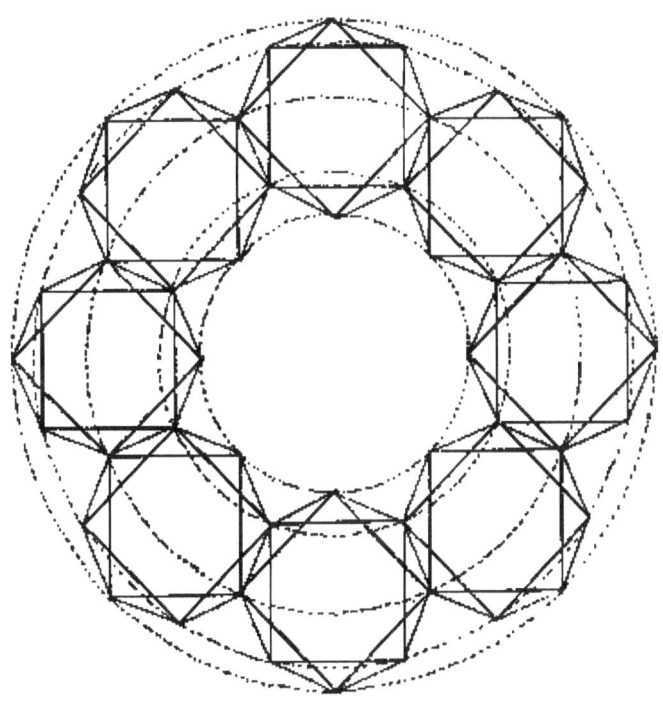

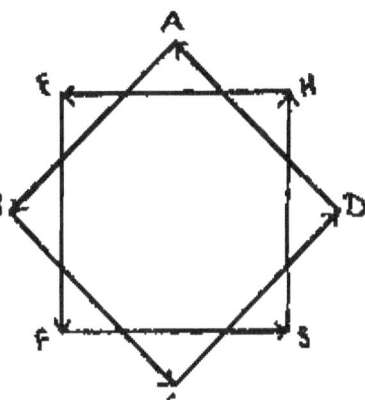

Interior movement: *A* to *B*, *B* to *C*, *C* to *D*, *D* to *A*'s former place; *E* to *F*, *F* to *G*, *G* to *H*, *H* to *E*'s former place.

Movement round circumference: *D* to *H*, *H* to *A*, *A* to *E*, *E* to *B*, *B* to *F*, *F* to *C*, *C* to *G*, *G* to the apex.

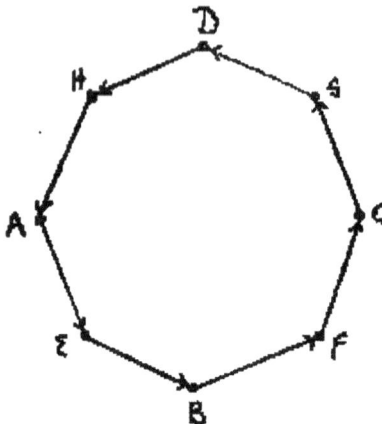

Transition: G, *D*, *H* go towards the left, G on the outermost, *D* on the second, *H* on the third circle; *C*, *F*, *B*, *E* go towards the right, C on the second, *F* on the third, *B* on the fourth, *E* on the innermost circle. *A* on the fourth circle, remains stationary (or shifts along as the case may be).

Four Octagons in a Circle

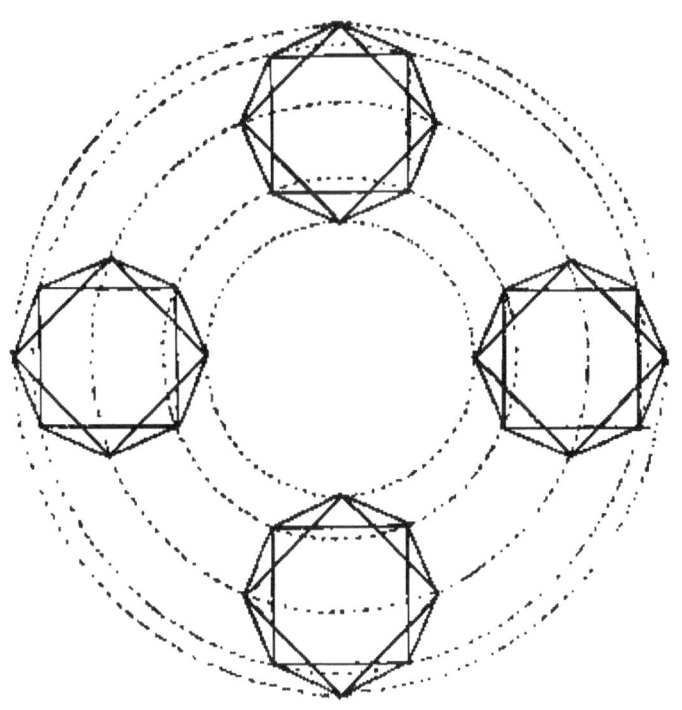

TRANSITIONS

1. Transition:

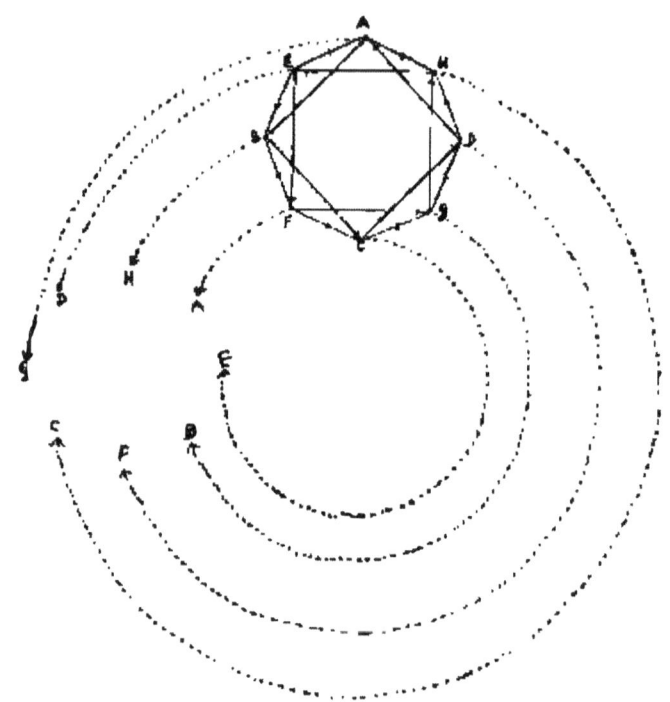

2. Transition:

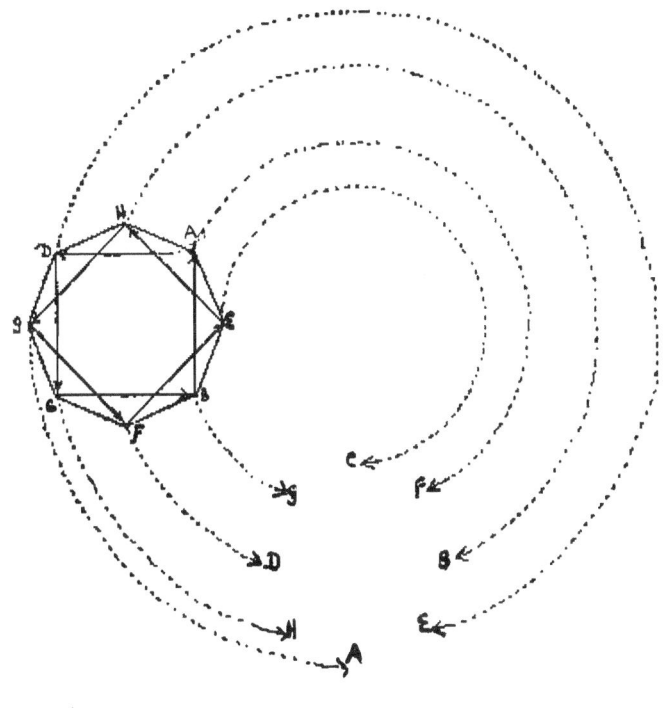

3. Transition :

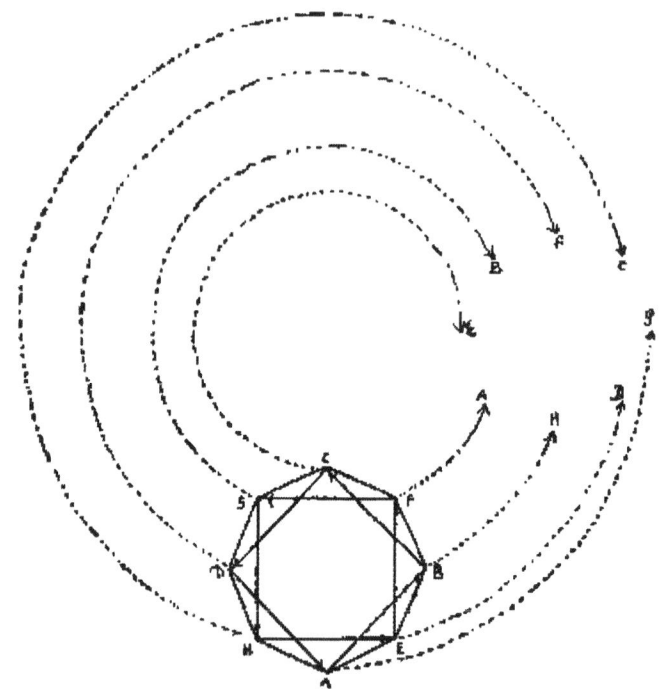

4. Transition:

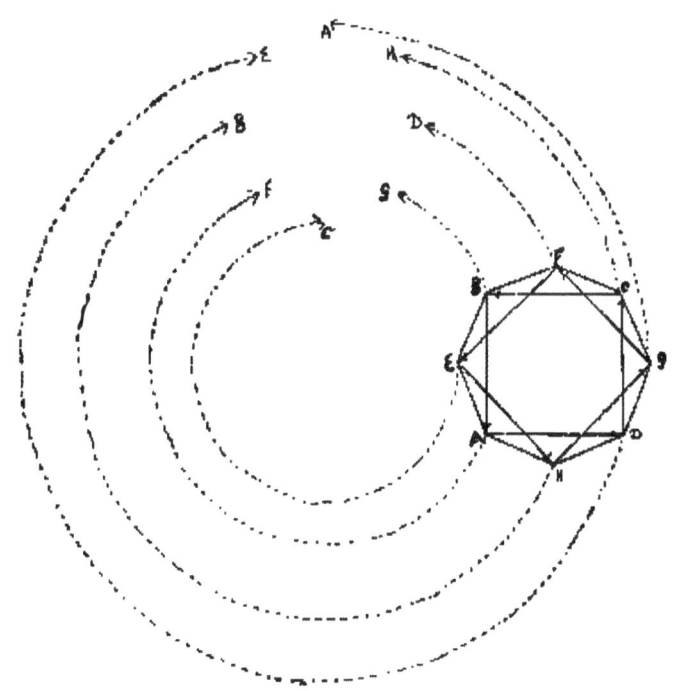

Another method of arrangement, in which the interior movement is carried out in small curves:

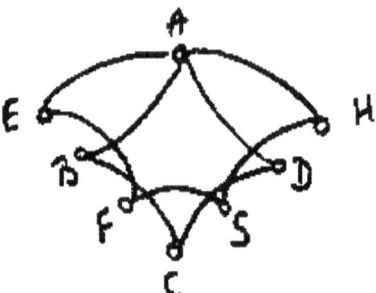

Should one wish to accompany the transitions with definite sounds, in the case of the interior movement, those on the first square can form the sound o, those on the second square e, and then allow them to dissolve. During the transitions everyone does the sound i, each one raising the arm in the direction in which he is going.

XVIII

FORMS FOR CHILDREN

These forms, which are carried out to the accompaniment both of recitation and music, were originally given by Dr. Steiner as educational exercises 'for children and young people'; they can, however, also be used in a purely artistic way as preludes to poems where the mood is merry and lighthearted.

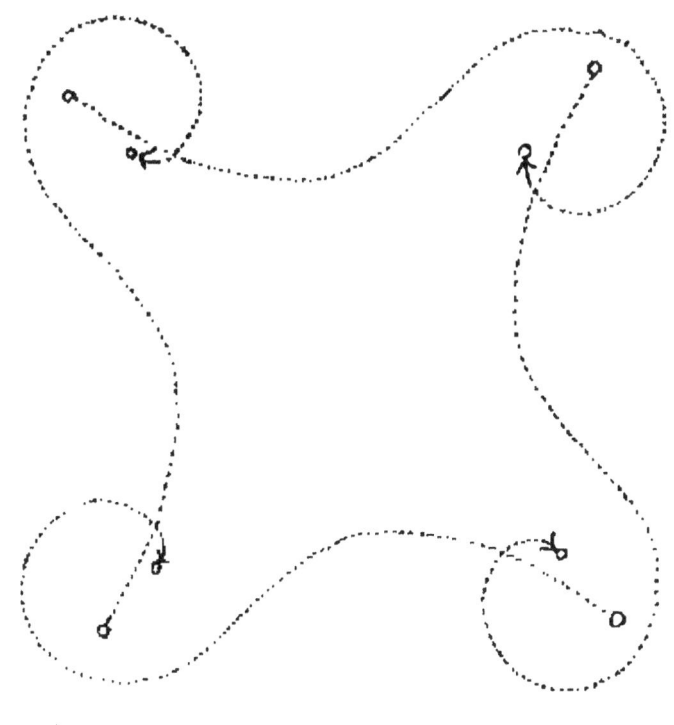

There are three forms of this type and to these Dr. Steiner himself added the words.

I. Behold Thyself—Behold the World.
(Schau in dich—Schau um dich.)

During the first sentence each of the four children runs to the next place in the spiral form shown in the diagram, at the same time doing the vowel-sounds for these three words. With 'Behold the World', first making the small curve as though beginning an evolving spiral, they run back to their places, at the same time doing the movements for the consonants. On the forward journey the head is somewhat lowered and the gaze of the eyes turned inwards, while the movements for the sounds are led over towards the interior, towards the central point of the form. On the way back: 'Behold the World', the head is raised up with a free glance of the eyes, and the movements for the consonants are made to radiate outwards into space.

When this exercise is made more artistic in character, it can be arranged thus: 'Behold thyself' is first recited (while the eurythmists remain quietly standing). Then follows the movement of the form (together with the gestures for the sounds) accompanied by suitable music*. Now the text is again recited: 'Behold the World', and it is only with the ensuing music that the Eurythmy form is concluded. In the two following forms also there can be a similar alternation between the recitation and musical accompaniment.

---

* See catalogue at end of book.

II. We seek one another—We feel one another—quite near.
(Wir suchen uns—wir leben uns—ganz nah.)

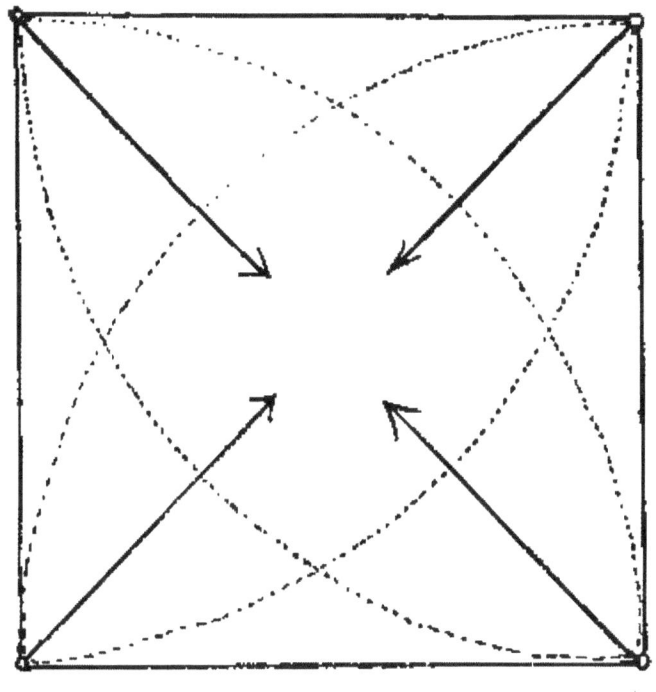

BASIC PRINCIPLES OF EURYTHMY

*We seek one
another :*

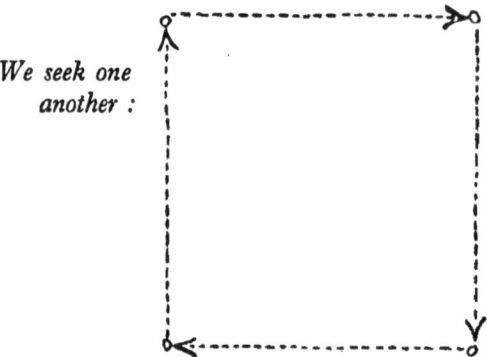

Here again the movement in space is combined with the gestures for the sounds. With 'We seek one another' everyone runs to the next place (in this exercise the form is run facing the direction in which the line leads); with 'We feel one another', the places are exchanged diagonally from point to point.

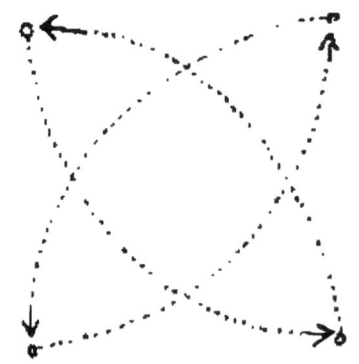

*We feel one
another:*

And with 'quite near' everyone comes together in the centre, so that with the movement for i^* the hands nearly touch.

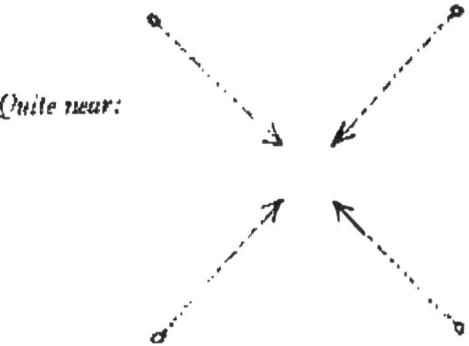

Then comes a short intermediate movement, the last steps being retraced (without turning round) so that the position in the square is again reached.

The whole form can be done in reversed sequence (the words also), producing in this way a 'satirical form' for humorous poems.

---

* a if the text is being recited in German. (Translator's Note.)

BASIC PRINCIPLES OF EURYTHMY

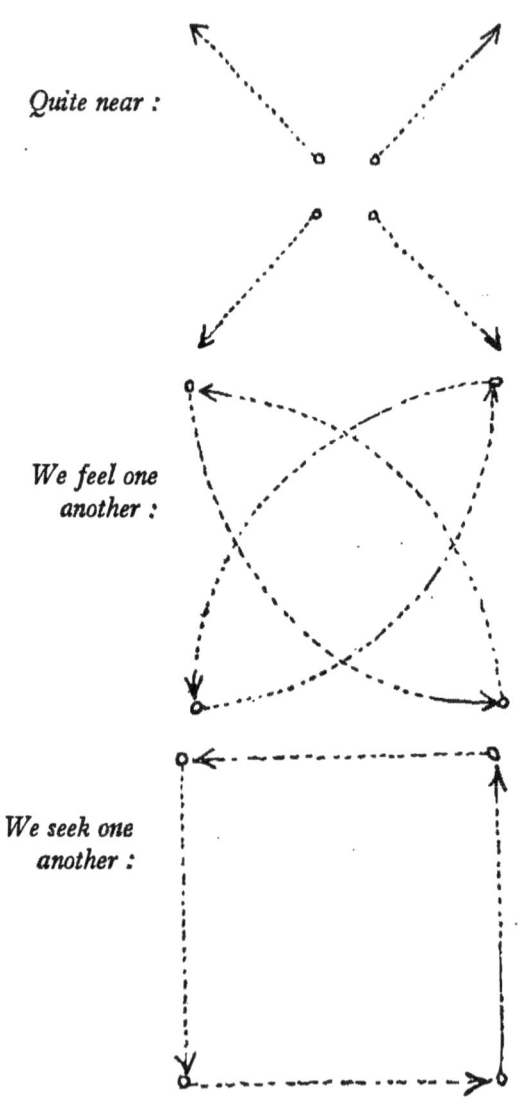

Now everyone runs swiftly to the centre, beginning again with 'quite near'. When the words are done in German—'ganz nah'—the angle of the *a* is specially marked at the elbow, and the forearm turned outwards.

III. *We will seek one another—we feel near one another—we know one another well.*
(Wir wollen suchen—wir fühlen uns nah—wir kennen uns wohl.)

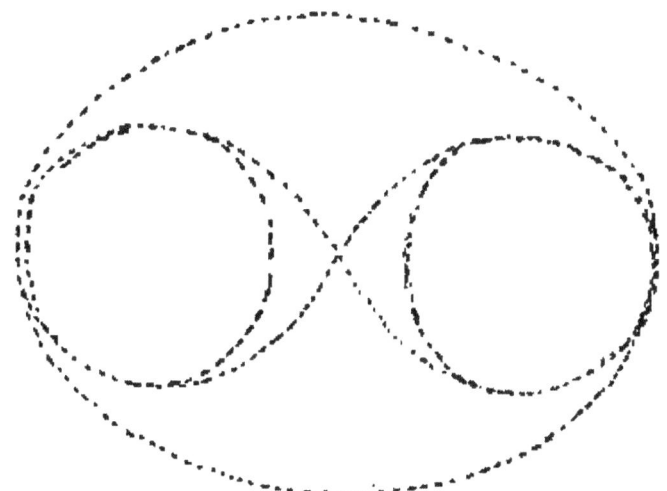

This exercise can also be done by four children. A beginning is made with the first sentence (once or twice repeated), to which the outer ellipse-form is run once and half round again. Then begins the lemniscate; here everyone simply runs round one after the other. Two children must remain somewhat behind, so that, when the first two have reached the left side (as seen from the audience) for the second time, those who have remained behind will just have arrived at the right side. The small circular forms are begun on the left side towards the left and on the right side towards the right, and are twice completed. If this form is made artistic in character, it can also be carried out by two people only. One begins on the left, the other on the right side. The repetition of the lines of the form can be determined by the length of the music.

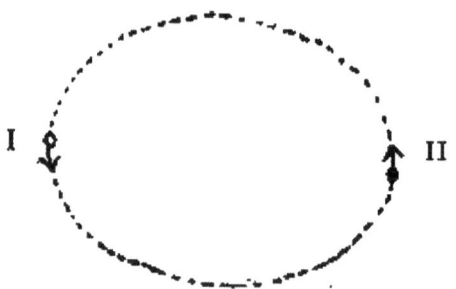

We will seek one another:

We feel near one another:

We know one another well:

FORM FOR POEMS OF HAPPY MOOD

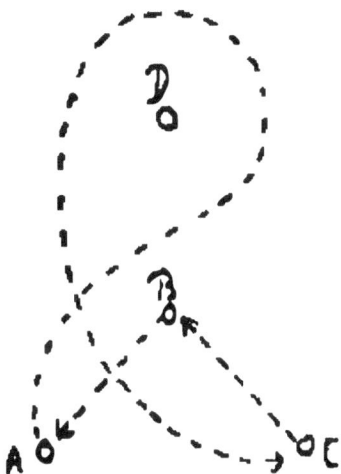

This form can be used as a prelude to lyrical poems where the mood is bright and happy. Three people form a triangle in the foreground, while a fourth stands the whole time in the background, in the posture for 'merriment' (which posture is also taken up by the other three). *A* begins the form and runs swiftly, in twenty-four small steps, along the line which, as shown in the diagram, leads round *D*, standing still when *C* is reached.

Then in four small steps, *C* moves to point *B*, *B* to point *A;* and now the latter *(B)* begins the long run round. The next time, after the changing of places, it is *C*'s turn to run, and so on.

* * *

FORM FOR POEMS OF MELANCHOLY MOOD

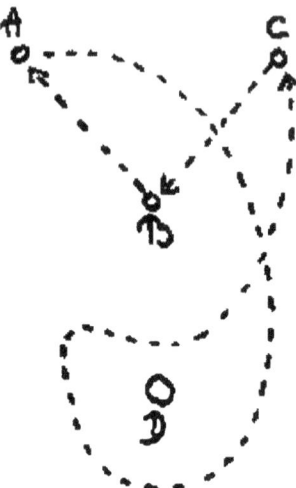

In this case the stationary figure is in the foreground, the triangle at the back. The whole form is a reversal of the previous merry form, but with a slight indentation of the line which leads round the standing figure. This small deviation must be felt as essential: it is as if something had bored its way into the form and at the same time there is, as it were, a feeling of retardation, of protraction. The movement of the form is quiet and leisurely and is carried out in twenty-eight steps in accordance with the music. It can be so divided that after twelve steps A has reached the right side of D (as seen from the audience), after six further steps the place where the indentation begins is reached; and then, with the remaining ten steps, the backward journey is concluded. During the first twelve steps A does the movement for the vowel-sound i, passes round the stationary figure in the gesture for o, carrying out the indentation and final line in u. Then comes the hanging of places:

C to point *B*, in four steps in the *e*-gesture, *B* to point *A*, again in four steps in the *e*-gesture; and now, with the same division of steps, *B* moves the long form to the sounds *a, i, o*. The changing of places is again accompanied by the movement for *e*. During the whole of the circuit round *C* does the movement for *a* (here, however, an inner tension, an intensification of the mood, must naturally be brought to expression). After the places have been changed round for the last time, this time in *a*, everybody passes over into the posture for *o*, which has been retained by *D* during the entire form.

A THREEFOLD FORM

I. *The Riddle of Destiny* or the *Spirit of Nature*.
   (Schicksalsfrage, oder auch *eine Naturstimmung),*
II. Intensification (Verinnerlichung),
III. Elegiac Relaxation (Elegische Lösung).

Six eurythmists take up their places in the following group-form and to the consonants *B, M, D, N, R, L,*

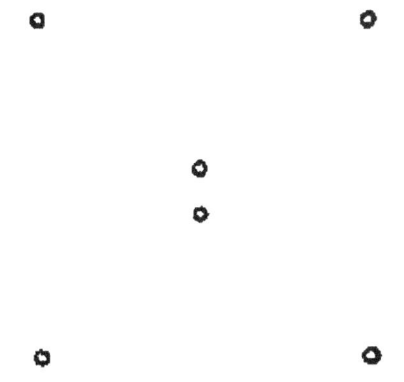

(other consonants or gestures can also be selected) pass over to the following formation:

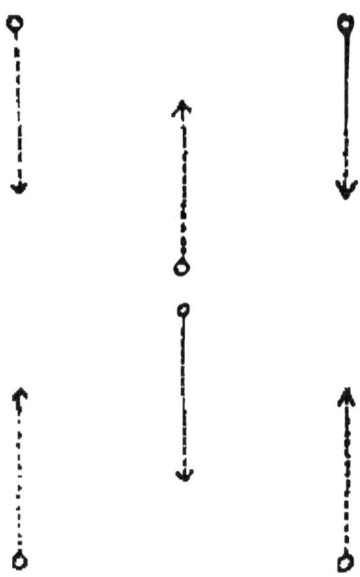

In this contraction of the outer square and expansion outwards from the two inner points, the feeling of *intensification* is expressed. This grouping is now retained for a time, while a definite sequence of eurythmy color-impressions is represented. As the basic posture the sound *e* is indicated and then the colors *white, yellow, red, green* are shown one after the other. This can be repeated three times.

Now follows the *elegiac relaxation*.

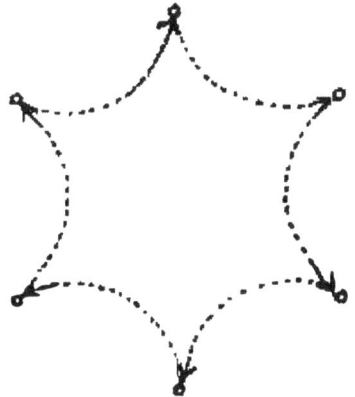

This is expressed in a tranquil and solemn circuit round the form. Everybody begins to move at the same time, walking round the hexagon in lines which are arched somewhat inwards towards the center. During the transition from place to place (6 steps), one sound must be slowly formed and the relative grouping steadily maintained. During the contraction of the form (the *intensification*) the first six sounds of the 'evolution of man' are carried out; and now this circular movement can be accompanied by the six following sounds: G, CH, F, S, H, T. With the T everyone will have returned to his original place.

XIX

TIAOAIT

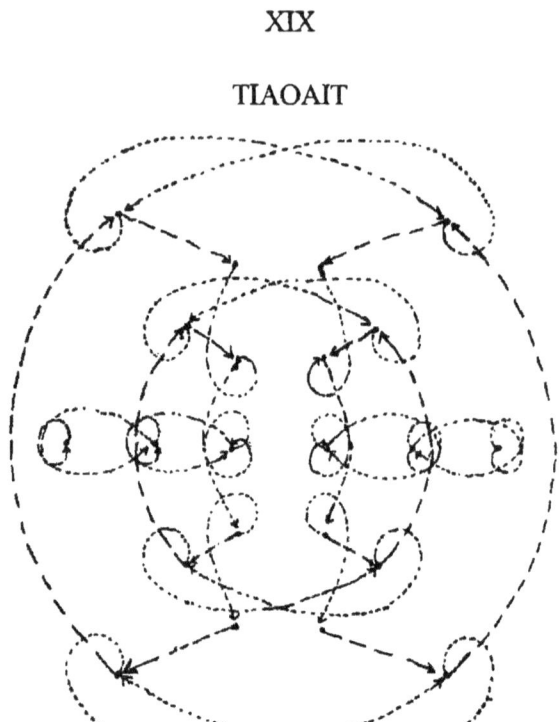

This form, which is built up on a definite combination of eurythmy sounds: *TIAOAIT—is* suited to poems of a certain solemnity and exaltation, or to poems of cosmic character, to *Odes, Hymns* or *Psalms*. During the recitation, at intervals either of one or more lines of the poem, a pause must be made in which the transition to the next metamorphosis of the group-form is carried out. (The text itself is done to Apollonian forms, which each eurythmist must start from his own spot, and which must, naturally, be carried out in a very limited space.)

The form begins with six eurythmists standing side by side in a line, quietly holding the gesture for *T*.

The first movement is a spiral-form, which leads from one place to the next. This is accompanied by the movement for *I*. The same spiral-form, again in *I*, is repeated, and now, with the sound *A*, the two front pairs part outwards away from each other, thus forming an angle:

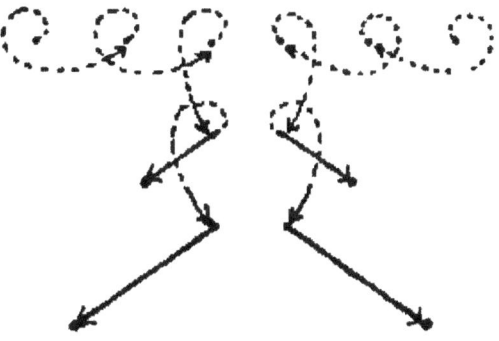

There now follows, always in the A-gesture, a double transition on the part of both front pairs; V and VI remain standing:

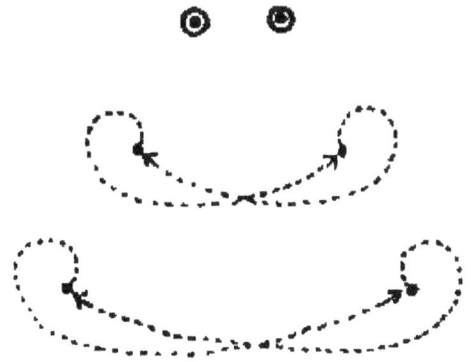

At this point everybody passes over into the O-gesture, I, II, III, IV moving in a semi-circle backwards. (In this exercise the movements in space closely resemble the formation of the sounds.)

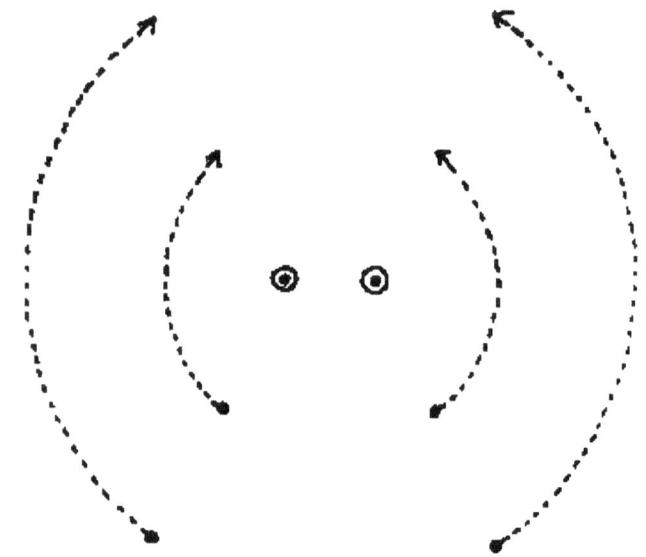

The second half of the form is an exact reflection of the first part (the sounds always corresponding to the sequence *TIAOAIT**).

It begins with the transition in *A*, the lines this time being curved outwards towards the background.

* See Appendix.

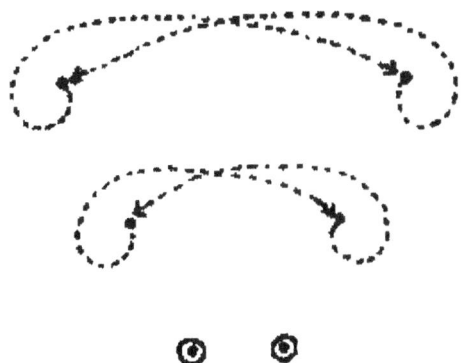

The angle is now drawn together again, and then, with two involving spirals in the I-movement, the original position is reached, where the sound *T* is formed again as a conclusion.

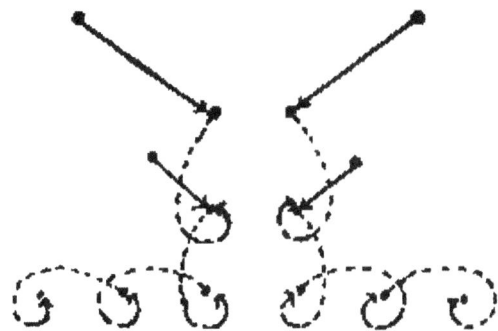

The direction of the eyes is also important in this exercise: with the first position the gaze is directed straight ahead with *I* upwards; with *A* slightly upwards, but *less* than with the *I*, and with the *O* the eyes are lowered.

* * *

FORM FOR POEMS OF A COSMIC CHARACTER

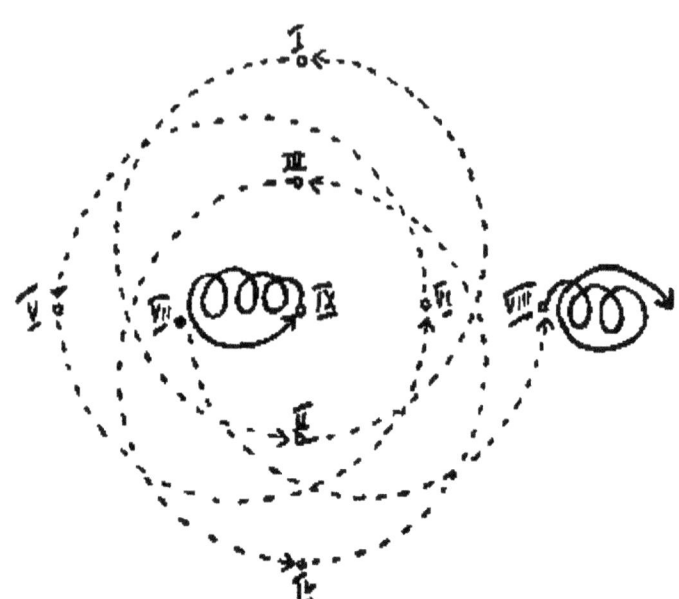

Dr. Steiner, when speaking of this form, said that it is the expression of an inner *movement forwards*—such as everywhere presents itself invisibly in the etheric world; like an advancing wave it flows onward in spirals, circles, or even in straight lines.

In the first place seven lines are moved; added to this we have the movement of the one who is standing in the center and the one who is standing on the right side. It is in fact these two who cause the whole wave to advance; the central figure urges, as it were, from inside, and it is the right-hand figure who 'seeks for the new'.

The form is carried out as follows: I moves to II; as soon as he has arrived II runs to place I; then III to IV, IV to place III ; V to VI, VI to place V ; and now VII to VIII at this very instant VIII and IX simultaneously begin to move, but in opposite vortex-like directions. These eddying forms can be varied in such a way, for instance, as the following

VIII is now standing somewhat further towards the right; the others catch up by means of two or three steps.

This can be repeated three times or oftener as a prelude to the performance of poems which bring mankind nearer to things of a *cosmic nature*.

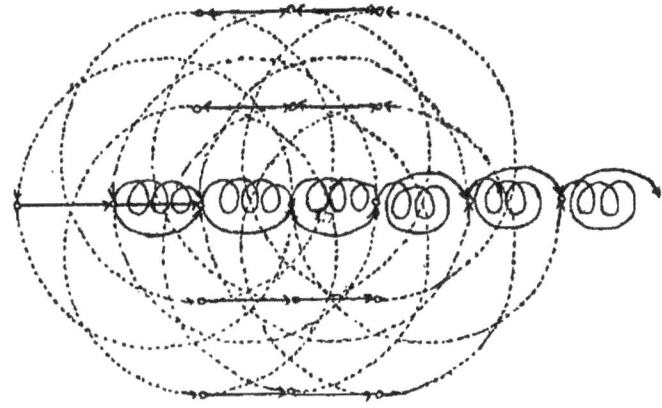

XX

PRESENTATION OF A POEM ON THREE LEVELS

'In this mode of presentation we have something closely bound up with the organism, for it is a presentation of speech itself. Here we are nearest the microcosm, just as in the Dance of the Planets* we are nearest the macrocosm. For the human being, as regards head and larynx, is actually organized in this way.'†

The eurythmists are divided into three half-circles, arranged at different levels. Those standing on the highest level express all the vowels of the poem which is to be presented. On the second level stands another group, and these do the movements for the lip-sounds: *B, P, M, V, F, W* (English *V*), and any *R*-sounds occurring after the vowel A, at the end of a word or before a consonant; added to these the dental sounds *S, SCH, Z*. On the third level the lingual and palate sounds are represented: *D, T, N, L, G, K, H, CH*, and the rolled *R* (which occurs before a vowel).

---

* See following Chapter
† From a lecture on eurythmy by Dr. Steiner to a small and intimate audience in 1915.

Let us take, for instance, the word *Morgen*; here *M* would be expressed on the second level, the *o* on the first, the *r* (which tends in sound towards *a*) again on the second, g on the third, *e* on the first, and *n* on the third. The individual movements must naturally play one into the other, and for this reason it is wise first to practice this distribution of sounds in such a way that everyone really looks in order to follow how the others are forming their sounds and the exact moment at which they are completed. Only then will they be able to retain the feeling of the whole, so that even those in the front will be able to fit their movements harmoniously into the movements of those standing behind their backs.

The onlooker then has before him a complete picture of the way the sounds are produced out of the organism of speech.

Here again Apollonian forms are made use of on the three levels. On the first level, in conjunction with the vowels that is to say, all straight and angular forms are carried out; all concrete nouns or nouns of condition, and all verbs, whether the mood is active, passive or of duration. On the second level all prepositions, conjunctions and interjections are shown; here, then, no forms are moved, but the corresponding gestures of the upper part of the body and head must be fitted into the presentation of the text in accordance with the sense of the words. And on the lowest level all the curved forms are moved, all such forms as express what is of a soul-nature, spiritual or abstract.

For this method of presentation only poems of a cosmic character should be selected, or nature-impressions having a certain magnitude and objectivity.

XXI

A DANCE OF THE PLANETS

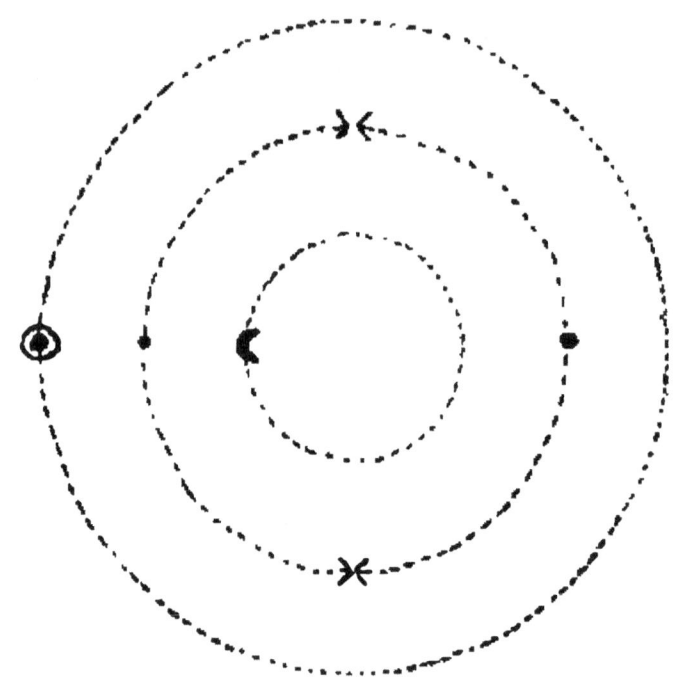

Es leuchtet die Sonne—
Was traget ihr Strahlen
Zu Blüten und Steinen
So machtvoll daher?

Es webet die Seele—
Was hebet das Leben
Aus Glauben zum Schauen
So sehnend hinauf?

O suche, du Seele,
In Steinen den Strahl
Im Blüten das Licht—
Du findest dich selbst.

Es blauet der Himmel—
Was sendet die Tiefe
Aus Fernen zur Erde
Geheimnisvoll her?

Es wirket der Geist—
Was schaffet der Starke
Aus wollendem Sein
Zur scheinenden Kraft?

So lenke, O Geist,
Zur Ferne den Blick,
Zur Tiefe dich selbst—
Du findest die Welt.

Es funkeln die Sterne—
Was breitet das Glänzen
Aus Weiten zur Mitte
Enthüllend daher?

Es fraget der Mensch—
Was rätselt im Innern
Aus bänglichem Streben

Zum Wissen sich hin?
So lenke, du Mensch,
Zur Weite dich selbst
Zur Mitte das Sein—
Du findest den Geist.

Es waltet die Nacht—
Was dämpfet die Wesen
In endlosem Raum
Zum lastenden Nichts?

Es weset das All—
Was waltet, sich hüllend
Im Dunkel der Gründe,
Verborgen atmend?

Es ahnet des Geistes
Erbrennendes Dursten
In Welten die Wesen,
In Wesen die Welten.

      RUDOLF STEINER.

 The structure of this poem conforms to cosmic laws. From the first line of each verse speak sun-forces, from the last line the backward-streaming forces of the moon. The whole poem, with its four times three verses, increases in movement, followed by a gradual relaxation. The mood of sunrise, of spring, which colors the opening verses, reaches full development in the second group of three verses, and then falls back towards the mood of night, towards the spiritualisation of everything external.
 The eurythmy form is carried out along three circles. On

the outermost circle the sun-aspect is expressed—the sun in the twelve aspects of the zodiac. (Here, on this circle, can stand either one eurythmist, or else twelve, as representatives of the zodiacal signs.) On the intermediate circle two eurythmists carry out lines two and three, the planetary aspect; the inner circle is the path of the 'Moon,' which moves in the opposite direction to the 'Sun' (which begins the circle backwards). Both 'Sun' and 'Moon' complete their circle once during the twelve verses. The two 'Planets' move in semicircles which swing backwards and forwards. One begins with the second line in the direction of the Moon, the other with the third line in the direction of the Sun.

The first position :

⊚ • ❰ •

After three verses :

⊚

•

⌄
•

After the sixth verse :

• ❱ • ⊚

After the ninth verse :

■
⌃

■
●

After the twelfth verse :

The 'Sun' does the movements for all the sounds of the first line (vowels and consonants), at the same time expressing all the nouns in Apollonian forms. The actual circuit round the circumference is moved with a measured step during the lines of the others. (This latter also holds good for the circular motion of the Moon and the backward and forward motion of the Planets.) The 'Moon' has to portray all the vowels and consonants of the fourth line, and, in addition, does all the movements for verbs, prepositions, conjunctions and interjections contained in these lines. The 'Planets' do the movements for the vowels—each one his own line; and, as everything adjectival or adverbial falls to their lot, they need add no other forms to their movement round the circle.

These were the original indications; but, in order to bring more life into the movement, it can also be done in such a way that the eurythmists do the Apollonian forms for all the words of their own line, so dividing these in space that they gradually move round their own form.

If, instead of the Sun, twelve eurythmists represent the zodiacal signs, number I, during the first line of the verse, does the vowels and forms (for the nouns), while II, standing still accompanies this with the consonants; with the second verse II undertakes the vowel-sounds and forms of the first line, while III accompanies with the consonants, and so on.

The 'Sun' as soon as his line of the text is completed, passes every time into the gesture for au, the 'Moon' into the gesture for ei; the two 'Planets' do the movements for a and e while the others are carrying out their lines.

The 'Sun' in his sounds must express something protective. Something invigorating.

The 'Moon' must express the motive-force of desire; thus all his movements must tend towards the will-zone.

For all those taking part the most important thing to bear in mind with regard to the sounds is that the first of every three verses must express the mood of love. The second verse must be carried out in the mood of yearning, the third in the posture for exclamation (Ruf). This threefold differentiation of mood is shown four times in succession.

XXII

THE ORIGIN OF THE SOUNDS IN THE MACROCOSM

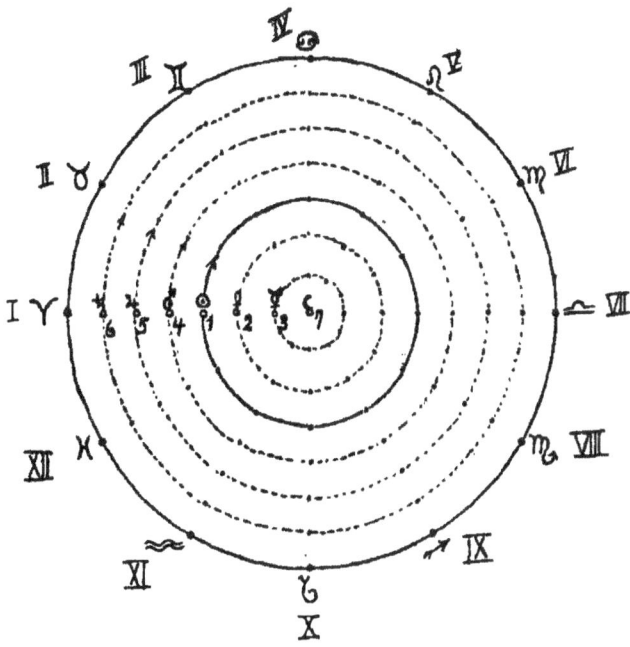

Here again in the eurythmy gestures and forms in space cosmic events are brought to expression.

Let us first quote the poem by Dr. Steiner upon which this whole series of movements is based:

Zwölf Stimmungen[*]

Erstehe, O Lichtesschein *(Sun)*
Erfasse das Werdewesen, *(Venus)*
Ergreife das Kräfteweben, *(Mercury)*
Erstrahle dich Sein-erweckend. *(Mars)*
Am Widerstand gewinne, *(Jupiter)*
Im Zeitenstrom zerrinne. *(Saturn)*
O Lichtesschein verbleibe! *(Moon)*
                                              (Aries.)

Erhelle dich, Wesensglanz,
Erfühle die Werdekraft,
Verwebe den Lebensfaden
In wesendes Weltensein,
In sinniges Offenbaren,
In leuchtendes Seins-Gewahren.
Owes Wesensglanz, erscheine!
                                           (Taurus.)

Erschliesse dich, Sonnesein
Bewege den Ruhetrieb,
Umschliesse die Strebelust
Zu mächtigem Lebewalten,
Zu seligem Weitbegreifen
Zu fruchtendem Werdereifen.
O Sonnesein, verharre!
                                           (Gemini.)

---

[*] Translation available from Mercury Press as *The Twelve Moods*.

THE ORIGIN OF THE SOUNDS IN THE MACROCOSM

Du ruhender Leuchteglanz,
Erzeuge Lebenswärme,
Erwärme Seelenleben
Zu kräftigen sich Bewähren
Zu geistigem sich Durchdringen
In ruhigem Lichterbringen.
Du Leuchteglanz, erstarke!
(Cancer.)

Durchströme mit Sinngewalt
Gewordenes Weltensein,
Erfühlende Wesenschaft
Zu wollendem Seinentschluss.
In strömendem Lebensschein,
In waltender Werdepein,
Mit Sinngewalt erstehe!
(Leo.)

Die Welten erschaue, Seele!
Die Seele ergreife Welten,
Der Geist erfasse Wesen,
Aus Lebensgewalten wirke,
In Willenserleben baue,
Dem Weltenblüh'n vertraue,
O Seele erkenne die Wesen!
(Virgo.)

Die Welten erhalten Welten,
In Wesen erlebt sich Wesen,
Im Sein umschliesst sich Sein,
Und Wesen erwirket Wesen
Zu werdendem Tatergiessen,
In ruhendem Weltgeniessen.
O Welten, traget Welten!
(Libra.)

Das Sein es verzehrt das Wesen
Im Wesen doch hält sich Sein.
Im Wirken entschwindet Werden,
Im Werden verharret Wirken.
In strafendem Weltenwalten,
In ahndendem Sich-Gestalten.
Das Wesen erhält die Wesen.
(Scorpio.)
Das Werden erreicht die Seinsgewalt,
Im Seienden erstirbt die Werdemacht.
Erreichtes beschliesst die Strebelust
In waltender Lebenswillenskraft.
Im Sterben erreift das Weltenwalten
Gestalten verschwindet in Gestalten.
Das Seiende fühle das Seiende!
(Sagittarius.)
Das Künftige ruhe auf Vergangenem.
Vergangenes erfühle Künftiges
Zu kräftigem Gegenwartsein.
Im inneren Lebenswiderstand
Erstarke die Weltenwesenwacht,
Erblühe die Lebenswirkensmacht.
Vergangenes ertrage Künftiges.
(Capricorn.)

Begrenztes sich opfere Grenzenlosem.
Was Grenzen vermisst, es gründe
In Tiefen sich selber Grenzen;
Es hebe im Strome sich,
Als Welle verfliessend sich haltend,
Im Werden zum Sein sich gestaltend.
Begrenze dich, O Grenzenloses.
(Aquarius.)

THE ORIGIN OF THE SOUNDS IN THE MACROCOSM

> Im Verlorenen finde sich Verlust,
> Im Gewinn verliere sich Gewinn,
> Im Begriffenen suche sich das Greifen
> Und erhalte sich im Erhalten.
> Durch Werden zum Sein erhoben,
> Durch Sein zu dem Werden verwoben,
> Der Verlust sei Gewinn für sich!
>
> *(Pisces.)*

In the strict exactitude of their structure the "Zwölf Stimmungen" conform exactly to the content they express; movement and rest—the twelvefold circle which appears in the universe as the Zodiac and the sevenfold circle which appears as the sequence of the planets. We have twelve verses, each of seven lines, an exact image of what takes place in the universe. This is, as it were, the outer scaffold; but built into it are all the details which manifest themselves in the flood of movement of our solar system. This is shown in the rising and falling line of the individual verses, in the rising and falling line of the entire poem; in the general atmosphere of each verse, as it corresponds to a definite heavenly body, a correspondence brought about by the whole manner in which the words of the verse in question are put together, and also by the part played by each separate line as it corresponds to the movements of the planets; for one may feel: Here is the energetic movement of Mars, here the majesty of Jupiter, there we have the forces of Saturn, mature to ebbing-point, finally the confirming rays thrown back from the Moon—rays which in the first Sun-line are a direct radiance, then to pass over to the gentle warmth of Venus and the weaving activity of Mercury. And this sevenfold inner soul-experience, descending from the Sun through Venus, Mercury, Mars, Jupiter, Saturn, as far as the Moon, is woven into the mood-content of the verse corresponding to each sign of the Zodiac through which the Sun passes. It is a veritable "one-ness" with the laws of the universe, the polar opposite of anything subjective or arbitrary.' (From Marie Steiner's 'Preface to the collection Wahrspruchworte by Rudolf Steiner.') Twelve eurythmists, representing the Zodiac, form the circumference of a circle; the seven planets* move from one zodiac-sign to the next. A beginning is made with Aries. The first line of each verse, which corresponds to the Sun, is expressed in vowels by the eurythmist representing the Sun. The second line, which manifests the inward qualities of Venus, is carried out by number 2; 3 does the Mercury-line; the Mars-; 5 the Jupiter-; 6 the Saturn-; 7 the Moon-line. During the interval the Sun has made a complete circuit through the zodiac, and, by the end of the verse, has regained his original place. At this point the whole line moves onto the next sign of the zodiac,and now it is the verse portraying what takes place under th sign of Taurus which is brought to expression.

During the first verse the eurythmist representing Arie (I) does all the consonants contained in the text; then th consonants are done by 'Taurus' (II); during the third verse by 'Gemini' (III), and so on. In this way we hay visibly expressed in eurythmy movement how each zodiac sign is related to the separate planets as they speak in turn During the time taken by each verse all the others form th sounds corresponding to their individual signs, 'The Word surges through the world and the world-structure holds the word fast.'

The planets represent the vowel-element, the zodiac represents the element of the consonants; and indeed, at the beginning of every verse, each one of the twelve eurythmists must make a point of sounding his consonant again finally,

---

* See Appendix.

THE ORIGIN OF THE SOUNDS IN THE MACROCOSM

while forming it (thus not completely finishing th movement) passing over into and retaining the movement for his sign.

The sequence of the sounds is as follows:

Aries	— v (a)
Taurus	— r (a)
Gemini	— h
Cancer	— f
Leo	— t
Virgo	— b
Libra	— c (ts)
Scorpio	— z
Sagittarius	— g
Capricorn	— l
Aquarius	— m
Pisces	— n
Sun	— au (and i)
Venus	— e (and o)
Mercury	— a (and u)
Mars	— i
Jupiter	— o (and e)
Saturn	— u (and a)
Moon	— ei (and i)

The planets, on completing the movements belonging to their line, remain standing in their own special sound. (Where a choice of vowel has been indicated, the eurythmist must let feeling guide him as to which sound to select.) The Sun does the whole circuit in the gesture for *au*.

In the Speech-Eurythmy Course, in another context, Dr. Steiner indicated certain differentiations in the sounds related to the planets. In such a case one must not bring to these differing points of view ordinary thought merely; but one must approach them with a definite realization of the different constellations, of the different epochs of civilization, of the changes also which may have taken place in cosmic relationships, in the spiritual utterances of star to star. The one method of presentation refers to one moment in evolution, the other to some other moment.

The colors worn by the eurythmists, and which should be allowed to play into the whole manner in which the sounds are formed, are these:

    Sun — *white*
    Venus — *green*
    Mercury — *yellow*
    Mars — *red*
    Jupiter — *orange*
    Saturn — *blue*
    Moon — *violet*

The zodiacal circle, in so far as the colors are concerned, must be pictured as divided into two halves. If one imagines a line drawn between Aries and Libra, then those standing in the half-circle in the background, beginning with Aries, appear in the seven colors of the spectrum:

    Aries — *red*
    Taurus — *orange*
    Gemini — *yellow*
    Cancer — *green*
    Leo — *blue*
    Virgo — *indigo*
    Libra — *violet*

In the case of the five standing in the foreground, this violet-color is played upon in varying tones and shades; in the sign of Capricorn it pales to the color of peach-blossom, assuming in its passage through Aquarius and Pisces a more intense shade, until it finally leads over into the red of Aries. Here we have the day- and night-aspect of the colors, the physically visible, and—in the varied shades of violet—the spiritually supersensible.

The way in which the whole group gradually assembles on the stage is also given in strict detail. The first to appear is the 'Moon', who moves to the center-point, making the movement for the corresponding vowel-sound. Then follow:

> *Saturn with Aries and Libra.*
> *Jupiter with Virgo and Taurus.*
> *Mars with Gemini and Leo.*
> *Sun with Cancer and Capricorn.*
> *Venus with Pisces and Scorpio.*
> *Mercury with Aquarius and Sagittarius.*

At the conclusion the eurythmists taking part make their exit in the reversed order.[*]

* * *

These cosmic group-dances were first presented on the stage in Dornach, August the 29th, 1915. On this occasion Dr. Steiner gave a lecture, the main part of which he concluded with the following reference to the tremendous significance such presentations, indeed, such poetical forms in themselves, can have for the history of spiritual development.

Thus the attempt was made to draw out from the mysteries of the universe poems whose form of expression is equally adapted either to speech or the movements of

---

[*] See Appendix.

eurythmy. Now when the time arrives in which people will have learned to read the meaning of these things, one will, after seeing such a performance as this, know, really know, what such a system of movement brings to expression. Some people might of course hold the opinion that such things are quite unnecessary; but opinions can differ, can they not? It would also be possible for someone to hold the opinion that it would be better for the human being to remain silent, that there is no need to speak. And, if everyone in the world were dumb and only a few people began to speak, all the rest would certainly regard speech as something highly unnecessary. It is simply a question of relative opinions. One only needs to admit the possibility of relative opinions to realize the fact that true progress in the evolution of humanity will only be achieved when people perceive the necessity of drawing out from human nature *all* the possibilities inherent in it.'

XXIII

PRESENTATION OF A SCENE FROM A PLAY

Preceded by the Mercury-Prelude

7th Scene from the 'Portal of Initiation' by Rudolf Steiner.

THE MERCURY-PRELUDE.

This form is based upon the design of the Seal of Mercury:

An occult seal should be understood as a 'hieroglyph', which expresses facts, occurrences of the super-sensible worlds. An inner connection exists between the Mercury-Seal and the spiritual events described in the seventh scene of the *Portal of Initiation*. In this scene *tidings* are brought and received; and everywhere where the bringing-of-tidings—where anything in the nature of a message—is contained in a poetical work (also, for instance, in certain scenes from *Faust*), the Mercury-Prelude may be introduced.

In this scene Maria, who plays the principal feminine role, appears, together with the beings who represent the forces of her own soul. From what we know of the basic laws of eurythmy-forms, we are able, just by the direction taken by the lines of this form, to see how it is connected with the three soul-forces, thinking, feeling and willing, enclosed as these are by the unity of the circle, the line taken by Maria. Astrid moves the straight lines, which ray out from the center and return to the same point ; Luna winds in and out of this 'staff-form' with the doubly curved line ; Philia accompanies Maria, the lines of her form continually passing over from the curved to the straight. During the entire form, Philia does the movement for *i* in the upper-, the feeling-zone; Astrid does a in the thought-zone ; Luna *u* in the zone of will. Maria unites these three sounds, carrying out in succession: one *i-movement,* one *u-movement,* (the hands touching each other at the breast and pointing to the heart) and one *stretched movement for a.*

The form of this prelude is carried out to music in three-part form by L. van der Pals. (Astrid and Luna can, if space-conditions render it advisable, lay their form into the circle three times only.)

With the first bars of the music Philia appears alone; with the beginning of the eighth bar Astrid also makes her appear-

PRESENTATION OF A SCENE FROM A PLAY

ance; with the twelfth bar (somewhat faster than the others) Luna; then, with the thirteenth and fourteenth bars, appears Maria. At this point there is a pause of two bars in the following position.

The actual form begins with the new entry of the music. During the third 'movement-round', where the first motif re-enters (seventy-eighth bar), a chorus appears in the background. After the last note of the music has sounded, the four characters move to the places from which they start the scene itself; the chorus is divided into three groups.

BACKGROUND.

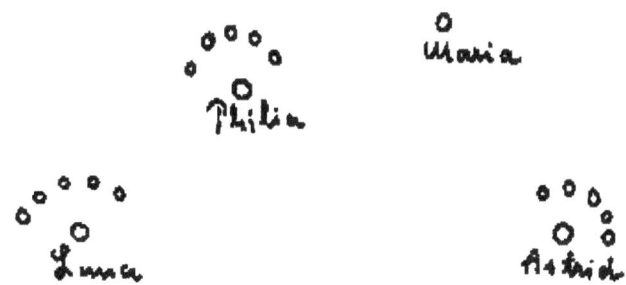

Seventh Scene from the 'Portal of Initiation.'

MARIA:

    Ihr, meine Schwestern, die ihr
    So oft mir Helferinnen wart,
    Seid mir es auch in dieser Stunde,
    Dass ich den Weltenäther
    In sich erbeben lasse.
    Er soll harmonisch klingen
    Und klingend eine Seele
    Durchdringen mit Erkenntnis.

Ich kann die Zeichen schauen,
Die uns zur Arbeit lenken.
Es soll sich euer Werk
Mit meinem Werke einen.
Johannes, der Strebende,
Er soll durch unser Schaffen
Zum wahren Sein erhoben werden.
Die Brüder in dem Tempel
Sie hielten Rat,
Wie sie ihn aus den Tiefen
In lichte Höhen führen sollen.
Von uns erwarten sie,
Dass wir in seiner Seele heben
Die Kraft zum Höhenfluge.
Du, meine Philia, so sauge
Des Lichtes klares Wesen
Aus Raumesweiten,
Erfülle dich mit Klangesreiz
Aus schaffender Seelenmacht,
Dass du mir reichen kannst
Die Gaben, die du sammelst
Aus Geistesgründen.
Ich kann sie weben dann
In den erregenden Sphärenreigen.
Und du auch, Astrid, meines Geistes
Geliebtes Spiegelbild,
Erzeuge Dunkelkraft
Im fliessenden Licht,
Dass es in Farben scheine.
Und gliedre Klangeswesenheit;
Dass webender Weltenstoff
Ertönend lebe.
So kann ich Geistesfühlen

Vertrauen suchendem Menschensinn.
Und du, O starke Luna,
Die du befestigt im Innern bist,
Dem Lebensmarke gleich,
Das in des Baumes Mitte wächst,
Vereine mit der Schwestern gaben
Das Abbild deiner Eigenheit,
Dass Wissens Sicherheit
Dem Seelensucher werde.

PHILIA:
Ich will erfüllen mich
Mit klarstem Lichtessein
Aus Weltenweiten.
Ich will eratmen mir
Belebenden Klangesstoff
Aus Ätherfernen,
Dass dir, geliebte Schwester,
Das Werk gelingen kann.

ASTRID:
Ich will verweben
Erstrahlend Licht
Mit dämpfender Finsternis,
Ich will verdichten
Das Klangesleben.
Es soll erglitzernd klingen,
Es soll erklingend glitzern,
Dass du, geliebte Schwester,
Die Seelenstrahlen lenken kannst.

LUNA:
: Ich will erwärmen Seelenstoff
: Und will erhärten Lebensäther.
: Sie sollen sich verdichten,
: Sie sollen sich erfühlen,
: Und in sich selber seiend
: Sich schaffend halten,
: Dass du, geliebte Schwester,
: Der suchenden Menschenseele
: Des Wissens Sicherheit erzeugen kannst.

MARIA:
: Aus Philia's Bereichen
: Soll Strömen Freudesinn;
: Und Nixen Wechselkräfte
: Sie mögen öffnen
: Der Seele Reizbarkeit,
: Dass der Erweckte
: Erleben kann
: Der Welten Lust,
: Der Welten Weh.—
: Aus Astrids Weben
: Soll werden Liebelust:
: Der Sylphen wehend Leben,
: Es soll erregen
: Der Seele Opfertrieb,
: Dass der Geweihte
: Erquicken kann
: Die Leidbeladenden,
: Die Glück Erflehenden.—
: Aus Luna's Kraft
: Soll strömen Festigkeit
: Der Feuerwesen Macht

Sie kann erschaffen
Der Seele Sicherheit;
Auf das der Wissende
Sich finden kann
Im Seelenweben,
Im Weltenleben.

PHILIA:
Ich will erbitten von Weltengeistern,
Dass ihres Wesens Licht
Entzücke Seelensinn,
Und ihrer Worte Klang
Beglücke Geistgehör;
Auf dass sich hebe
Der zu Erweckende
Auf Seelenwegen
In Himmelshöhen.

ASTRID:
Ich will die Liebesströme,
Die Welt erwärmenden,
Zu Herzen leiten
Dem Geweihten;
Auf dass er bringen kann
Des Himmels Güte
Dem Erdenwirken,
Und Weihestimmung
Den Menschenkindern.

LUNA:
Ich will von Urgewalten
Erflehen Mut und Kraft,
Und sie dem Suchenden

In Herzenstiefen legen;
Auf dass Vertrauen
Zum eignen Selbst
Ihn durch das Leben
Geleiten kann.
Er soll sich sicher
In sich dann selber fühlen.
Er soll von Augenblicken
Die reifen Früchte pflücken,
Und Saaten ihnen entlocken
Für Ewigkeiten.

MARIA:
Mit euch, ihr Schwestern,
Vereint zu edlem Werk,
Wird mir gelingen,
Was ich ersehe...

* * *

MARIA:
My sisters who of old
So oft my helpers were;
In this hour help me too
That Ether of the worlds
May quiver in itself;
Resound in harmony,
And thus resounding reach
And permeate a soul
With knowledge that is true.
I now can see the signs
Which guide us to our work;
For your work must to-day
Unite itself with mine.

Johannes who doth strive
Must be by our designs
To real existence raised.
Within the temple walls
The Brethren counsel took
How they should raise him up
From depths to heights of light;
From us do they expect
To fill the soul with power
For such high spirit flight.
From breadths of space shalt thou,
My Philia, win for me,
Clear essence of the light;
And fill thyself with all
The charm of sound which wells
From soul-creating power.
That thou mayst give to me
Gifts gathered by thyself
From out the spirit's depths.
Then can I weave for him
Their perfect harmonies
In the soul-stirring dance
And rhythm of the spheres.
And thou, my Astrid,
Dear image of my spirit,
Shalt cause within the light
The power of shade to grow
That colors may shine forth.
To formless harmonies
Thou shalt give shape, and thus
World-substance, weaving life,
May sound upon its way.
So can I give to man

When he doth seek therefor
A spirit consciousness.
And thou, strong Lima, too,
So firm in thine own self;
E'en like the living sap
Hid deep within the tree,
To these thy sister's gifts
Do then unite thine own.
Impress thyself thereon
That he who seeks may find
True wisdom's surety.

PHILIA:
I will myself imbue
With clearest rays of light
From cosmic spaces wide.
I will breathe deep within
Sound-substance that gives life
From distant ether-bounds,
Dear sister, that thou mayst
Succeed in this thy work.

ASTRID:
Through all the streaming light
I will weave darkness in
To cloud its radiant beam.
I will make dense and thick
The living life of sound;
That glowing it may sound
And sounding it may glow,
Dear sister, that thou mayst
Direct the soul-life's rays.

LUNA:
>   Soul-substance will I warm,
>   Life's ether harden too.
>   That they may thus condense
>   And may thus feel themselves
>   As living in themselves
>   And powerful to create,
>   Dear sister, that thou mayst,
>   Prove wisdom's certainty
>   To mankind's seeking soul.

MARIA:
>   From Philia's realm
>   Shall stream forth delight;
>   And transforming powers
>   Of Undines arouse
>   The sensitive soul.
>   That he who is roused
>   May feel all the mirth
>   And feel all the woe
>   In cosmic domains.
>
>   From Astrid's close web
>   Love's joy shall come forth.
>   The Sylphs airy life
>   Shall rouse in the soul
>   Self-sacrifice true;
>   That consecrate man
>   May rouse to new life
>   Souls laden with grief,
>   Souls yearning for joy.
>
>   From Luna's domain

Shall firmness stream forth.
And Fire-beings might
Shall form in the soul
Security's strength.
That he who doth know
May find his own self
In weaving of souls
And life of the worlds.

PHILIA:
From cosmic spirits I
Will beg their being's light
The soul-sense to enchant,
The sound too of their words
To charm the spirit's ear;
That he, who wakening hears
May raise himself aloft
Upon the paths of soul
Unto celestial heights.

ASTRID:
> The love-streams will I guide
> That fill the world with warmth
> Unto the heart of man
> Who is initiate;
> That thus he may bring down
> Into his work on earth
> The grace of heaven, and give
> The joy of holy rite
> Unto the sons of men.

LUNA:
> From primal powers will I For might and courage pray
> And lay them deep within
> The human seeker's heart:
> That so trust in himself
> May guide him through his life,
> Then shall he feel secure
> In his own self, and pluck
> Each moment ripened fruit
> And draw the seeds therefrom
> For all eternity.

MARIA:
> With you, my sisters, joined in noble work I shall succeed in what I long to do.

(At this point ends that part of the scene which is presented in Eurythmy.)

In this scene, which is enacted in spirit-realms, we have the sole example of 'dramatic Eurythmy' in which Rudolf Steiner gave definite indications as to how one single performer may endeavor to unite the gesture of Eurythmy with the spoken word. Whereas the three soul-powers accompany their part of the text, which is spoken from behind the scenes, with Eurythmy movements, Maria herself speaks, accompanying her words with gestures which are not related to the actual spoken sounds but to the thought- and mood-content of the individual sentences. The moods to be expressed pass over from 'Exclamation' or 'Appeal' (Ruf) to 'Yearning' (Sehnsucht), then from 'Knowledge' (Erkenntnis) to the 'Bringing-of-tidings' (Mitteilung). Wherever the mood of *Exclamation* occurs it is accompanied by an *i;* thus during the first three lines of the text, as far as 'help me too' (see text), Maria carries out only one *i*. Differentiation must be brought into this one sound according to the emphasis laid upon the words, and also the direction taken by the form. Apollonian forms are here employed. They can, however, be very much curtailed, in accordance with the meaning and significance of the text; it is enough, for instance, to fit a whole sentence into one line-of-duration, or one soul-form. With the mood of *Yearning* Maria passes over to *u* (with touching hands), *Knowledge* and the *Bringing-of-Tidings* are expressed by a. Variety is introduced by means of the different postures of the body corresponding to the various moods. (See 'Various Aspects of Artistic Production.')

My sisters who of old	
So oft my helpers were,	*Appeal*
In this hour help me too	
That ether of the worlds	
May quiver in itself	*Yearning*
Resound in harmony	
And thus resounding reach	*Knowledge*

And permeate a soul
With knowledge that is true.

I now can see the signs
Which guide us to our work;   *Bringing-Tidings*

For your work must to-day
Unite itself with mine.   *Appeal*

Johannes who doth strive
Must be by our designs   *Yearning*
To real existence raised.

Within the Temple walls
The Brethren counsel took   *Tidings*
How they should raise him up
From depths to heights of light.

From us they do expect
To fill the soul with power   *Yearning*
For such high spirit-flight.

From breadths of space shalt thou,
My Philia, win for me
Clear essence of the light;
And fill thyself with all
The charm of sound which wells   *Appeal*
From soul-creating power.
That thou mayst give to me
Gifts gathered by thyself
From out the spirit's depths.

Then can I weave for him
Their perfect harmonies   *Tidings*
In the soul-stirring dance

And rhythm of the spheres.

And thou, my Astrid,
Dear image of my spirit,
Shalt cause within the light
The power. of shade to grow
That colors may shine forth. *Appeal*
To formless harmonies
Thou shalt give shape, and thus
World-substance, weaving life,
May sound upon its way.

So can I give to man
When he doth seek therefore *Tidings*
A spirit consciousness

And thou, strong Luna, too
So firm in thine own self;
E'en like the living sap *Appeal*
Hid deep within the tree,
To these thy sisters' gifts
Do then unite thine own.

Impress thyself thereon
That he who seeks may find *Tidings*
True wisdom's surety.

    As soon as Maria addresses one of the Soul-forces she carries her gestures over into the zone in question. The whole of her second speech—'From Philia's'— is carried out in the mood of *Appeal*. As long as she is speaking to Philia she directs the i-movement upwards; immediately Astrid is mentioned the sounds are transferred to the middle zone, and where Luna is mentioned to the lower. The 'Soul-forces' must endeavor to bring all their movements into an attitude of *response,* of *expectation fulfilled.* Apart from this they retain their individual zones and direction of the glance of the eyes. The space-forms carried out in this scene by the soul-forces, when answering Maria, are also in the nature of Apollonian forms.*

The exact division of this scene among the soul-forces and their choruses is as follows

During Maria's first speech, Philia, Astrid and Luna stand in their respective sounds; the three choruses carry out the accompaniment, those in the Philia-chorus with consonants in the upper zone; of those in the Astrid-chorus some do vowels, the others consonants, in the zone of thinking; the Luna-chorus does vowels in the zone of will. While the soul-forces are carrying out the Eurythmy movements for their part of the text (Philia vowels, Astrid vowels and consonants, Luna consonants) the chorus belonging to the one who is speaking remains quiescent, the other choruses carrying out the accompaniment.

During Maria's second speech the soul-force who is being addressed carries out a few sounds standing still. The chorus belonging to the character momentarily speaking remains quiescent, while the two other choruses carry out the accompaniment. (In this case the Luna-chorus does consonants.)

When the soul-forces answer for the second time, each one is accompanied by her own chorus, the other choruses remaining quiescent. (In this case the Philia-chorus does the consonants.)

---

* See Appendix.

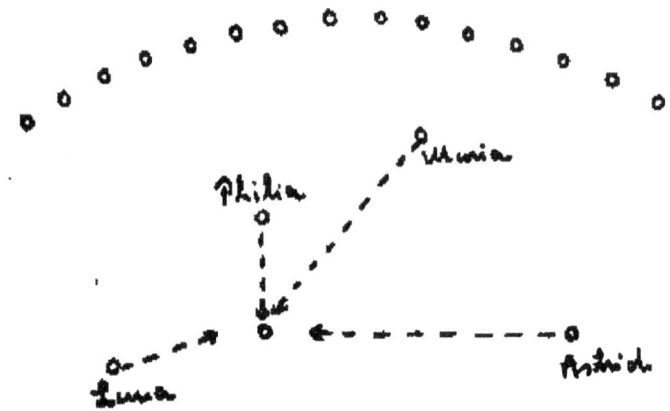

With Maria's final sentence the movements are done by everybody together.

After Maria has spoken her last word, all those taking part group themselves as follows: Philia takes a few steps forwards in the i-movement, Maria, with a protecting gesture taking up her position behind her; Luna and Astrid approach from either side, making their sounds—Luna *u* and Astrid *a*—towards Philia. The choruses group themselves together in the background.*

* * *

Many other scenes from Rudolf Steiner's Mystery Plays have either been produced in Eurythmy, or else Eurythmy has been introduced into them. Wherever events of the spiritual world come into the action, where beings from the supersensible worlds make their appearance, the movements of Eurythmy play their part. For certain scenes of *Faust* also (the Prologue in Heaven, Faust's Awakening, and so on), as well

---

* See Appendix

as for the chorus of elves from *A Midsummer Night's Dream,* Dr. Steiner designed the group-movements, wonderful creations, which, together with solo-and group-forms for poems and piece of music, multiplied from year to year, accumulating an unbelievable treasure. Dr. Steiner gave the key to the cosmic depth and beauty of these mighty creations, when, at the end of his life, he delivered the lectures contained in the two courses of eurythmy-the Tone-Eurythmy Course and Speech-Eurythmy Course of the year 1924.

APPENDIX

Page 22. This rhythm may at first make unwonted demands; it is, however, as can be learned from Spiritual Science, deeply rooted in the human organization, and can be discerned by finer observation in many human activities.

Page 24. Dr. Steiner once pointed out, when looking at a Greek statue, that the freeing of the foot should really be looked upon as a 'Luciferic revolt' against being earthbound; resting on both feet expresses the purely human connection with the earth.

Page 26. With a view to developing this delicate faculty of perception in the feet, one may here practice writing with the toes; the right and left foot alternately should accurately describe the forms of the letters, the left foot, indeed, writing in symmetry.

Page 33. The movements carried out by the fingers are, in a certain sense, the most significant of all.

Page 36. The 'human proto-form', as Dr. Steiner called it. In the sketch which he drew, this picture, which arises through the move-

ments of the bodily-physical limbs, is enclosed in an egg-form:

We know from Spiritual Science that the human aura —the astral sheath surrounding the physical human body— appears to clairvoyant vision as an egg-shaped form. At the beginning of earth-evolution everything physical still appeared in astral form. Thus the definite physical body we possess to-day was first developed out of

APPENDIX

this egg-shaped sheath. (See *An Outline of Occult Science*, by Dr. Rudolf Steiner.)

Page 40. The colors of the eurythmy-figures are selected more in accordance with the soul-mood of the sound, as may be seen from Lecture VI.

Page 45. The etheric body—the supersensible member of the human being, which, in that it permeates the entire physical body, works upon it with formative and life-giving effect. 'All the organs are held together in their shape and form by the currents and movements of the etheric body.' (Dr. Rudolf Steiner, *An Outline of Occult Science*.).

Page 45. 'As the physical body cannot retain its form by means of the mineral matter and forces to be found in it, but must, in order to retain this form, be penetrated throughout by the etheric body, so the forces of the etheric body cannot of themselves be illumined by the light of consciousness. An etheric body left entirely to itself would find itself in a continual state of sleep. It might also be said that an etheric body in a physical body could only maintain a plant-existence. A waking etheric body is illumined by an astral body. (*An Outline of Occult Science*.)

Page 45. When teaching children yet another indication of Dr. Steiner's must be borne in mind: at the conclusion of the lesson all the children should be gathered together, in a circle, for instance, and remain for a few moments in absolute silence. All that has been taken in the lesson then re-echoes in the children and is still more firmly established.

Page 49. When a beginning is made at point c, the active element, the resolve, as one might say, is emphasized by walking backwards (see Apollonian forms); then, with the second line, one has the feeling of actually striving towards something; when beginning at point b, one would end with this striving and with the attainment of the goal. The essentials, therefore, remain the same; they are only experienced in another order.

Page 94. The 'Atlantean Age' was a very early epoch of earthly evolution, which ran its course on a continent situated where the Atlantic Ocean now is. (Plato, in legendary form, speaks in 'Timaios' and 'Kritias' of the ancient 'Island of Atlantis'.)

Page 116. For all pronouns as well—reflexive pronouns excepted—the form of the angle backwards was originally given; but it is apparent from what Dr. Steiner says in this connection in the Speech-Eurythmy Course, that these words can also simply be passed over. At most, when a pronoun bears special emphasis, the angle can be applied; for instance: 'Tauchen auf und heben tragend *Ihn*, den schönen, aufgefrischten.' (Goethe, *Pandora*.)

Special attention must be directed to the impersonal 'Es': Es schneit, es regnet, es war, etc. This *Es* is always carried out standing still, with the arms crossed *over the head (e)*.

Page 121. In the XIV Eurythmy Lecture Dr. Steiner gave additional, though slight, differences of posture, according to whether a preposition governs the genitive, dative or accusative.

Page 134. Mention may here be made of an indication given by Dr. Steiner on some special occasion, namely, that the cause must always be expressed with bigger and more significant movements than the effect.

Page 161. This experience of the relationship of chin to shoulder was once characterised by Dr. Steiner as: 'Ich will mich.'

Page 204. This sequence is not invariably binding; one of those standing in the front can also begin. The same thing holds good for the following studies.

Page 212. The apex should in fact always lie on the outermost circle. But with a view to making things more easily apparent it is

APPENDIX

generally carried out with the back point as the apex, thus with the form turned towards the audience. Thus the inner movements and transitions must be correspondingly described. A diagram drawn so that one may see the forms with their apex laid on the outside would show the corresponding way of making the transitions.

Page 248. This exercise can also be done in shorter form as Tiait; in this case the transition in *o* and the second half of the form lying in the background are omitted; instead, after the two first transitions in a, the form contracts again and the two spiral forms in *i* are retraced winding inwards, until finally one is again standing in *t*.

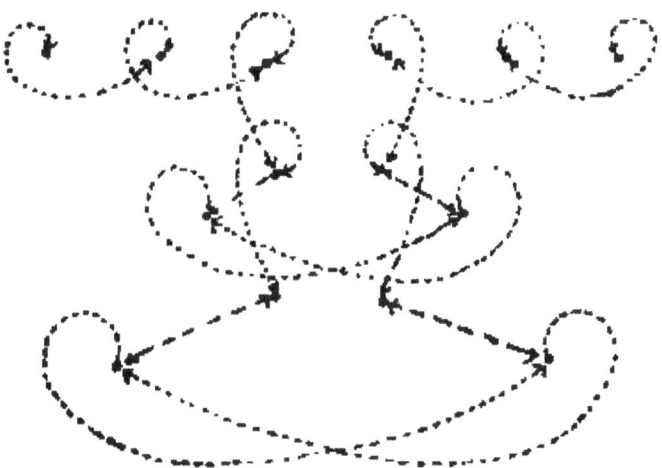

The A spirals at the back of the TIAOAIT, may also be reversed, that is inwinding.

Page 266. These descriptions of the planets, determined as they are by essential spiritual facts, agree with the old systems which were based upon spiritual vision.

Page 269. These 'Zwölf Stimmungen' were re-cast by Dr. Steiner as satire, and form a cutting criticism of mystical, over-intense conceptions of the path of knowledge. When presented in eurythmy they retain the same fundamental form and movements in space, the only difference being that, on the transition from one zodiac sign to another, the separate planets gradually get left behind; they get caught, as it were, between certain signs. Only the Sun completes the entire circle.

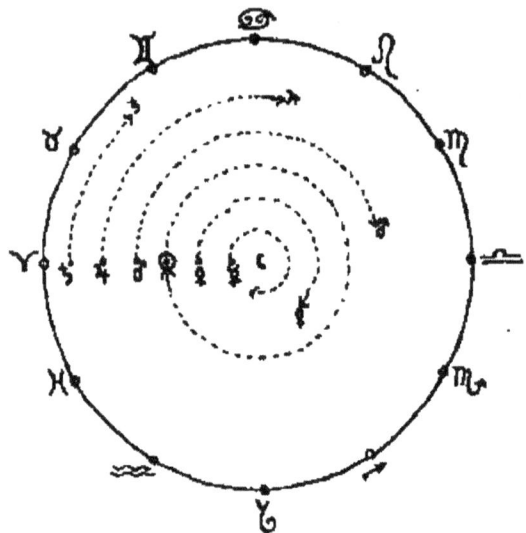

The text of this satire, 'The Song of Initiation' as Dr. Steiner sarcastically named it, runs as follows:

> Die Augen leuchten ihm helle,
> Im Kopfe stolpert sein Denken
> Vom Glück des Sinnens berauscht.
> Im Sturme folgt er der Erinnerung
> Des wunderbaren Traumes,
> Der Blüte der Erkenntnisbaumes
> In mystisch schwüler Nacht erlebt. (Aries.)
>
> Schon spukt in wirren Hirne
> Possierlich grüblerisch verträumt
> Vom Herzen aus mit Wohlgefühl begleitet
> Im Traumgaloppe geisterwärts

Gewichtig Schauen, kühn erspähend,
Wie aus dem Kosmos, deutlich krähend,
Ein Geisterchor sich offenbart. (Taurus.)

Entrissen fühlt das helle Ich
Dem Denken sich, das physisch nur,
Und drum vom hohen Geistestrieb,
Mit einem Seelentritte mächtig,
Vom Pfade edlen Strebens
Und kosmisch hohen Lebens
Wird kühnlich weggeschmissen. (Gemini.)

Ganz aus dem Leibe fühlt sich schon,
Durch Geistesboten recht geführt,
Durch Geistesliebe wohlgeflegt,
Von weiser Torheit stark gestossen,
Der Seele dunkles Schauen—
In den weiten Geistesauen
Ganz kosmisch geistgenährt. (Cancer.)

Was wirkt so mächtig wundersam,
Gedankenlos und Geistesträchtig,
Von Weltenliebe prächtig triefend,
Im kühnen Herzen ihm so ahnungsvoll?
Er ist zum Löwengrade
Auf dem steilen Wissenspfade
Ja klärlich nun schon vorgedrungen. (Leo.)

Nun muss er auch empfangen
Aus Weltgedanken würdevoll,
Aus Weltenliebe gnadereich,
Mit zuckendem Geistesblitz,
Aus hierarchischer Region—
Die hohe Seeleninitiation
Ganz ungeteilt und tief. (Virgo.)

Er lebt nun schon in Harmonie
Mit aller Weltenklarheit.
Empfinden kann in seinem Herzen er
Die Schwungkraft aller Wahrheit.
In sich fühlt er die Weltenwage,
Auf der des Daseins Rätselfrage
Von Geistern abgewogen steht. (Libra.)

Da zwickt und zwackt es ihn...
— Des Geistes Prüfung (findet er)
Scheint mir dies Prickeln in dem Leibe—
'Der Stich, der trifft ihn sicher!'
So grinzt verständing jetzt ein Ungelehrter,
Ein gänzlich mystisch Unverkehrter
Dem Mysterium ganz frech entgegen. (Scorpio.)

Er aber hat in Weltennacht erkannt,
Wie doch Homer und Sokrates, Goethe auch,
In seines Iches Wesensgründen
Die schärfsten Seelenpfeile schossen,
Und ihre unverfälschte Menschenwesenheit
Verkörpert wie mit Selbstverständlichkeit
In ihm zu neuer Daseinsgrösse sich. (Sagittarius.)

'Erfühlst du denn Homers Genie
In deinem Denken stark sich regen?'
'O, regt es sich, ich liebt es nicht,—
(So sprach mit spitzer Rede
Der Eingeweihte), das wäre Maya-Streben.
Homer will in meinem gegenwärtigen Leben
All sein Genie in Mystenschlafe pflegen!' (Cancer.)
'Dir fehlt, O mystisch ungeformter Sokrates,
Vom klügsten Griechen jede Spur.

APPENDIX

Dazu bist du so eitel, wie er weise war.'
'Erdrücke Lästerrede! (sagt der Myste)
Nichts zu wissen, liebte ich als dieser Mann
Und da ich jetzo gar nichts weiss und kann
Erfühl ich dieses Leben ganz sokratisch mystisch.'
(Aquarius.)

'Und welcher Sonnenstrahl von Goethe,
Als Bote führt er deine Seele
Zum Reifen hoher Wissenstriebe?'
Der Seher greift zu schärfsten Redepfeile.
'Es schuf' (so sagt er) 'Goethe viel zu helle.
Drum träum ich Goethes hohe Kunst und wähle
Des Schlafes Tiefen mir zum Arbeitsfeld.' (Pisces.)

Dr. Steiner said of this satire: It is in truth no game with serious matters when one gives rein to one's humour over the earnestness which, in many circles, fancies itself as 'mystical', which is fostered with trifling absurdities and bears a caricature-like mask of 'spiritual profundity', expressing itself in a pose of physical dignity, with tragically long faces; all this must indeed strike experienced people as a grotesque reversal of the spiritual life.... It is just where a spiritual knowledge is striven for that one must also be able to laugh at the absurdities of many 'seekers after the spirit'.

Page 287. A simpler method of presenting this scene would be for Maria to stand still, either doing the vowelsounds or reciting; Philia would also stand still and do the vowels, while Astrid, describing the following form, would at the same time do the consonants:

Luna does both vowels and consonants, at the same time moving this form there and back:

when the line goes forward she steps: — u —, when it goes backwards: — —

Page 288. In a similar way, with soloist and surrounding chorus, Greek Chorus Scenes could also be presented in eurythmy.

www.ingramcontent.com/pod-product-compliance
Lightning Source LLC
Chambersburg PA
CBHW052102230426
43671CB00011B/1909